99 Jumpstarts for Kids' Social Studies Reports

Research Help for Grades 3–8

Peggy J. Whitley and Susan Williams Goodwin

LIBRARIES UNLIMITED

A Member of the Greenwood Publishing Group

Westport, Connecticut • London

Library of Congress Cataloging-in-Publication Data

Whitley, Peggy.
  99 jumpstarts for kids' social studies reports : research help for grades 3-8 /
Peggy J. Whitley and Susan Williams Goodwin.
    p. cm.
  Includes bibliographical references and index.
  ISBN-13: 978–1–59158–403–2 (alk. paper)
  1. Social sciences—Study and teaching (Elementary) 2. Research—Methodology—
Study and teaching (Elementary) 3. Report writing—Study and teaching (Elementary)
4. Information retrieval—Study and teaching (Elementary) I. Goodwin, Susan Williams. II.
Title. III. Title: Ninty-nine jumpstarts for kids social studies reports.
LB1584.W488 2007
372.83—dc22   2006102884

British Library Cataloguing in Publication Data is available.

Library of Congress Catalog Card Number: 2006102884
ISBN-13: 978–1–59158–403–2

First published in 2007

Libraries Unlimited, 88 Post Road West, Westport, CT 06881
A Member of the Greenwood Publishing Group, Inc.
www.lu.com

Printed in the United States of America

∞™

The paper used in this book complies with the
Permanent Paper Standard issued by the National
Information Standards Organization (Z39.48–1984).

10 9 8 7 6 5 4 3 2 1

Contents

Preface

In our previous three books, *99 Jumpstarts to Research: Topic Guides for Finding Information on Current Issues*, *99 Jumpstarts for Kids: Getting Started in Research*, and *99 Jumpstarts for Kids' Science Research*, we focused on topics covering a variety of subjects from forensic science to children of India. In *99 Jumpstarts for Kids' Social Science Research* we focus on social science topics for students in grades 3 through 8. We have included jumpstarts from history, economics, psychology, geography, politics, and sociology. Except for a few ancient world jumpstarts, we have focused entirely on American history and events. Our goal in writing the *99 Jumpstarts* series is to promote improved information literacy by encouraging beginning researchers to evaluate their topic and to examine a variety of materials. We are very aware of how easy it is to go to the Internet for everything. We encourage teachers to require the use of books, newspapers, interviews, journals or magazines, other media, and other resources. It will improve student skills if they are required to search further than Google.

Today's students have to deal with information overload, and this makes it difficult to select the best information—or even determine where the best information can be found. Should I find this topic in the newspaper, in magazines, online, in videos, or in books? Each time these questions are asked, the answer may be different. So a little critical thinking about topics is an important starting point. We encourage the use of mind maps or other visual aids to refine a large topic down to one that is manageable. We believe that systematic planning, by teacher, librarian, and student, will make all the difference in the quality of the final product—and the way students feel about research. Help them get off to a good start, and you will reap the reward with well-organized papers and students who feel successful.

We continue to feel that the approach teachers take to research deeply affects the way students (young or old) react to the process. This attitude will influence students throughout their education. So help them enjoy the discovery process. Help develop the natural curiosity young students already have.

As college librarians who were school librarians in our past lives, Susan and I especially want to thank school librarians everywhere for introducing students to the research process. Every day we see college students who are clueless about gathering information, refining topics, and writing short reports. So believe us, when you have spent time developing research skills, we know and appreciate it. In our college library, we continue to encourage students to use a variety of formats—and to carefully evaluate the information they use. It is never too early to begin the process of critically analyzing information. We appreciate comments or suggestions.

Peggy Whitley
Dean of Educational Services
Kingwood College
peggy.whitley@nhmccd.edu
kclibrary.nhmccd.edu

Susan Goodwin
Reference Librarian
Kingwood College
sue.goodwin@nhmccd.edu
kclibrary.nhmccd.edu

Introduction: How This Book Is Organized

Each jumpstart is divided into the following sections:

- **A quotation about or introduction to the topic**

- **Words to Know,** introducing the students to words they will encounter when researching the topic

- **Related Jumpstarts,** which lead to other jumpstarts that are related to that era or subject

- **You Are There,** which puts the reader inside the topic by suggesting he or she become a part of the period or topic. We can introduce the topic painlessly by putting the reader there

- **Topics to Consider,** which include several suggestions for the budding researcher. Most topics are too broad for a short paper. These suggestions break the topic down and give interested students something they can handle.

- **Books,** which lists five to seven of the best books, both reference and circulating, on the topic. We know that students will use the books they can get their hands on. Hopefully, librarians will consider the books we have listed for collection development. All mentioned books received positive reviews and are appropriate for grades 3–8.

- **Internet,** which sends the researcher to kid-friendly sites with appropriate reading levels. The information found on these selected sites can be trusted for use in a research paper. We have attempted to choose organizations, education, and government sites, since they generally have the best staying power.

- **For the Teacher,** a lesson plan we have found online that is fairly comprehensive.

- **Student interactivity sections,** which give the students something to do that enhances their understanding of the topics they have chosen. We attempted to find enjoyable projects. Most are appropriate for family, friends, or even the classroom. We'd like to encourage the budding historian through activities.

We have not added newspapers or journal full-text databases. We hope teachers and students will use them if they are available. They are very useful and often contain the newest and best information on a topic. They are generally reliable, and online full-text databases are important for student learning.

Finally, we hope that teachers will celebrate the completion of the big research project. Allow the students to make oral reports and encourage them to bring in experiments and posters to show to the class. If the Internet is available, let the students share with their classmates the site that was most helpful to them. Think back on your own learning—and provide the kind of environment that you enjoyed. Celebrating new knowledge allows students to realize how important their curiosity is to the learning experience.

Search Engines Especially for Kids

Several very good search engines are available for kids of all ages. They are filtered and touted to be safe from pornography and suggestive advertising. The ones we list are chosen for entertainment and enlightenment. Bookmark the ones you like best, and use more than one when searching. We have also annotated specialized search engines that you may not find on your own, like ALA Great Websites for Kids (from American Library Association) and First Gov for Kids. These collections are generally hand-picked for their information and appropriateness for children. They may not have the high ranking of KidsClick or Yahooligans—but we encourage you to use them.

Major Kids' Search Engines

KidsClick!
http://www.kidsclick.org/

KidsClick lists about 5,000 Web sites in various categories. Librarians back these sites, and they are maintained by Colorado State Library. A click will take the student to the library version, arranged by Dewey Decimal number. Though it is a small collection, we usually start our search here because of the quality of the selections.

Yahooligans
http://www.yahooligans.com/

Yahoo for kids, designed for ages 7 to 12. Sites are hand picked to be appropriate for children. Yahooligans is the oldest major directory for children, launched in March 1996. It is arranged by subject headings and subheadings just like its grownup version.

Ask Jeeves For Kids
http://www.ajkids.com/

Ask Jeeves For Kids has been vetted for appropriateness. Sometimes the results are good. It may be best for more experienced searchers.

Looksmart's Kids Directory
http://search.netnanny.com/

The Kids Directory is a listing of over 20,000 kid Web sites that were hand picked by employees of Looksmart subsidiary Net Nanny and vetted for quality. Arranged by broad subject, this is a friendly Web site for the young. Family safe.

Kid's Search Tools
http://www.rcls.org/ksearch.htm

Dictionaries, encyclopedias, search engines, and Web sites for teachers and kids are on this search-friendly page. A keyword search line is right on the page. The collection is maintained by InfoPeople Project of California. Easy to use.

My Prowler

http://www.myprowler.com/kids.htm

This metasearcher finds and prioritizes sites on five of the major kids' search engines: Kids Click, Awesome Library, Yahooligans, SearchEdu, and CyberSleuth Kids. Save a little time and use a metasearch engine. You can narrow your search to images, MP3, audio, U.S. government, and Weblogs—before you put in your search words. Recommended.

TekMom's Search Engines for Kids

http://www.tekmom.com/search/

Starting with the big four, TekMom then gives immediate access to specialized search engines by topic: General, Science, History, Authors, Biographies, Encyclopedias, Dictionaries, Images, and Maps. Easy to use, and the search line is on the page

Ivy's Search Engines for Kids

http://www.ivyjoy.com/rayne/kidssearch.html

Listed are Internet search engine links (the big four), links to Web guides for kids, some specialized search engine forms, and specialized search engine links of interest to kids. Also included under 'family friendly' are search engines similar to Ivy's and engines where the user can set the filter.

Lesson Plans and Teaching Strategies

http://www.csun.edu/~hcedu013/plans.html

A huge collection of lesson plans for teachers of social studies. Marked by grade level. Alphabetized by topic rather than chronological. Each entry includes a brief summary.

The Teacher's Corner—Social Studies

http://www.theteacherscorner.net/lesson-plans/socialstudies/index.htm

A nice, long list of links to plans on the Internet. We particularly like the list of map sources.

Other Search Engines We Enjoy Using

ALA Great Web Sites for Kids

http://www.ala.org/greatsites

Collection of sites from the American Library Association. You can search by age or grade or browse through the subjects. Excellent site with strict guidelines for selection.

Social Studies: Federal Resources for Educational Excellence

http://wdcrobcolp01.ed.gov/cfapps/free/displaysubject.cfm?sid=9

Use this excellent collection of 884 Web sites from reputable organizations and government resources. This is the best for safe sites with quality information.

ThinkQuest Social Sciences and Culture

http://www.thinkquest.org/library/cat_show.html?cat_id=14.

The ThinkQuest Library provides innovative learning resources for students of all ages on a wide range of educational topics. Featuring more than 6,000 Web sites, the library is created by students from around the world.

Librarian's Index

http://lii.org/search/file/history

You can trust these sites to be good for kids and adults alike. Carefully selected by librarians for researchers, these 16,000+ sites are annotated, and review dates are listed.

Kid's World

http://www.northvalley.net/kids/index.shtml

Kid's World has an excellent collection of topics by subject, from government to vacation. Viewers can suggest sites, which are then carefully searched for appropriateness. Easy to use, colorful, and well organized. The only drawback is that the user has to search through the list of sites under broad subject. There is no keyword search. (An easy fix, which we hope they do soon.)

Awesome Library

http://www.awesomelibrary.org/

More than 26,000 reviewed sites have been classified into a directory, specifically organized for teachers, students, and parents. Browse or search, the "search engines" section is worth your time. Awesome Library is aptly named.

Education World

http://www.education-world.com/

This site features more than 500,000 sites of interest to educators. Browsable or searchable; users have the ability to narrow terms by appropriate grade level. Launched in spring 1996, this site is a an educator's resource. One problem is the number of ads on this page—and you will need an ad blocker to be able to use it.

FirstGov for Kids

http://www.kids.gov/

FirstGov provides links to federal kids' sites along with some of the best kids' sites from other organizations, all grouped by subject. You are invited to explore, learn, and have fun. The keyword search helps—but this site is great to browse for a topic you might like to learn about.

The Why Files from Google

http://whyfiles.org/search.html

A good place to search for answers. No filter, but the sites are some of the best.

How Stuff Works

http://howstuffworks.com

Unbelievably, this site tells how the government and economics work as well as science topics. This site is organized by broad subjects (electronics, health, home, people, science, computer) and is easily searched. Use the suggested Table of Contents topics that come with your search. Excellent, current information from howstuffworks.com.

Essortment: Information and Advice You Want to Know

http://www.essortment.com/history.html

Essortment's mission is to provide high-quality, free information to Web surfers. The information provided is concise, clear, and accurate.

10 Suggestions for Better Internet Searching

Entering your search terms may be enough. But the Internet is huge, and you can ensure that you find what you want by using these tips. Keep in mind that each search engine is different. Use the Help or Advanced Searching, too. These tips are generally good with all search engines. They help "limit" and improve your search.

1) Add as many appropriate search terms as you need to get the very best information. The Internet is so big that our problem is "too much information."

   Example: *explorer Fountain of Youth Ponce de Leon Florida*

2) Use the word "kids" in your search—for safer and easier sites.

   Example: cattle drives *kids.*

3) Prefixes often help your search. Do NOT put in spaces. If you do, this will not work.

   a. Definition:suffrage (find definitions of terms)

   b. URL:nhmccd (nhmccd will be part of the URL of all findings)

   c. Title:women's suffrage (the title is above the line)

   d. Domain:edu

4) Use math when adding and subtracting search words. Attach the + or - to the word.

   a. Use + to make sure your words are included in a search. You will find pages that have all of the words. Do not use a space between the symbol and the word you want to include or exclude

   Example: *American +revolution + kids*

   b. Use – to exclude words from your pages. You *will not* find the word *British* on your result pages.

   Example: *American + revolution + kids – British*

   c. If you want to find words together, like a phrase, surround them with quotation marks. You will find those words together.

   Example: *"American industrial revolution" + kids*

5) Use the asterisk to take the place of letters: *state (upstate) state* (statehood)

6) Boolean searching still helps exclude or include terms.
   Examples:
   a. *town **and** government **and** kids* (find all terms)
   b. *town **or** city* (find either one or the other term—helps poor spellers)
   c. "*mayor*" ***not*** *kids* (do not find pages with "*kids*")
   d. *explorer **near** LaSalle* (these terms will be within 10 to 25 words of each other, depending on the selected search engine.)

7) Use more than one search engine. We start with Yahooligans—but it is not the only good search engine for kids. Use another search engine—try one or two of the specialized ones listed above. Librarians have already collected safe and good sites for you in these specialized engines. Bookmark your favorites.

8) Be happy when you come across subject lists from which to choose. Start your search by using them, and then search within the subject with your terms.

9) Love any Web site that has its own search engine—one especially for the information on that site.

10) Be discriminating. You do NOT have to look at every site. Often, the search results are selected by popularity. A really good new site may not yet be popular. Use the descriptions and don't be afraid to go to page 2 or even page 15 of your search. You may discover a real jewel.

Suggestions for Class Projects

Following are 10 classroom projects provided for your units of study. We remember how much fun it was to work on these projects. We hope you will include the librarian, music, physical education, and art teachers, and as many others as you can. Grade level projects are very exciting for kids, and for older kids, too, if you approach this gingerly. Students remember projects done in class long after they have forgotten other things. Get students involved.

1. Life in the Middle Ages

The following is suggested as a classroom project during a study (including class reports) of the Middle Ages. Any time period would work; ours is just an example. Create a living village in your classroom. Spend a few weeks really learning about a period like the Middle Ages. Here are a few suggestions:

1. Have students research in the library for information and write brief reports on their own topic. Use the list of villagers and village life below for topics.

2. Create a large mural depicting the many aspects of village life. These can surround your walls. The Middle Ages is perfect for this because there is so much information about the village and the way it was created. Don't forget the manor house, peasant homes, mill, church, and open fields. And be sure you add villiens, the sheriff or reeve, the nun and monks, freemen, lords and ladies of the manor, the chapman, and others. For a more professional look, you can have the students draw the background and find pictures in books, scan or copy, enlarge, and glue them on the mural background. The librarian can help you gather materials. A large print glossary of terms is important and makes an excellent display.

3. There are many examples of music from the Middle Ages. Don't forget to include it in your study. Games children played are described, too. Have the PE teacher show the students how to play them.

4. Celebrate by having a "Day in the Life of the Middle Ages." Assign roles and have students come in costumes to take part in a day of life in the past. Suggestions for your day include a folkmoot (trial), creating illuminated texts, sharing food, and student oral reports. If you are brave, invite other classes or parents. And have your work ready for the big Open House.

2. The Age of Exploration

The exploration of America from Columbus to the settling of the West is exciting. Something in each of us springs to life when a discovery is made. We suggest you have students explore the past, learning about Columbus, LaSalle, Hudson, Lewis and Clark, and others. For a project, why not let them have an exploratory experience?

1. First, help the students understand why early explorers felt it was important to discover new worlds. Was it for personal advantage? What did they find? What were they looking for? How did they claim the new land for their country? Make a list of these important elements. Include the following elements (or others):

    a. Travel. Did the explorers travel by foot, in sailboats, canoes, etc.?

    b. Companions. How did they find sustenance? What did they take with them? Who did they take with them?

    c. Claiming the land by planting the flag. Laying claim for the home country.

    d. Indigenous people. Who was already there? What kind of reception did they get?

    e. Value, like gold or slaves. Exotic plants. Did they find gold? Did they find minerals?

    f. Creating a map of the area. Draw as accurate a map as possible.

    g. Naming the area, the country, place, rivers, archeological points.

    h. Biological interests. What plants thrive there?

    i. Zoological interests. What animals live there?

2. Now for your exploration! Divide your class into three or four groups. You will want between six and ten students per group. Students will become explorers and document the "new world" they discover. You may need volunteer parents for younger groups. If there are none, every group can work on the same area of discovery and exploration.

    a. Allow each group to choose a block of land. Or choose it for them. If your school is in the suburbs, they may take a square block; if in the city, a block or street. If you are lucky enough to have a park nearby, that would be a perfect area for discovery. If you can't leave the school grounds, let the groups discover and explore their school. The most important thing is that each group can discover and explore an identified area.

b. Each group will have a name (e.g., Christopher Columbus) and will make a flag. Dowels can be attached for "planting" the flag after the discovery.

c. Students will explore their block or street. They will make a journal that includes how they traveled to get to the new land, who accompanied them, a description of the area, a description of anything of value (a bank, a convenience store, a park with trees and swingsets, etc.), and the people indigenous to the area. Make a list of criteria before they set off. They should even try to do a population study. Each group will create an accurate map, naming the streets, lakes, or other features. They should report on the animals they find (cats, dogs) and the kinds of plants and trees that grow there. There are several examples online. Use the list above or create your own.

3. Final reports should look like a journal, with drawings throughout. Each group can decorate the journal and tie it together with string. Prizes can be given.

3. Colonial Life

Everyone loves learning about colonial life, and there is information available in books, in films, in journals, and online. Many elementary and middle schools have created Web sites that go along with their learning. Some are sponsored by local businesses or created by parents with web experience. Make your own. If you need someone to help get your information on the web and design your Colonial Life site, you probably will not have too much trouble finding a person to help. If there is a local college, you can always find "interns" ready to take this on. It would be a great service learning project. Your students should organize the information that will go on the site and create the documents.

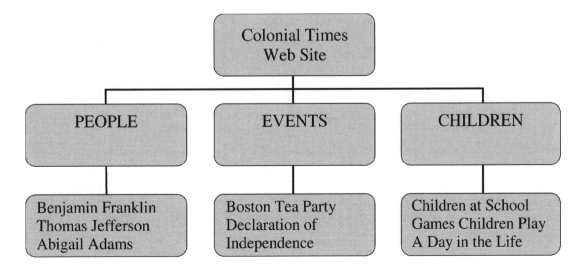

Directions

1. Have your Web designer come and talk with your students about their colonial Web site. They can discuss how important it is to make a plan before beginning.

2. Help the students create an outline, dividing topics or times. They should come up with topics to fit into the main headings, such as "People," "Events," "Government," "Entertainment," and "Education."

3. Have the students work in small groups. That will be more fun for them. Each student should contribute one paper, and it should be decorated with a drawing and signed.

4. The students should definitely find important documents or Internet links they want to link to on their Web site.

5. You will need a bibliography and a list of all contributors. Your Web designer can help with that. Remember, this should be fun and rewarding.

4. Broadsides of the Civil War

From colonial times through the early twentieth century, broadsides (or broadsheets) were popular as a means of communication. They were used for advertising, elections, announcements, news, government communications, weddings, funerals, odes, sales, song lyrics, addresses, and even poems. They were single sided and usually 18 to 20 inches long by 15 or 16 inches wide. They could be rolled up for carrying from place to place.

Have your class create their own broadside. Computer fonts and sizes are fun to change, and the content for these broadsides is generally brief. Additional fonts can be downloaded free from the Internet. First, have students research broadsides or broadsheets. There is excellent information at http://www. nls.uk/ broadsides/index.html.

Students should settle on the topic of their broadside. Then small groups team up to create an authentic work, using ideas from past creations. Both history books and the Internet have examples. Or, students can use their own research to create their broadside. Poems, odes, addresses, and elections are very good examples, with accompanying drawings. These work very well on large newsprint. The results can be posted in the classroom. What fun!

5. Westward Expansion

Immigrants, settlers, cowboys, explorers, Indian tribes, pony express coaches, railroads, stagecoaches, gold rushes, and cattle drives: There are so many topics of interest that help explain why the westward movement is a major era in American history. We like the idea of helping students understand the challenges faced by the brave pioneers who went west. There is a musical that aptly describes the opening of the Oklahoma territory and the differences between the settlers (farmers) and the cattlemen: *Oklahoma!*

Have a Friday movie festival. Tout it with posters placed around the room or school. Invite the whole grade level for an afternoon of movies and discussion. PTO parents can serve popcorn or hotdogs and soft drinks. Study the Oklahoma land rush (http://www.library.cornell.edu/ Reps/DOCS/landrush.htm).

Then show *Oklahoma!* It will be even more fun if your music teacher introduces the music to the group before film day. Print the lyrics and have the students sing along while they watch. If you have a gym, let different groups dance to some of the numbers. We have done this, and it is fun for everyone, especially on a snowy or rainy day. Keep in mind, a movie can always be paused while you discuss it—and refocus your group. All smart teachers start out with rules. If you really hate musicals, we suggest a Gene Autry movie, *The Oklahoma Cowboy,* or *Stagecoach* with John Wayne. You could even show Charlie Chaplin in *The Gold Rush.* Improve the learning experience by following the showing of the film with a panel of experts (teachers?) discussing the film and answering questions.

> The farmer and the cowman should be friends,
> Oh, the farmer and the cowman should be friends.
> One man likes to push a plough, the other likes to chase a cow,
> But that's no reason why they cain't be friends.
> Territory folks should stick together,
> Territory folks should all be pals.

> —**"The Farmer and the Cowman," from *Oklahoma!*** (Lyrics and music by Rogers and Hammerstein)

6. Children at the Turn of the Century

From 1880 to 1910, crucial inventions altered life as it was known. The automobile and the telephone totally changed life and brought people closer together. Mills and factories brought more families to the city. Problems we hadn't noticed much before were now apparent. Sweatshops and child labor became two of the biggest problems. Poverty spread. In the country, it became more difficult for farming families to keep workers. Young people left the farms for the city lights.

Have the students research these two groups. Help them step into the shoes of the children who lived at this time. Divide the class into two groups. Each group will find information on their topic and try to "experience" what the times must have been like for different families. They can write, draw, create a mural, do a computer project, or make charts. The more they find out, the better they will understand what life was really like for children at this time. A lively discussion should take place, with comparisons between the groups and an analysis of life for children in 1900.

Groups

1. The first group will "work in the city—in a factory." It should be pointed out that they will no longer go to school. They will work about 14 to 16 hours each day, six days a week, in a large room with other children and adults. During summer there is no air conditioning and in the winter the rooms are unheated. When workers get home, they will have chores to do.

    http://www.historyplace.com/unitedstates/childlabor/

    http://memory.loc.gov/learn/lessons/98/labor/resource.html

2. Group 2 will live on a farm. They rise early. They go to a one-room school after their morning chores are completed. When they get home from school, they do evening chores, play for a short time, and then do their homework around a table. In the country they may not have electricity or water. They use candles to study by. They go to bed early so they can get up for more chores. During "picking" time, the schools close so the children can work.

    http://www.eagle.ca/~matink/themes/Pioneers/farm.html

    http://www.ruralhillfarm.org/teachers.htm

7. Mid-Century America

Peggy Whitley (author), center

What was life like in America following World War II? Some consider it one of the best eras for families in our long history. Television shows like *Leave it to Beaver, Lassie, I Love Lucy, Andy Griffith, Father Knows Best,* and *The Adventures of Ozzie and Harriet* depicted family life. Stay-at-home moms cooked meals. Moms wore dresses and aprons (no robes or pants allowed) when they served the entire family breakfast. Everyone sat down to dinner together. Kids did chores without argument and were perfect in school. We look back with nostalgia at that period. Was it really that way? Find out.

Help your students delve into the past and discover what life was really like in the fifties and sixties. Grandparents can help. *American Cultural History: The Fifties* is a good place to start studying the period: http://kclibrary.nhmccd.edu/decade50.html.

Here are a few ideas we like:

⅄ Interview grandparents or older relatives.

⅄ Collect fifties memorabilia to share and discuss.

⅄ Compare a family show from the fifties (some are listed above) with one from today.

⅄ Research school life in the fifties and make a chart that compares with school today.

⅄ Have a fifties Christmas—do a little research into the toys that were available and popular in the 1950s. Create a wish list with photographs.

⅄ Cut out old magazine advertisements and make a poster of them.

⅄ Make a chart with prices of items in the fifties compared to today.

⅄ Create a 1950s scrapbook of memories of students' family members.

⅄ Have a Fifties Day. Make a list. Then invite everyone to join in the fun. The music, art, and PE teachers can plan events in their disciplines. Everyone can wear fifties clothes, and the librarian can share picture books written at that time. Grandparents can be invited as speakers. Family albums might be shared. The students can even write and perform a play. There are probably teachers who were alive during that time who can share their pictures and experiences with the class.

8. Creating a Digital Story

Digital storytelling can be several things. Generally it means telling a story using digitized photographs. A digital story project we like should work very well with young students. They can use a throwaway camera or a digital camera. You may need a scanner or other equipment if you use books. Internet pictures can be easily copied with a right mouse click. It is important to tell the students about copyright. With younger children this may be a perfect project to ask parents in to help. Many are experts at picture taking.

Directions

Have each student select a topic from the units you are learning in class. Have students research their topics and be sure they understand them so they can teach them through a digital story. Next, students should make a list of five pictures that would explain a process, relate an event, or tell the story. They will then take the five pictures that tell their story and arrange them in order of occurrence. The viewer should be able to "read" the story by looking at the pictures. Captions may be displayed for each picture, but the pictures should tell the story. A title is a must. Your students may want to post their stories online. (See example on the right.) Create a film strip template to put the pictures in.

Sample Digital Story: Michael Makes an A+: The Story of Success in the Library.

Students may need to scan pictures from books or copy them from the internet. If this is too difficult or the equipment is not available, you may just have them tell a story about their family, friends, activities, or school.

Have a contest. Give prizes and show the work.

(Fact sheets are fun to write, too. See a sample format at http://www.kidsplanet.org/factsheets/ map.html.)

9. Service Learning Projects

Volunteer hours and service learning projects are very popular in schools today. Students are never too young to learn the value of helping others. Through these projects students will gain a better understanding of self and their involvement in the community. By having them commit to a service learning project, you expose them to diverse populations and give them an experience that helps them develop a sense of responsibility. And if you follow these experiences with a means of reflection, students are more likely to make a lifelong commitment to helping others. There are many places in the school and in the community where even young children can contribute. Help the students in your class by requiring 10 or more hours of service during the semester. The librarian can help teachers find groups that will accept help. Students feel good about themselves when they know they have been able to help others. Promote this while they are young. Following are 10 project suggestions.

1. Working on Saturday to help clean up a park or an elderly person's yard.

2. Taking on a mile of the highway to keep clean. This is a great school project.

3. Helping a charitable agency or church to serve food to the poor at Christmas or Thanksgiving.

4. Collecting books for the children's hospital.

5. Working in an old cemetery. Looking up family history and documenting the past.

6. Passing out flyers or doing another job during an election.

7. Reading to the elderly or helping them learn about the computer.

8.   Serving at the public library by working in the ESL program, talking with non-native speakers of English.

9.   Walking dogs at the local humane society.

10.   Working with your family or church group on Habitat for Humanities houses or another major charitable project.

10. You Are There

Each jumpstart in this book has a section called "You Are There" designed to create a visual picture in the mind of students. What was it like to live during the time of Lindbergh or Jefferson? What if they had worked in a sweatshop in New York in the early twentieth century? What if their moms had attended the First Women's Rights Congress in Seneca Falls in 1848? What if they had been kids right after World War II? How would they have felt if they had marched with other suffragettes in 1920 when women finally got the vote? What would it have been like to go to school during colonial times, or to have been a child playing along the Nile during the time of the pharaohs?

A semester-long "You Are There" social studies project could lead to better understanding of the past for young students. Instead of writing the typical one- or two-page papers, students could keep a notebook that contains their own writings. Journal-like entries would include facts, people, and events and would focus on their own feelings about "being there." Each entry should be illustrated. Students should write a "You Are There" paper for each unit of study. Following is a sample story:

Life after the War

The war is finally over and our dad is home from the front. He served in Europe for the last two years of the war and fought at the Battle of the Bulge. We were so afraid, and now we are happy that our family is together. Our mom has quit her job at the factory, and dad has returned to his old job at the steel mill. The mill is running 24-hours a day, so dad works overtime. At night our family has dinner together. My brother and I do the dishes; then we join our parents in the living room to listen to Amos and Andy on the radio. On Saturday I listen to Let's Pretend with my girlfriends. We ride our new bicycles and we play outside until dark. We play games like Red Rover , jacks, and jump rope. On Sunday we go for a drive in the country in our new car. In town, we enjoy seeing the sailors and soldiers walking around town, proudly wearing their uniforms, with their arm around their girlfriends. Life is good.

99 Jumpstarts for Kids'
Social Studies Reports

9/11

The pictures of airplanes flying into buildings, fires burning, huge structures collapsing have filled us with disbelief, terrible sadness and a quiet, unyielding anger. These acts of mass murder were intended to frighten our nation into chaos and retreat. But they have failed. Our country is strong.—President George W. Bush, September 11, 2001

Words to Know

Disaster
Extremists
Flight 77
Ground Zero
World Trade Center
Pentagon
September 11, 2001
Terrorism
Twin Towers

Related Jumpstarts

Cold War

Disaster

The President Has Been Shot!

Telling America's Story with Photographs

You Are There

When something terrible happens, you remember it forever. It is September 11, 2001. It is 9:00 A.M., and you are concentrating on your schoolwork when the teacher tells you that a plane has just flown into the World Trade Center tower in New York City. Your teacher turns the television on to let you see what's happening. You see the smoke coming out of one building. As you watch, another plane flies into the twin tower. It takes a little time before you really believe what you have just seen. During the days to come you, your family, and the rest of America watch in awe at the horror of what has happened. On the other hand, you are proud of the heroes and the stories of many firefighters and others who endanger their own lives to save others. 9/11 is an event that no one will forget. Years later we will recall where we were when planes demolished the twin towers.

Topics to Consider

9/11: A Day to Remember	A Memorial for 9/11
9/11 at the Pentagon	People Helping People after a Disaster
American Airlines Flight 77	Rebuilding at Ground Zero
Firefighters of 9/11	Security Measures Following 9/11
Ground Zero	U.S at War in Afghanistan
Heroes of 9/11	U.S. at War in Iraq

Books

Search Words: September 11 Terrorist Attacks, 2001; War on Terrorism

Gard, Carolyn. *The Attack on the Pentagon on September 11, 2001.* (Terrorist Attacks). New York: Rosen, 2003.

Kelley, Allison. *First to Arrive: Firefighters at Ground Zero.* (United We Stand). Philadelphia: Chelsea House, 2003; Peachtree City, GA: Gallopade International, 2001.

Marquette, Scott. *America under Attack.* (America at War). Vero Beach, FL: Rourke, 2003.

Marsh, Carole. *The Here and Now Reproducible Book of the Day That Was Different: September 11, 2001: When Terrorists Attacked America.* (Here and Now). Peachtree City, GA: Gallopade International, 2001.

Valdez, Angela. *We the People: The U.S. Government's United Response Against Terror.* (United We Stand). Philadelphia: Chelsea House, 2003.

Internet

Helping Kids Heal discusses using art to come to terms with tragedy—http://news.nationalgeographic.com/news/2002/09/0910_kidsart.html.

ThinkQuest shows September 11 through children's eyes—http://library.thinkquest.org/CR0211220/.

A Day That Changed America by Scholastic explores the heroes and recovery from the attacks—http://teacher.scholastic.com/scholasticnews/indepth/911/.

Learn about firefighters' protective clothing, including the materials and how it all works, at the Davis, California Fire Department; video included—http://www.ci.davis.ca.us/fire/pct/.

Test of Courage: The Making of a Firefighter from PBS—http://www.pbs.org/testofcourage/.

Life After 9-11 contains news, stories, and videos—http://www.pbs.org/newshour/extra/features/after911/.

Five Years + After: Pictures, news, videos covering the attacks, remembrance of victims and rebuilding—http://www.nytimes.com/pages/nyregion/nyregionspecial3/ index.html.

For the Teachers

Young Heroes of History has pulled together a list of resources for teaching students about terrorism, patriotism and the 9/11 attacks—http://www.youngheroesofhistory.com/sept11links.htm. See also http://www.cyfernet.org/warres.html and http://www.scils.rutgers.edu/~kvander/911/.

Express Your Feelings

When you feel so much emotion that it's difficult to put it into words, sometimes it's best to express your feelings in other ways. Try expressing yourself with art, as these students did—http://www.fema.gov/kids/nse/drawing_911.htm. Draw your impressions of 9/11 or of an incident in the news that is important to you.

13 Original Colonies (1607–1776)

The first colonies in North America were along the eastern coast. Settlers from Spain, France, Sweden, Holland, and England claimed land beginning in the 17th century. The struggle for control of this land would continue for more than a hundred years. By (1776), the English colonies numbered 13. They were Massachusetts, New Hampshire, Connecticut, Rhode Island, New York, New Jersey, Pennsylvania, Maryland, Delaware, Virginia, North Carolina, South Carolina, and Georgia.—The Thirteen American Colonies, Social Studies for Kids

Words to Know

Colonial
Colonial America
Colonies
Independence
States

Etiquette
Founding Fathers
King George
Plantation

Related Jumpstarts

Abigail Adams
Aboard the *Mayflower*
Benjamin Franklin, Statesman
Boston Tea Party
Colonial Williamsburg
Declaration of Independence
Pilgrim Harvest

You Are There

You are lucky enough to belong to an upper-class family in colonial days. Your education is strict. You have a tutor and you study higher math, Greek, Latin, science, celestial navigation, geography, history, fencing, social etiquette, and plantation management. You memorize your lessons by reciting them over and over. When you are older, you will go with the other sons of wealthy planters to boarding school in England for a higher education. Your sisters are learning to assume the duties of the mistress of a plantation. They will be able to record household expenses. A governess teaches them art, music, French, social etiquette, needlework, weaving, cooking, and nursing. No pranks, or you wear a dunce cap.

Topics to Consider

13 British Colonies	The Founding Fathers
British Citizens in Early America	Life in America in Early Virginia
Biography of Any Founder	Living in Colonial America
Early American Music	New England Colonies
Farming in Colonial America	Pilgrims in Plymouth
Focus on One State, Like Georgia	Revolutionary War

Books

Search Words: 13 Colonies; Colonial Life; Georgia—History; A Person's Name

Note: Scarborough ISD has an excellent bibliography of books for study of colonial America at http://www.scarborough.k12.me.us/wis/teachers/dtewhey/webquest/colonial/children's_literature.htm.

Fradin, Dennis B. *The Thirteen Colonies*. Chicago: Children's Press, 2000.

Hakim, Joy. *The Thirteen Colonies: From Colonies to Country*. (A History of U.S.). New York: Oxford, 1996. (See also books 1 and 2 of this series.)

McCarthy, Pat. *The Thirteen Colonies from Founding to Revolution in American History*. (In American History). Berkeley Heights, NJ: Enslow, 2004.

Internet

Use this Early America life site as your starting point—http://www.cybrary.org/colonial.htm.

13 Colonies from The Time Page has information about states. Use the links to maps and other information—http://www.timepage.org/spl/13colony.html.

This *Archiving Early America* Web site has original sources—http://www.earlyamerica.com/.

About.com has a chart of each state and time lines. If you can ignore the advertising, this is a good starting point—http://americanhistory.about.com/library/charts/blcolonial13.htm.

Intolerable Acts (use links for further study)—http://www.historywiz.com/intolerable.htm.

This page is for kids—http://www.socialstudiesforkids.com/articles/ushistory/13colonies1.htm.

Outline of the colonial period has excellent information by subheading—http://www.usemb.se/usis/history/chapter2.html.

Colonial era—http://www.scarborough.k12.me.us/wis/teachers/dtewhey/webquest/colonial/index.htm.

Flags of the American Revolution—http://www.foundingfathers.info/American-flag/Revolution.html.

Everything you wanted to know about colonial America—http://falcon.jmu.edu/~ramseyil/colonial.htm.

American music before 1900, chronological listings—http://kclibrary.nhmccd.edu/music-1.html.

For the Teacher

Let this Pennsylvania school district make your lesson plans. This projects looks interesting for all grade levels. includes grading rubrics—http://www.tesd.k12.pa.us/vfms/shaughnessy/intro.htm.

The History Detective

Do some research into what family life must have been like in early America. Research the Daggetts at http://www.hfmgv.org/education/smartfun/colonial/intro/. Make a poster or chart or write a story about a family that lived at that time. Where did the dad work? What did the mom do? What was school like? Did the kids have chores? What did they play? Where did they live? You might even create a diary.

Abigail Adams (1744–1818)

Remember, all men would be tyrants if they could. If particular care and attention is not paid to the ladies, we are determined to foment a rebellion, and will not hold ourselves bound by any laws in which we have no voice or representation.—Abigail Adams, March 31, 1776

Words to Know

Continental Congress   Militia
Patriot   Rebellion
Representation   Saltpeter
Tyrant

Related Jumpstarts

Boston Tea Party
Right to Vote
Women at War
Women Get the Vote
Women on the Home Front
Writing the Constitution

You Are There

You lie awake in bed at night listening to the cannons roar and the shells burst. Your heart beats in time with the guns, and you feel as if you were in the middle of the battle. Finally, around six in the morning, there is quiet. You hurry out to learn what has happened. Only one man was killed, and the militia were able to take Dorchester Hill. Hooray! But there is little time to celebrate. You still have a farm to run and a sick mare to tend. When that is done, you give your four children their lessons. You need to keep up on the news of the battle so you can write to your husband, who is trying to form the new government. At night you settle down to write a letter using your last piece of paper. You're almost too tired to write, but writing helps you to feel that you are talking to your husband, who is hundreds of miles away. When, you wonder, will it all end? And when it does, will anything be left of the life you knew?

Topics to Consider

Abigail Adams as a Child	John and Abigail's Children
Communication Before Electricity	Making Saltpeter, Candles
Compare Living in Massachusetts and in Virginia in the Eighteenth Century	Running a Farm in the Eighteenth Century
Daily Life in the Eighteenth Century	Women During the War
Education for Girls in Colonial Times	Women Soldiers in the Revolution
First Lady	Women's Rights

Books

Search Words: Adams, Abigail, 1744–1818; First Ladies

Ching, Jacqueline. *Abigail Adams: Revolutionary Woman.* (Library of American Lives and Times). New York: Power Books, 2002.

Ferris, Jeri. *Remember the Ladies: A Story about Abigail Adams.* (Creative Minds Biography). Minneapolis: Carolrhoda, 2001.

Glass, Maya. *Abigail Adams: Famous First Lady.* (Primary Sources of Famous People in American History). New York: Rosen, 2004.

McCarthy, Pat. *Abigail Adams: First Lady and Patriot.* (Historical American Biographies). Berkeley Heights, NJ: Enslow, 2002.

Internet

Biography of Abigail Adams from the White House—http://www.whitehouse. gov/history/firstladies/aa2.html.

The National First Ladies Library gives more details about Abigail Adams's involvement in politics—http://www.firstladies.org/biographies/firstladies.aspx?biography=2.

PBS offers a behind-the-scenes look at John and Abigail Adams. Listen to excerpts from their letters—http://www.pbs.org/wgbh/amex/adams/.

Copies of the letters Abigail and John Adams wrote to each other, from the Massachusetts Historical Society—http://www.masshist.org/digitaladams/aea/ letter/.

Revolutionary War: The Home Front, from the Library of Congress—http://rs6.loc. gov/learn/features/timeline/amrev/homefrnt/homefrnt.html.

Women During the American Revolutionary War, by the New York Historical Society—http://independence.nyhistory.org/museum/subtopic.cgi?page_id=14388.

For the Teacher

The National First Ladies Library has an extensive resource for classroom exploration of first ladies and related diplomats—http://www.firstladies.org/curriculum/choose.aspx.

A Taste of History

Abigail Adams is famous because of her letters. Certainly she would still be in history books if she hadn't written her thousands of letters; after all, she was the wife of a president. But how many other first ladies are actually famous? Try to make your place in history by writing a diary. Be sure to make it a diary worth reading. Rather than saying, "Today we went to the movies," write about the movie and how it made you feel. For ideas on descriptive writing and keeping a diary, check http://teacher.scholastic.com/writewit/diary/index.htm.

Aboard the Mayflower (1620)

After a long beating at sea they fell with that land which is called Cape Cod: they were not a little joyful! After some deliberation amongst themselves and with the master of the ship, they resolved to sail southward to find someplace about Hudson's river for their habitation. But after they had sailed that course about half a day, they fell amongst dangerous shoals and roaring breakers, and resolved to bear up again for the Cape, and thought themselves happy to get out of those dangers before night overtook them.
—William Bradford, 1620 (http://www.eyewitnesstohistory.com/mayflower.htm)

Words to Know

Chamber Pots	Patuxets
Comers	Pilgrims
Covenant	Protestant Reformation
Emigrant	Seasick
Immigrant	Squanto
Leiden	Separatists Wampanoag Indians
Miles Standish	

Related Jumpstarts

13 Colonies

Colonial Williamsburg

Columbus Discovers America

Coming to America

The Fountain of Youth

Pilgrim Harvest

Religions of the World

You Are There

It's dark and damp and cold in the hold of the *Mayflower*. You have been seasick for so long that you can hardly remember what it feels like to enjoy your food. Ever since the weather turned stormy, no one has dared to make a cooking fire, and that was weeks ago! You'd like to go up on the deck where you could smell something besides chamber pots and mold, but you don't dare. Yesterday John Howland went out for a little fresh air, and before he knew it, he had been swept overboard into the ocean! He grabbed onto that rope that was hanging over the side, even when it dragged him under the water. The sailors were able to pull him up with a boathook. You can't wait to reach the land! No matter how scary it is to go to a new land where Englishmen have never lived before, it can't be worse than the journey!

Topics to Consider

Any Individual Pilgrim	The *Mayflower*
Building Houses	Religious Freedom
Clothing of the Pilgrims	Thanksgiving
Compare the Saints and the Strangers	Tisquantum (Squanto)
The Courtship of Miles Standish	Wampanoag Indians
Food on the *Mayflower*	William Bradford

Books

Search Words: *Mayflower* (Ship); Pilgrims, New Plymouth Colony; Thanksgiving Day; Wampanoag Indians

Carter, E. J. *The* Mayflower *Compact.* (Heinemann Know It). Chicago: Heinemann, 2004.

Osborne, Mary Pope, and Natalie Pope Boyce. *Pilgrims: A Nonfiction Companion to Thanksgiving on Thursday.* (Magic Tree House Research Guide). New York: Random House, 2005.

Plimouth Plantation. Mayflower *1620: A New Look at a Pilgrim Voyage.* Washington, DC: National Geographic, 2003.

Poolos, J. *The* Mayflower: *A Primary Source History of the Pilgrim's Journey to the New World.* (Primary Sources in American History). New York: Rosen Central Primary Sources, 2004.

Santella, Andrew. *The First Thanksgiving.* (Cornerstones of Freedom). New York: Children's Press, 2003.

Internet

William Bradford's account of the journey aboard the *Mayflower*—http://www.eyewitnesstohistory.com/mayflower.htm.

This informative page tells about the voyage, with links to the Mayflower Compact and some of the more famous passengers—http://pilgrims.net/plymouth/ history/mayflower.html.

Full text of *The Courtship of Miles Standish* by Henry Wadsworth Longfellow—http://www.mainehistory.org/PDF/poem_Miles_Standish.pdf.

Plimouth Plantation explains the living conditions on the *Mayflower* and in the new colony—http://www.plimoth.org/learn/education/kids/homeworkHelp/mayflower.asp.

Books and letters written by the Pilgrims, a passenger list, and a genealogy—http://www.mayflowerhistory.com/PrimarySources/primarysources.php.

The Pilgrim story, illustrated by artifacts, tells about the Leiden Separatists in Holland, chartering the ships, the journey, and the Indians, by the Pilgrim Museum—http://www.pilgrimhall.org/museum.htm.

For the Teacher

Scholastic has online activities and teaching strategies for earning about the *Mayflower* and the first Thanksgiving—http://teacher.scholastic.com/thanksgiving/mayflower/index.htm.

Walk in Their Footsteps

Visit the Plimouth Plantation, where you can experience life much as the original pilgrims did. You can board the *Mayflower II*, a recreation of the original *Mayflower*, and visit a 1627 pilgrim village. If you can't get there, check out this Web site, and you may feel as though you were there—http://www.plimoth.org/visit/what/. It offers a virtual tour.

All Roads Lead to Rome (753 BC–AD 1453)

All roads lead to Rome. All paths or activities lead to the center of things. This was literally true in the days of the Roman Empire, when all the empire's roads radiated out from the capital city, Rome.—The New Dictionary of Cultural Literacy, bartleby.com

Words to Know

Aqueduct
Amphitheater
Chariot
Gladiator
Litter Roman
Patricians

Pedagogue
Plebeians
Praetorian
Roman Emperors
Senate
Villa

Related Jumpstarts

I Am the Pharaoh

Life Along the Nile

Life in Ancient Greece

Mayan Mathematicians

Mesa Verde Cliff Dwellings

You Are There

It is the first century AD, and you live in Rome. Your father is very rich. Your home is a beautiful villa, high on a hill. Your mother takes care of the family and slaves do the work at your house. Rome is a busy city, and many soldiers walk through the streets, past the beautiful temples, shops, and public buildings. You don't walk; you have a covered litter, with curtained couches carried on poles by slaves. At home you enjoy eating wonderful foods—with your fingers. You go to school to study reading, writing, and counting. When you get home you play many games with friends, like tic-tac-toe, hoops, walking on stilts, hobby horses, and kites. You even have a pet goose and two dogs.

Topics to Consider

All about Ancient Rome	Going to School in Rome
Children of the Rich in Rome	Roman Gods
Clothing in Ancient Roman Times	Roman Roads (or Its Aqueducts)
Compare Rich and Poor in Rome	Roman Towns and Cities
Everyday Life in Rome	Technology in Ancient Rome
Food and Farming	Who Were the Romans?
Games People Played	Women in Ancient Rome

Books

Search Words: Ancient Rome; Ancient Rome, Children; Aqueducts; Baths, etc.; Life in Ancient Rome; Technology

Burgan, Michael. *Empire of Ancient Rome.* (Great Empires of the Past). New York: Facts on File, 2005.

Carlson, Laurie. *Classical Kids: An Activity Guide to Ancient Greece and Rome.* Chicago: Chicago Review, 1998.

Green, John, and William Kaufman. *Life in Ancient Rome.* New York: Dover, 1997.

Kops, Deborah. *Ancient Rome.* (Civilizations of the Ancient World). Berkeley Heights, NJ: MyReportLinks.com, 2005.

Nardo, Don. *Roman Roads and Aqueducts.* (Building History). San Diego: Lucent, 2001.

Nicolet, Claude. *The World of the Citizen in Republican Rome.* Berkeley: University of California Press, 1988.

Internet

Social Studies for Kids Ancient Rome—http://www.socialstudiesforkids.com/articles/worldhistory/introancientrome1.htm.

The Romans, from BBC for schoolchildren. Find background—http://www.bbc.co.uk/schools/romans/.

Who were the Romans? This is a good place to begin—http://www.brims.co.uk/romans/index.html.

PBS Roman Baths—http://www.pbs.org/wgbh/nova/lostempires/roman/.

Mr. Donn wrote this interesting Web site for kids—http://ancienthistory.mrdonn.org/AncientRome.html.

ThinkQuest *Daily Life in Rome* is an excellent place to start. Good place to compare rich and poor in Ancient Rome—http://library.thinkquest.org/22866/English/FRAME.HTML.

Teacher's Oz has links—most topics are here. The home page shows you how to cite the source (MLA)—http://www.teacheroz.com/romans.htm.

Draper Middle School Librarian page for sixth graders in Schenectady, N.Y. From architecture to technology—http://www.mohonasen.org/dmslib/ancient%20rome.htm.

For the Teacher

Check out Mr. Donn's lesson plans. They are thorough and interesting for young kids. You can also buy other curriculum plans at his Web site—http://ancienthistory.mrdonn.org/AncientRome.html.

When in Rome

Look at this Roman games site and see if you can make a Roman board game to play with your friends. We like Pettela—http://www.personal.psu.edu/users/w/x/wxk116/roma/rbgames. html.

The American Industrial Revolution

The Industrial Revolution itself refers to a change from hand and home production to machine and factory. The first industrial revolution (Britain) was important for the inventions of spinning and weaving machines operated by water power which was eventually replaced by steam. This helped increase America's growth. However, the second industrial revolution (America) truly changed American society and economy into a modern urban-industrial state.—Martin Kelly, about.com

Words to Know

Alexander Graham Bell
Assembly Line
Eli Whitney
Immigration
Inventors

Mass Production
Migration
Patent
Samuel Slater
Thomas Edison

Related Jumpstarts

American Sweatshops
Atchison, Topeka, and Santa Fe Railroad
Brooklyn Bridge
Child Labor
Coming to America
Rosie the Riveter
Where Cities Bloom

You Are There

It is 1794 and you live in Georgia, working on a cotton plantation. You have heard that a wonderful invention is about to be patented by its creator, Eli Whitney. The cotton gin is a machine that separates seeds and hulls from cotton after it has been picked. Mr. Whitney plans to own all the cotton gins and to gin all the cotton in the country, creating a huge monopoly. But he has miscalculated; the cotton plantation owners do not want to give up their ownership. It is soon clear that Mr. Whitney cannot make the machines fast enough to meet all the needs. Further, it seems this machine has industrialized the cotton industry. You are there from the beginning and see all the changes the cotton gin brings about. Wow!

Topics to Consider

Edison vs. Whitney: Whose Invention Most Changed the World?	Immigration and the Industrial Revolution
From Field to Factory	Inventors of the Industrial Revolution
From Hand Made to Machine Made	Mills, Mines, and Factories
Henry Ford and the Assembly Line	Samuel Slater, Father of America's Industrial Revolution
How the Industrial Revolution Changed Us	The Steam Engine (etc.)
How the Cotton Gin Changed America	What Is Mass Production?

 From *99 Jumpstarts for Kids' Social Studies Reports: Research Help for Grades 3–8* by Peggy J. Whitley and Susan Williams Goodwin. Westport, CT: Libraries Unlimited. Copyright © 2007.

Books

Search Words: American Inventors; Individual Names; Industrial Revolution—United States

Arnold, James R., and Roberta Weiner. *The Industrial Revolution.* Danbury, CT: Grolier, 2005.

Lewis, Cynthia Copeland. *Hello, Alexander Graham Bell Speaking: A Biography.* Minneapolis, MN: Dillon, 1999.

McCarthy, Pat. *Henry Ford: Building Cars for Everyone.* (Historical American Biographies). Berkeley Heights, NJ: Enslow, 2002.

Sioux, Tracee. *Immigration, Migration, and the Industrial Revolution.* (Primary Sources of Immigration and Migration in America). New York: PowerKids, 2004.

Stein, Conrad. *The Industrial Revolution: Manufacturing a Better America.* (American Saga). Berkeley Heights, NJ: Enslow, 2006.

Internet

Industrial Revolution Inventors—http://americanhistory.about.com/library/charts/blchartindrev.htm.

Industrial Revolution links—by subheading. Stick with American Industrial Revolution topics—http://www.kidinfo.com/American_History/Industrial_Revolution.html.

By the authors, *19th Century American Cultural History*—http://kclibrary.nhmccd.edu/19thcentury.html.

About.com's *Industrial Revolution* has it all if you can maneuver through it. Try not to get lost and you will get good info—http://americanhistory.about.com/od/industrialrev/.

Samuel Slater: Father of the American Industrial Revolution—http://www.woonsocket.org/slater.htm.

Eli Whitney and the Cotton Gin—http://www.whitneygen.org/archives/biography/eli.html.

Edison's Miracle of Light—http://www.pbs.org/wgbh/amex/edison/.

Way Back—*Technology in 1900* will be fun and helpful—http://pbskids.org/wayback/tech1900/.

Cotton Times Industrial Revolution can be very helpful if you take time to look for what you want using the index at the side. Easy to understand—http://www.cottontimes.co.uk/timeline1.html.

Henry Ford's Assembly Line—http://www.aeragon.com/02/02-04.html.

Answers.com pulls it all together for the older student—http://www.answers.com/topic/industrial-revolution.

For the Teacher

Industrial Revolution theme, with plans. Excellent organization for the teacher, from bulletin boards to activities to interactive sites—http://www.att.com/history/milestone_1892.html.

Invention Factory

Try your hand at inventing and learn the whole process from idea to patent to creation—http://www.nps.gov/archive/edis/inventionprocess/ENHS.html.

American Sweatshops: Yesterday and Today

When it's busy, we work up to sixty to sixty-three hours. The conditions in the factory are not very good. There's no air circulation. The bathrooms are outside on our floor. . . . Almost no one goes to the bathroom, they feel embarrassed. The bathroom is outside. You have to leave the factory, go to the hallway. It's a bit dangerous because anyone can enter the bathrooms. Also, there is a part in the building that is unprotected. You can easily fall into that empty space.—Jaclyn Smith, apparel worker

Words to Know

Immigrants	Sweatshops
International Ladies' Garment	Workers' Union
Poverty Triangle	Shirt Factory
Secretary of Labor	Unfair and Unsanitary Conditions

Related Jumpstarts

The American Industrial Revolution
Border Patrol
Child Labor
Coming to America
I Want That! Needs vs. Wants
Poverty in America
Rosie the Riveter
Wal-Mart Comes to Our Town

You Are There

It is 1912, you are 15 years old, and you work in the garment industry in New York. Day after day you add collars to dresses—a tiresome job. Your eyes hurt and your back is sore. You work 15 hours a day in a hot, dark, poorly ventilated, and unsafe building, with only a short break for lunch. You earn much less than 25 cents an hour. (It will be 20 years before you can be guaranteed that much money.) Many other workers are there as well. Many groups have tried to make things better for you and your workmates, but no changes have been made. A factory nearby burned down last year, and more than 100 workers were killed. Still nothing has changed. Is this all there is to your life? What can you do?

Topics to Consider

Anti-Sweatshop Movement	Sweatshops in Mexico (or China, or Japan, or elsewhere)
Henry Ford and Factories	Sweatshops Today—Why?
Nineteenth-Century Garment Industry	Triangle Factory Fire
A Person Who Worked in a Sweatshop	United Students Against Sweatshops
Sweatshops and the Gap and Old Navy	
Sweatshops in America, 1900–1920	

Books

Search Words: Child Labor; Sweatshops; Triangle Factory Fire

Featherstone, Liza. *Students Against Sweatshops.* New York: Verso, 2002.

Kyi, Tanya Lloyd. *Blue Jean Book: The Story behind the Seams.* Toronto: Annick, 2005.

Lieurance, Suzanne. *The Triangle Shirtwaist Fire and Sweatshop Reform in American History.* Berkeley Heights, NJ: Enslow, 2003.

Manheimer, Ann. *Child Labor and Sweatshops.* (At Issue). Detroit: Greenhaven, 2006.

Woog, Adam. *A Sweatshop During the Industrial Revolution.* (Working Life). San Diego: Lucent, 2003.

Internet

Between a Rock and a Hard Place: A History of American Sweatshops, 1820–Present is a good place to begin. See also the Web version with pictures—http://historymatters.gmu.edu/d/145.

Cornell University Web site about the Triangle Factory Fire—http://www.ilr.cornell.edu/trianglefire/

A college essay by Todd Pugatch has good information about the history of the sweatshops in America and England—http://www.unc.edu/~andrewsr/ints092/sweat.html.

Global Exchange Sweatshops information contains background information and campaign links to sweat-free environments—http://www.globalexchange.org/campaigns/sweatshops/.

The Gap's Global Sweatshop is a report with statistics and photographs of sweatshops making Gap's clothing—http://www.behindthelabel.org/pdf/Gap_report.pdf.

Answers.com has good background information and links—http://www.answers.com/topic/sweatshop.

The Smithsonian Institution has an interactive exhibit on the history of American sweatshops from 1820 to the present—http://americanhistory.si.edu/sweatshops/.

Sweatshop Watch explores modern-day sweatshops here and abroad—http://www.sweatshopwatch.org/.

For the Teacher

NEH has created lesson plans for sweatshop study. *The Industrial Age in America: Sweatshops, Steel Mills, and Factories* includes studies from the past and future. Good links and activities—http://edsitement.neh.gov/view_lesson_plan.asp?id=430 (grades 6–8).

Sweatfree Zone

Take a look at the agencies that work against sweatshops and find a way you can help. You may write a letter or get friends to join in a Free the Children or Adopt a Village campaign. If you live in a large city, you may even find something closer to home—http://www.heartsandminds.org/links/sweatlinks.htm.

America's Melting Pot

America has traditionally been referred to as a "melting pot," welcoming people from many different countries, races, and religions, all hoping to find freedom, new opportunities, and a better way of life.—Joyce Millett, *Understanding American Culture*

Words to Know

Assimilation
Diversity
Ellis Island
Homogeneous

Immigrants
Melting Pot
Multicultural
Refugees

Related Jumpstarts

American Sweatshops

Border Patrol

Child Labor

Coming to America

Cultures and Cuisines

Fighting Prejudice

The Great Depression

You Are There

It is 1947. You are the father of three small children. You and your wife were born in Germany and left there just before the Second World War. Jews were not welcome in Germany, and you came to America to escape the concentration camps. You want to be free and to educate your family. You live in the Jewish area in New York City. All of your friends from the old country live there. Your English is still very poor. Your children go to the Jewish schools and continue to speak German and Yiddish. You have been thinking that it may be better for your children to grow up in another part of America. They would learn English and have a better chance to live the "American dream." Is this true? What should you do?

Topics to Consider

Advantages of the Melting Pot Today	My Own Melting Pot: A Study of My Family
The Americanization of My Family	Should Ethnic Groups Maintain Their
Disadvantages of the Melting Pot Today	Own Culture and Language?
Does the Melting Pot Still Work?	A Subway Ride into the Melting Pot of
Italians (or Another Group) in Philadelphia	America
Melting Pots Make America Great	What Is a Melting Pot?
Miami and Its Many Cultures	Your Own Ethnic Background

Books

Search Words: Immigrants; Italian Americans (or Other Groups); Melting Pot

Note: Several publishers have series on Swedish Americans (and other groups). Find them in your library.

Franklin, Paula. *Melting Pot or Not?: Debating Cultural Identity.* (Multicultural Issues). Springfield, NJ: Enslow, 1995.

Jocoby, Tamar. *Reinventing the Melting Pot: The New Immigrants and What It Means to Be American.* New York: Basic, 2004.

Sioux, Tracee. *Immigration, Migration, and the Growth of the American City.* (Primary Sources of Immigration and Migration in America). New York: PowerKids, 2004.

Internet

Understanding American Culture: From Melting Pot to Salad Bowl should be helpful for background—http://www.culturalsavvy.com/understanding_american_culture.htm.

The Myth of America's Melting Pot—history lesson from 1900 to present, with statistics. For older students—http://www.washingtonpost.com/wp-srv/national/longterm/meltingpot/melt0222.htm.

A Subway Ride into America's Melting Pot—a report describing the many ethnic neighborhoods of New York, or any other large city—http://www.planetizen.com/node/20147.

Census 2000—a look at ethnic diversity, and a good place to draw your own conclusions about it—http://www.pbs.org/newshour/extra/features/jan-june01/census_newdata.html.

Compare the three Americas described in *The Heartland, Melting Pot and Suburbs*—http://www.milkeninstitute.org/publications/publications.taf?function=detail&ID=242&cat=Arts.

Melting Pot America has a good article from the British Broadcasting Company—http://news.bbc.co.uk/1/hi/world/americas/4931534.stm.

For the Teacher

Stirring the Melting Pot lesson plans are designed to help students explore their roots—http://www.nytimes.com/learning/teachers/lessons/20040804wednesday.html.

The Melting Pot in My Town

Have fun doing some research on immigrants in American and "America in the Immigrant." This site gives you ideas for New York, but they can be used in any part of the country. Activity 2B looks like fun. Use the phone book to collect data about your community. This would be fun to do with a friend—http://pbskids.org/bigapplehistory/activities/a_life/activity3/index.html.

Ancient Greece (800–323 BC)

I saw how ideally politics filled the Greek definition of happiness: "A full use of your powers along lines of excellence in a life affording scope."—John F.Kennedy, "Politics and Public Service," 1960, tapes.millercenter.virginia.edu/exhibits/jfk_politics

Words to Know

AD
Aristotle
BC
City-states
Epicureans
Helen of Troy
Hellenic
Mercenaries

Mycenaean
Mythology
Olympics
Parthenon
Philosophy
Skeptics
Spartan
Stoics

Related Jumpstarts

All Roads Lead to Rome
I Am the Pharaoh
Life Along the Nile
Mayan Mathematicians
Mesa Verde Cliff Dwellings

You Are There

What a day! You live in Sparta but have traveled by foot to Olympia to participate in the Games. The festival of games honors Zeus, the chief Greek god. It is your first time so far away from home, but you have a mission. You know you're the fastest runner in all of Sparta. Today, at the Olympic Games, you hope to prove that you're the swiftest boy in all of Greece. You look around you at all the people wearing togas, talking and laughing together. There are people here from Athens, Pella, and Eretria, but you don't need to worry about anyone fighting. That's one of the most exciting things about the Olympic Games: the truce. There can be no fighting from the time it's announced until the Games are over. But now it's almost time to begin. Time to see if you can win the garland of olive leaves.

Topics to Consider

Alexander the Great	Iliad
Ancient Greek Drama	Olympics
City-states	Oracle of Delphi
Clothing of the Time	Origins of Democracy
Food in Ancient Greece	Philosophy: Socrates, Plato, and Aristotle
Greek Architecture	Trojan War
Greek Mythology	Weapons and Armor

Books

Search Words: Greece, Civilization; Greece, History

Ackroyd, Peter. *Ancient Greece.* (Voyages Through Time). New York: DK Publishing, 2005.

Kirby, John T. *World Eras.* Vol. 6, *Classical Greek Civilization 800–323 BCE.* Detroit: Gale, 2001.

Lassieur, Allison. *The Ancient Greeks.* (People of the Ancient World). New York: Franklin Watts, 2004.

Powell, Anton. *Ancient Greece.* (Cultural Atlas for Young People). New York: Facts on File, 1989.

Sacks, David. *Encyclopedia of the Ancient Greek World.* 2d ed. New York: Facts on File, 2005.

Williams, Jean Kinney. *Empire of Ancient Greece.* New York: Facts on File, 2005.

Internet

History for Kids has information about architecture, sports, language, food, and much more—http://www.historyforkids.org/learn/greeks/.

Social Studies for Kids tells you about Athens and Sparta, the Olympics, and the law. It includes a time line and maps—http://www.socialstudiesforkids.com/subjects/ancientgreece.htm .

History of the ancient Olympic Games from the Olympic Organization—http://www.olympic.org/uk/games/ancient/index_uk.asp.

Classical Orders of architecture by Charlotte-Mecklenburg Historic Landmark Commission —http://www.cmhpf.org/kids/dictionary/ClassicalOrders.html.

Learn about Greek mythology—http://www.mythweb.com/.

ThinkQuest has a study of ancient Greece by middle school students, with games and activities—http://library.thinkquest.org/CR0210200/ancient_greece/greece.htm.

Ancient Greek civilizations, including the *Iliad,* the *Odyssey,* the role of medicine, and the various cultures—http://www.mnsu.edu/emuseum/prehistory/aegean/.

For the Teacher

The *Internet Ancient History Sourcebook* has translations of original ancient Greek texts—http://www.fordham.edu/halsall/ancient/asbook07.html#Crete. For lesson plans on all matters of Greek civilization, check out http://www.archaeolink.com/ancient_greece_lesson_plans.htm.

A Taste of History

Many Greek children's games were similar to games that kids still play today. Some of their games resembled jacks and football, and they even had board games. Read up on Greek games—http://hoodmuseum.dartmouth.edu/exhibitions/coa/re_high_games.html—and learn to play one or more of them. You can teach a game to your class and have a competition.

Atchison, Topeka, and Santa Fe Railroad

Do yuh hear that whistle down the line?
I figure that it's engine number forty nine,
She's the only one that'll sound that way.
On the Atchison, Topeka and the Santa Fe.
See the ol' smoke risin' 'round the bend,
I reckon that she knows she's gonna meet a friend,

Folks around these parts get the time o' day
From the Atchison, Topeka and the Santa Fe.

—Lyrics, "On the Atchison, Topeka and the Santa Fe"

Words to Know

Cyrus Holiday
Depots
Engineers
Harvey Girls

Philip Pullman
Santa Fe Chiefs
Transcontinental

Related Jumpstarts

The American Industrial Revolution
Brooklyn Bridge
Coming to America
Go West, Young Man
Oklahoma Land Rush
Reshaping the Land
Route 66
Underground Railroad
Where Cities Bloom

You Are There

It is 1908, and this summer you and your whole family are taking a trip from your home in San Diego to Santa Fe. You will travel by train. You are taking the scenic route past the Grand Canyon. You will eat in the elegant train restaurant and sleep in Mr. Pullman's sleeper compartment with fine sheets and pillows. What a treat! What luxury! Along the way you will stay at hotels owned by Fred Harvey and meet the Harvey Girls. Many interesting people will be traveling on the train with you. You will even meet several artists who are painting the beautiful scenery along the way. How lucky you are!

Topics to Consider

Building the Railroad	The Old Santa Fe Trail
The First Transcontinental Railroad	Pullman Cars and the Presidents
The Harvey Girls	Riding a Passenger Train
History of Atchison, Topeka and Santa Fe	Santa Fe Chiefs
History of Railroad in Your State	Surviving Train Depots—research one
History of Railroad Maps	close to where you live
Merging the Atchison with the Santa Fe	Why Build Railroads?

From *99 Jumpstarts for Kids' Social Studies Reports: Research Help for Grades 3–8* by Peggy J. Whitley and Susan Williams Goodwin. Westport, CT: Libraries Unlimited. Copyright © 2007.

Books

Search Words: Atchison, Topeka, and Santa Fe Railroad; Westward Expansion

Armstrong, John H. *Railroad: What It Is, What It Does.* 4th ed. New York: Simmons-Boardman, 1998.

Bryant, Keith. *History of the Atchison, Topeka and Santa Fe Railway.* (Railroads of America). New York: Macmillan, 1974.

Ducker, James H. *Men of the Steel Rails: Workers on the Atchison, Topeka and Santa Fe Railroad, 1869–1900.* Lincoln: University of Nebraska Press, 1983.

Halpern, Monica. *Railroad Fever: Building the Transcontinental Railroad 1830–1870.* (Crossroads America). Washington, DC: National Geographic Children's, 2004.

McBride, Bill. *Santa Fe Railroad: A History in Advertising 1937–1961.* (CD-ROM). Hartford, CT: Archives of Advertising, n.d.

Speaker-Yuan, Margaret. *Philip Pullman.* (Who Wrote That?) Philadelphia: Chelsea House, 2006.

Yenne, Bill. *Santa Fe Chiefs.* (Great Passenger Trains). St. Paul, MN: Motorbooks International, 2005.

Internet

Atchison, Topeka, and Santa Fe by Wikipedia is a good starting point, with history and helpful links—http://en.wikipedia.org/wiki/Atchison,_Topeka_and_Santa_Fe_Railway.

Littleton, Colorado Train Depot—http://www.littletongov.org/history/histlandmarks/atchisondepot.asp.

History of the Atchison, Topeka and Santa Fe from an article in *Cosmopolitan* in 1893—http://www.catskillarchive.com/rrextra/statsf.html.

Suite 101 often has good information. Follow the links and related articles and discussion boards—http://www.suite101.com/article.cfm/old_west/93512.

Railroads and Mapping by Library of Congress—What is the connection between building railroads and creating maps? Find out—http://memory.loc.gov/ammem/gmdhtml/rrhtml/rrintro.html.

History of Railroad Maps—http://worldmapsonline.com/History/historyofrailroadmaps.htm.

Links to railroad information from the University of Connecticut—http://railroads.uconn.edu/links.htm.

For the Teacher

I Hear the Locomotives has links to other lesson plans on transcontinental railroads —http://edsitement.neh.gov/view_lesson_plan.asp?id=253.

Trademarks of the Santa Fe

The Santa Fe used this trademark in the late 1800s because the British had supported the building of the rail lines. Put on your detective hat and find as many trademarks of the Santa Fe Railway as you can. Get pictures and make a collection board or notebook. See if you can find out why and how the trademarks you collect were used. This would be fun to do with a friend.

Banking

Banks put a community's surplus funds (deposits and investments) to work by lending to people to buy homes and cars, to start and expand businesses, to put their children through college, and for countless other purposes. Banks are vital to the health of our nation's economy. For tens of millions of Americans, banks are the first choice for saving, borrowing, and investing.—Office of Comptroller of the Currency, www.occ. treas.gov

Words to Know

Bank Note	Inflation
Budget	Interest
Checking	Investing
Credit	Legal Tender
Debit	Lending
Depression	Mutual Funds
Federal Reserve	Savings
Financial Security	Stock Market

Related Jumpstarts

The Great Depression

I Want That! Needs vs. Wants

Making Money

Marketing to Kids

Stocks and Bonds

You Are There

You have just received your inheritance, a sack full of gold. What are you going to do with it? Carrying it around with you is a nuisance. It's much too heavy. If you hide it under your mattress, thieves might find it while you're off at work. You could bury it in the ground, but then you'd have to dig it up whenever you needed to use it. But there is that bank in town . . . .

You take your sack of gold into the bank, and they give you a bank note to prove that the gold is yours. The bank holds on to the gold until you are ready to take it back. Meanwhile, the bank can lend your gold to other people. Those other people have to pay interest, a certain amount of money, for being allowed to borrow. In return, the bank gives you interest, too.

Topics to Consider

Bank Robbery	History of Banking
Budgeting	Interest Rates
Certificates of Deposit	Loans
Checking Accounts	Pros and Cons of Credit Cards
Federal Reserve	Savings
Financial Security	Savings Bonds

Books

Search Words: Banks and Banking; Finance, Personal

Giesecke, Ernestine. *Everyday Banking: Consumer Banking.* (Everyday Economics). Chicago: Heinemann, 2003.

Giesecke, Ernestine. *Money Business: Banks and Banking.* (Everyday Economics). Chicago: Heinemann, 2003.

Harman, Hollis Page. *Money Sense for Kids.* 2d ed. Hauppage, NY: Barrons, 2004.

Tattersall, Clare. *Young Zillionaire's Guide to Money and Banking.* (Be a Zillionaire). New York: Rosen, 2000.

Thomas, Keltie. *The Kids Guide to Money Cent$.* Tonawanda, NY: Kids Can Press, 2004.

Internet

XAT3 explains the history of money, banking, and money lending—http://www.xat.org/xat/moneyhistory.html.

What does a bank do with your money? Let the FDIC show you—http://www.fdic.gov/about/learn/learning/index.html.

Banking for Kids explains the basics with Flash and games, at various age levels—http://www.bankingkids.com/.

The basics of monetary policy, banking supervision, and financial services, for older students—http://www.federalreserveeducation.org/fed101/index.htm.

Sovereign Bank uses cartoons to illustrate banking for kids. Check them out—http://www.kidsbank.com/.

The history of banking in the United States, from the Comptroller of the Currency—http://www.occ.treas.gov/exhibits/histor1.htm.

Zing the spaceman helps younger students, and Angie helps middle school students, learn all about banking and money—http://www.handsonbanking.org/.

For the Teacher

Banking on Kids offers materials to establish a student-run bank to get kids started saving from a young age, intended for elementary school and middle school students—http://www.bankingonkids.com/.

An Account of Your Own

Visit a bank with your parents. Start a savings account of your own, and try to deposit money into it regularly. Check About.com's Compound Interest Calculator—http://math.about.com/library/blcompoundinterest.htm—to see how your money will grow.

Battle of New Orleans (1815)

Remember New Orleans I say,
Where Jackson show'd them Yankee play,
And beat them off and gain'd the day.

And then we heard the people say
Huzza! For Gen'ral Jackson
—"The Eighth of January"

Words to Know

Andrew Jackson
Artillery
Creole(s)
Earthworks
Formation
Fort McHenry
Francis Scott Key

Jean Lafitte
Militia
Muskets
National Anthem
Privateers
Reenactors
Troops

Related Jumpstarts

Abigail Adams
Boston Tea Party
Lewis & Clark Expedition
Mighty Mississippi
Women on the Home Front

You Are There

You've been waiting all night for the arrival of the British troops. In the fog, you reinforced the earthworks, or walls of dirt, and waited for orders. With you are other soldiers and militia from all over the south, including Choctaw Indians, pirates, and free men of color. Just as the fog lifts, a cannon roars and you look across the fields at rows and rows of colorful British soldiers. They're marching straight across the field toward you! You feel fear growing inside you at the sight of thousands of well-trained troops, but General Jackson said to wait. They come closer and closer. Suddenly the American cannons and artillery begin firing. British soldiers fall, but the rest continue marching. Some are finally in your firing range. It's time to join the fight! In less than two hours it's all over. The British troops are running away, and General Jackson declares victory.

Topics to Consider

Andrew Jackson	Louisiana Territory
"The Battle of New Orleans," by Jimmy Driftwood	Military Uniforms
	Militia
Black Soldiers	Piracy
Causes of the War of 1812	"Star-Spangled Banner"
Creoles	Treaty of Ghent
Jean Lafitte	Weapons of the Nineteenth Century

Books

Search Words: New Orleans, Battle of; Privateering; Pirates; War of 1812

Figley, Marty Rose. *Washington Is Burning.* (On My Own History). Minneapolis, MN: Millbrook Press, 2006.

Gonzalez, Catherine Troxell. *Lafitte: The Terror of the Gulf.* Burnet, TX: Eakin, 1981.

Nardo, Don. *The War of 1812.* (World History). San Diego: Lucent, 1991.

Sonneborn, Liz. *The War of 1812: A Primary Source History of America's Second War with Britain.* (Primary Sources in American History). New York: Rosen, 2004.

Whitelaw, Nancy. *Andrew Jackson: Frontier President.* (Notable Americans). Greensboro, NC: Morgan Reynolds, 2001.

Internet

Eyewitness accounts of the battle and preparations from Galafilm—http://www.galafilm.com/1812/e/events/orl_battle.html.

The Battle of New Orleans—An overview by the Cabildo, the Louisiana State Museum—http://lsm.crt.state.la.us/cabildo/cab6.htm.

Music and words to "The Battle of New Orleans" by Jimmy Driftwood, a high school history teacher—http://www.niehs.nih.gov/kids/lyrics/battleof.htm.

Weapons, people, forts, and reenactments of the War of 1812—http://members.tripod.com/~war1812/.

The Library of Congress has a recording of "The Eighth of January" and sheet music celebrating the victory—http://memory.loc.gov/ammem/today/jan08.html.

Battle of New Orleans Research at the Historic New Orleans Collection has artifacts and maps for the serious researcher—http://www.hnoc.org/BNO/bnopathindex.htm.

Answers.com has a readable account of the battle, with maps—http://www.answers.com/topic/battle-of-new-orleans.

For the Teacher

The War of 1812 for Kids has links to Web sites, lesson plans, and links to music, weapons, pirates, and more about the war and the times—http://www.kathimitchell.com/1812war.html.

Act Out the War

The war is long since over, but the battle still goes on, with reenactor groups who dress in uniforms of the time and have mock battles. You may already know who won the battle, but it doesn't matter when you are in the thick of it. Check out reenactor groups near you for an upcoming battle, or, better yet, join one! Get more information —http://members.tripod.com/~war1812/.

Becoming a Citizen

I hereby declare, on oath, that I absolutely and entirely renounce and abjure all allegiance and fidelity to any foreign prince, potentate, state, or sovereignty of whom or which I have heretofore been a subject or citizen; that I will support and defend the Constitution and laws of the United States of America against all enemies, foreign and domestic; that I will bear true faith and allegiance to the same; that I will bear arms on behalf of the United States when required by law; that I will perform noncombatant service in the Armed Forces of the United States when required by the law; that I will perform work of national importance under civilian direction when required by the law; and that I take this obligation freely without any mental reservation or purpose of evasion; so help me God. In acknowledgement whereof I have hereunto affixed my signature.—
"Oath of Citizenship"

Words to Know

14th Amendment   Immigrants
Aliens   Nationals
Bill of Rights   Naturalization
Citizens   Oath
Citizenship   Refugees
Duties and Responsibilities

Related Jumpstarts

America's Melting Pot
Becoming a State
Border Patrol
Coming to America
Constitution
Cultures and Cuisines

You Are There

Imagine this: You have lived in the United States for five years. You and your family want to become citizens and you have all learned to speak English. At night, you study together to learn about American history and government. You know the examination will be difficult. When you are through taking it, you will probably know more about America than many of its natural citizens. What a day it will be when you stand before the judge, raising your right hand, and swearing to support and defend your new country. What a photo op! This is an event you will remember all your life.

Topics to Consider

Becoming a U.S. Citizen	What Is a Green Card?
Compassion, Respect, Responsibility, and Courage	What Is Dual Citizenship
Five Themes of Good Citizenship: Honesty,	What Is Good Citizenship?
History of Citizenship in America	Who Is a Natural Born Citizen?
The Rights and Responsibilities of American Citizens	Why Should I Become a Citizen?

Books

Search Words: Citizenship—U.S.; Civics—Juvenile literature

American Citizenship. (videorecording). (American Government for Children). Wynnewood, PA: Schlessinger Media, 2005.

Boy Scouts of America. *Citizenship in the Community.* (Merit Badge). Irving, TX: Boy Scouts of America, 2005.

Boy Scouts of America. *Citizenship in the Nation.* (Merit Badge). Irving, TX: Boy Scouts of America, 2005.

De Capua, Sarah. *Becoming a Citizen.* (True Books: Civics). Danbury, CT: Children's Press, 2002.

Shuker-Haines, Frances. *Rights and Responsibilities: Using Your Freedom.* (Good Citizenship Library). Austin, TX: Raintree Steck-Vaughn, 1993.

Teitelbaum, Michael. *The Bill of Rights.* (Our Government and Citizenship). Chanhassen, MN: Child's World, 2005.

Internet

Ben's Guide to the U.S. Government for kids has basic information about becoming a citizen—http://bensguide.gpo.gov/9-12/citizenship/oath.html.

PBS for Kids created an excellent page of information—http://pbskids.org/democracy/educators/citizenshipcity.html.

Learn about U.S. citizenship—http://www.uscitizenship.info/.

Puertoricousa.com discusses the status of Puerto Rican citizens and the United States. Good links—http://www.puertoricousa.com/.

A government booklet listing reasons to become a U.S. citizen—http://uscis.gov/graphics/lawsregs/handbook/m618-7.pdf.

For the Teacher

Citizenship City: Lesson plans on learning about citizenship and democracy. This site includes activities—http://pbskids.org/democracy/educators/citizenshipcity.html.

Who Are You?

If someone in your family arrived in America through Ellis Island, have fun searching for that person. There is a lot of information about Ellis Island and immigrants on this site—ellisisland.org. You could spend lots of time—and we hope you will. This is a good family project. Create a family scrapbook online. For older students, if working alone.

Becoming a State

Congregate a hundred Americans anywhere beyond the settlements and they immediately lay out a city, frame a state constitution and apply for admission into the Union, while twenty-five of them become candidates for the United States Senate.
—D. Richardson, journalist, 1859

Words to Know

Act of Admission   Northwest Ordnance
Admission   Representative Government
Citizen   Rights and Responsibilities
Commonwealth   States' Rights
Constitution   Territory
Enabling Act

Related Jumpstarts

Donkeys and Elephants
Go West, Young Man
Lewis & Clark Expedition
Missouri Compromise
Oklahoma Land Rush
Rough Riders

You Are There

You are a citizen of Puerto Rico. That also makes you a citizen of the United States, but Puerto Rico is not a state. Instead, it is a commonwealth. In 1998 the United States Congress passed a law allowing Puerto Ricans to vote on whether they would like to become an independent country, to become a state, or "none of the above." Since half the people voted for "none of the above," Puerto Rico is still a commonwealth, enjoying the protection of the United States but not all the rights and responsibilities. For instance, you don't have any voting members of Congress. And your parents don't have to pay federal income tax. Every 10 years, Puerto Ricans will vote again. You aren't old enough to vote this time, but you listen to all the arguments. You can't wait until it is your turn to vote for statehood!

Topics to Consider

Compare a State to a Territory	Puerto Rico
Constitutional Rules	Should We Have More States?
The District of Columbia	State Constitution
Meaning of Your State Flag	States and the Stars and Stripes
Missouri Compromise	States' Rights
Northwest Ordnance	Your State's Path to Statehood

Books

Search Words: Statehood (American Politics); Your State's Name

Laney, Garrine P. *Statehood Process of the Fifty States.* Hauppage, NY: Nova Science, 2002.

Schomp, Virginia. *New York.* (Celebrate the States). New York: Benchmark, 2006. (See other books in this series.)

Shearer, Benjamin F., ed. *The Uniting States: The Story of Statehood for the Fifty United States.* (3 vols.). Westport, CT: Greenwood, 2004.

Yorinks, Adrienne. *Quilt of States.* Washington, DC: National Geographic, 2005.

Internet

To find a Web site on how your state became a state, try a search for your state name, statehood, and site:.gov. For example, "California Statehood site:.gov" will take you to government sources on how California became a state.

The Arizona State Library briefly explains the Northwest Ordnance and the statehood process—http://www.lib.az.us/text/museum/statehood.htm.

The Enabling Act and other details about territories and how they become states are explained more thoroughly—http://www.thegreenpapers.com/slg/explanation-statehood.phtml.

The Northwest Ordnance, full text without interpretation—http://www.yale.edu/lawweb/avalon/nworder.htm.

Information Please explains the Missouri Compromise—http://www.infoplease.com/ce6/history/A0833427.html.

The Library of Congress exhibit on the Missouri Compromise includes background letters and primary documents—http://www.loc.gov/rr/program/bib/ourdocs/Missouri.html.

The US50 has basic historical information about each state—http://www.theus50.com/.

For the Teacher

Study tools for the 50 states include worksheets on capitals, blank maps, drill sheets, and links to lesson plans—http://www.50states.com/tools/.

Tell a Story

Every state has its own special tales and folklore. Learn some from your state. The best way to tell a story is to read it several times until you learn it by heart. Don't memorize it. The words don't have to be exactly right. Then practice with a tape recorder until you like the way you tell the story. Be sure to make it sound scary, exciting, and funny at the right times. Get some ideas for folktales from your state—http://www.americanfolklore.net/ss.html.

Benjamin Franklin, Statesman (1706–1790)

If you would not be forgotten,
as soon as you are dead and rotten,
either write things worth the reading,
or do things worth the writing.

—Ben Franklin, 1738

Words to Know

Ambassador
Benjamin Franklin
Broadside
Declaration of Independence
Historical Documents
Historian Statesman

Inventor
Junto or Leather Apron Club
King George
Poor Richard's Almanack
Silence Dogood

Related Jumpstarts

13 Colonies
Abigail Adams
Boston Tea Party
Declaration of Independence
Writing the Constitution

You Are There

Imagine yourself in June 1776. You are a young lad and you work for one of the most famous statesmen of the period, Dr. Benjamin Franklin. He and five others have been appointed to write a draft document presenting to the world the colonies' case for independence and freedom from England and King George. You are present with Dr. Franklin, John Adams, Roger Sherman, Robert R. Livingston, and Thomas Jefferson, when the committee of five meets. You hear them ask Thomas Jefferson to write the initial draft. You are privy to all the conversations of these famous founding fathers. You serve tea, run small errands, and do anything else that Dr. Franklin requires. You are in a place where history is being made. How lucky you are.

Topics to Consider

About *Poor Richard's Almanack*	Diary of the Life of Ben Franklin in 1776
Ben Franklin, Framer of the Constitution	Franklin, Ambassador to England
Ben Franklin, Signer of Historical Documents	The Life of Benjamin Franklin
Benjamin Franklin, Inventor	Silence Dogood
Benjamin Franklin, Printer and Librarian	Wit and Wisdom of Ben Franklin
Benjamin Franklin, Statesman	Young Ben Franklin

Books

Search Words: Franklin, Benjamin—Juvenile

D'Aulaire, Ingri, and Edgar Parin D'Aulaire. *Benjamin Franklin.* New York: Doubleday, 1987.

Franklin, Benjamin. *The Autobiography and Other Writings.* New York: Penguin, 2003. Also available as an e-book at http://www.earlyamerica.com/lives/franklin/index.html.

Fritz, Jean. *What's the Big Idea, Ben Franklin?* New York: Putnam, 1976.

Marcovitz, Hal. *Benjamin Franklin: Scientist, Inventor, Printer and Statesman.* (Leaders of the American Revolution). West Langhorn, PA: Chelsea House, 2006.

Satterfield, Katherine Hoffman. *Benjamin Franklin: A Man of Many Talents.* (Time for Kids). Scranton, PA: HarperTrophy, 2005.

Scarf, Maggi. *Meet Benjamin Franklin.* New York: Random House, 2002.

Internet

Ben's Guide to U.S. Government—select information by your grade level—http://bensguide.gpo.gov/.

PBS really knows how to make an exciting and educational site. Take time to explore all the information you will find here—http://www.pbs.org/benfranklin/index.html.

Benjamin Franklin: Documentary History. Enjoy this—http://www.english.udel.edu/lemay/franklin/.

World Almanac has biographical information on Franklin, nicely arranged—http://www.worldalmanacforkids.com/explore/inventions/franklin_benjamin.html.

Ben Franklin site at *US History* is an excellent guide, includes video, audio, and even games. (I played checkers with Ben)—http://www.ushistory.org/franklin/info/index.htm.

Benjamin Franklin and the American Revolution has excellent links, a time line, and biographical information—http://www.americanrevolution.com/BenjaminFranklin.htm.

Benjamin Franklin, an Enlightened American—http://library.advanced.org/22254/home.htm.

For the Teacher

PBS has eight plans with activities and assessment, and offers the rights for K–12 to copy the Ben Franklin video series and use it free in the classroom for one year—http://www.pbs.org/benfranklin/teachersguide.html.

Create a Broadside

In the colonial period, "broadsides" provided inexpensive information and entertainment to the masses. Broadsides were a single sheet of paper (20 by 15 inches) that generally contained print on one side only. Do some research and create your own broadside about what was happening during Franklin's life. Pick a "week," perhaps July 4, 1776. Make it entertaining. Add a poem, cartoon, and something from *Poor Richard's Almanack.* Start here—http://www.mass.gov/lib/collections/dc/broadside.htm.

Border Patrol

We are the guardians of our Nation's borders. We are America's frontline. We safeguard the American homeland at and beyond our borders. We protect the American public against terrorists and the instruments of terror. We steadfastly enforce the laws of the United States while fostering our Nation's economic security through lawful international trade and travel. We serve the American public with vigilance, integrity and professionalism.—Customs and Border Protection Mission Statement, http://www.cbp.gov/xp/CustomsToday/2003/April/core.xml

Words to Know

Coast Guard
Coyotes
Customs
Homeland Security
Illegal Alien
Immigrant
Mesquite
Minutemen
Terrorists
U.S. Customs and Border Protection (CBP)
War on Drugs

Related Jumpstarts

9/11

America's Melting Pot

Becoming a Citizen

Coming to America

Cultures and Cuisines

Poverty in America

Underground Railroad

You Are There

When you get the call that a group of illegal aliens are on the trail through the Lopez Ranch, you know just where the trail leads. You drive along the road until you see fresh tracks, then you park your Border Patrol car and follow them. It's hot and barren out here in south Texas. There are tufts of long grass sprouting out of the dry, light brown dirt. Prickly pear cactus dot the landscape. You walk on, looking for signs that the people recently passed that way: scuffed dirt, broken twigs, sometimes discarded trash. Up ahead there's a stand of mesquite trees, short and twisted. You decide to rest a few minutes in the shade. You sit down and take a long swig of water from your canteen. As you lower it, you notice a shoe just a few feet away. You look up. There, hiding in the scrub brush, is a man. Although you have a gun, you don't have to use it. You call out, "Let's go," and he comes out of the trees. With him come four others.

Topics to Consider

Border Patrol	Illegal Immigration
Border Patrols and the Drug War	Minutemen
Green cards for Immigrants	Preparing in Case of Terrorism
Guest Worker Program	Serving Your Country
Homeland Security Department	Should We Build a Wall Along the Border?
Identification of Citizens	Visas for Hispanic Workers

Books

Search Words: Alien Labor; Immigrants, United States; Law Enforcement; Terrorism

Bloom, Barbara Lee. *The Mexican Americans.* (Immigrants in America). San Diego: Lucent, 2004.

Cothran, Helen, ed. *National Security: Opposing Viewpoints.* San Diego: Greenhaven, 2005.

Haerens, Margaret, ed. *Immigration: Opposing Viewpoints.* San Diego: Greenhaven, 2006.

Talwar, Jennifer Parker. *Fast Food, Fast Track: Immigrants, Big Business and the American Dream.* Boulder, CO: Westview, 2002.

Woolf, Alex. *Why Are People Terrorists?* (Exploring Tough Issues). Chicago: Raintree, 2005.

Internet

The U.S. Border Patrol's home page gives you facts and news releases—http://www.cbp.gov/.

The U.S. Department of Homeland Security has information on border security—http://www.dhs.gov/dhspublic/.

Ready Kids has preparation plans to help you be prepared in any disaster, as well as fun and games—http://www.ready.gov/kids/home.html.

While the Border Patrol guards the land border, the Coast Guard guards the border along the oceans—http://www.uscg.mil/USCG.shtm.

Securing America's Borders fact sheet from the White House—http://www.whitehouse.gov/news/releases/2002/01/20020125.html.

NIDS (National Identification Scheme) or national identity cards are being considered—http://www.cpsr.org/issues/privacy/natidfaq.

The Office of Immigration Statistics will help you find the facts to support your paper—http://www.uscis.gov/graphics/shared/statistics/.

For the Teacher

The Immigration Debate in the Classroom links to a variety of Web sites and gives ideas for incorporating immigration reform into lesson plans—http://score.rims.k12.ca.us/score_lessons/immigration_debate/.

Law Enforcement

Learn more about being a law enforcement officer. You can go to a Law Enforcement Summer Camp, where you'll learn about crime scene investigation, police tactics, and emergency medical treatment. There are many camps, so you'll have to look for one in your area. Or, once you're 14, you can join a Law Enforcement Explorer Post and be trained to ride with a police officer. For more information—http://www.learning-for-life.com/exploring/lawenforcement/index.html.

Boston Tea Party (1773)

Conflict with colonists and the British Government grew worse in the 1760s and 1770s when the British Parliament imposed new tax laws on the colonists. Samuel and the members of the Country Party opposed these laws. Samuel organized a group called the "Sons of Liberty," who resisted the tea tax by secretly dumping tea into Boston harbor in the famous "Tea Party."—White House Dream Team, http://www.whitehouse.gov/kids/dreamteam/samueladams.html

Words to Know

American Revolution
Boston Massacre
British East India Company
Continental Congress
Intolerable Acts
King George III

Mohawks
Samuel Adams
Sons of Liberty
Taxes
Tea Act

Related Jumpstarts

Abigail Adams
Benjamin Franklin, Statesman
Declaration of Independence
Taxes
Writing the Constitution

You Are There

You are a colonist, and the colonists are angry. King George III of England has imposed new taxes on you. Why should you pay taxes to a country across the ocean? What will you gain sending hard earnings away from your new land? Just last night, December 16, 1773, you were part of a group of more than 5,000 angry colonists gathered at Old South to protest a tax on tea. You debated for hours, then Samuel Adams gave the secret signal that launched the Boston Tea Party. The Sons of Liberty (and you were part of the group,) disguised as Mohawk Indians, raced to Griffin's Wharf and dumped 342 chests of tea into Boston Harbor. You will never forget the jubilation! The fight for freedom has begun.

Topics to Consider

Boston Massacre	Sons of Liberty
Boston Tea Party	Stamp Act
Continental Congress	Tea Act
Events Following the Tea Party	The Tea Party and the Revolution
Events Leading up to the Boston Tea Party	Townsend Act
Importance of Tea	What Were the Intolerable Acts?
Samuel Adams	

Books

Search Words: American Independence; Boston Tea Party; Samuel Adams

Burgan, Michael. *Samuel Adams: Patriot and Statesman.* (Signature Lives). Minneapolis, MN: Compass Point, 2005.

Herbert, Janis. *American Revolution for Kids: A History with 21 Activities.* Chicago: Chicago Review, 2002.

Hull, Mary. *The Boston Tea Party in American History.* (In American History). Springfield, NJ: Enslow, 1999.

Landau, Elaine. *Witness the Boston Tea Party with Elaine Landau.* (Explore Colonial America with Elaine Landau). Berkeley Heights, NJ: Enslow, 2006.

Rosen, Daniel. *Independence Now: The American Revolution 1763–1783.* (Crossroads America). Washington, DC: National Geographic, 2004.

Trueit, Trudi Strain. *The Boston Tea Party.* (Cornerstones of Freedom). New York: Children's Press, 2005.

Internet

Revolutionary America Online Exhibit details events leading to the Revolutionary War. Includes photographs of documents. YES!—http://hoover.archives.gov/exhibits/RevAmerica/index.html.

The History Place's *Prelude to Revolution 1763–1776.* Links to the Boston Massacre and Boston Tea Party. Important events—http://www.historyplace.com/unitedstates/revolution/rev-prel.htm#tea.

Samuel Adams biographical information includes *Prelude to Revolution* and the *Boston Tea Party*—http://www.patriotresource.com/people/samadams.html.

Boston Massacre Trail. See images, remarks by Samuel Adams and other patriots, firsthand accounts—http://www.law.umkc.edu/faculty/projects/ftrials/bostonmassacre/bostonmassacre.html.

For the Teacher

Boston Tea Party: Costume Optional from the National Endowment for the Humanities has excellent plans—http://edsitement.neh.gov/view_lesson_plan.asp?id=397. Grades 6–8.

Boston Massacre

Read about the Boston Massacre trial. Write newspaper articles about the trial. Include interviews with the key figures. Don't forget to report on Crispus Attucks. Find out whether your teacher will take these articles in place of a report. Add pictures for interest—http://www.law.umkc.edu/faculty/projects/ftrials/bostonmassacre/bostonmassacre.html.

Brooklyn Bridge (1870–1883)

*And that's all I can
recall of Brooklyn Bridge,
tonight, John A Roebling
and Washington Roebling*
*built it, and it hath cables
and it does one good
to cross it everyday.*
—Jack Kerouac, *The Brooklyn Bridge Blues*, 1956

Words to Know

Anchorage
Boatswain's Chair
Cables
Caisson
Caisson's Disease
Concrete

Diagonal Stays
Engineer
John Roebling
Pedestrian Walkway
Suspension Bridge
Washington A.
    Roebling

Related Jumpstarts

The American Industrial Revolution

Atchison, Topeka, and Santa Fe Railroad

Reshaping the Land

Where Cities Bloom

You Are There

You live in Brooklyn in 1883. You are 12 years old, and throughout your entire life there have been men working to build a bridge across the East River, one that will allow you and your family to walk or ride when crossing the wide river. The bridge they are building will be named the Brooklyn Bridge and will be the longest suspension bridge in the world. Currently, if you want to go into New York, you have to ride the ferry. In the winter it is a treacherous trip. Sometimes the river is frozen and the ferry cannot maneuver through the ice. After school, you and your friends go to the river's edge to watch as the men work. Soon the bridge will open. You are hoping to be one of the first to go across. How exciting to be part of history!

Topics to Consider

Brooklyn Bridge Today	People Who Built the Bridge
Building the Brooklyn Bridge	Planning the Brooklyn Bridge
The Caisson and Caisson's Disease	Suspension Bridges
History of the Brooklyn Bridge	Who Was John Roebling?
Joseph Stella's Brooklyn Bridge	Who Was Washington A. Roebling?

Books

Search Words: Bridges—History; Brooklyn Bridge; Roebling, Washington; Stella, Joseph

Curlee, Lynn. *The Brooklyn Bridge.* New York: Atheneum for Young Readers, 2001.

Kent, Zachery. *The Story of the Brooklyn Bridge.* Chicago: Children's Press, 1988.

Mann, Elizabeth. *The Brooklyn Bridge: A Wonders of the World Book.* New York: Mikaya, 1996.

Pascoe, Elaine. *Building America: The Brooklyn Bridge.* San Diego: Blackbirch, 1999.

Reier, Sharon. *The Bridges of New York.* Mineola, NY: Dover, 2000.

St. George, Judith. *The Brooklyn Bridge: They Said It Couldn't Be Built.* New York: Putnam, 1982.

Weiner, Vicki. *The Brooklyn Bridge: New York's Graceful Connection.* Chicago: Children's Press, 2004.

Internet

Basic facts about the bridge—http://www.pbs.org/wgbh/buildingbig/wonder/structure/brooklyn.html.

John Roebling's Sons. Take your time. See the history of the family, inventions, and oral histories of employees—http://www.inventionfactory.com/history/index.html.

Brooklyn Bridge Historic Overview—http://www.nycroads.com/crossings/brooklyn/.

Brooklyn Bridge Web site—history, photos—http://www.endex.com/gf/buildings/bbridge/bbridge.html.

Engines of Our Ingenuity presents audio and transcript of John Roebling and the building of the Brooklyn Bridge—http://www.uh.edu/engines/epi87.htm.

The Brooklyn Bridge, articles and photographs written at the opening and during the next 20 years—http://www.catskillarchive.com/rrextra/bbpage.Html.

For the Teacher

PBS presents a lesson plan for educators—http://www.pbs.org/kenburns/brooklynbridge/educators/. Another plan with links—http://www.thirteen.org/edonline/ntti/resources/lessons/h_brooklyn_bridge/.

Building Your Own Bridge

Build your own suspension bridge. Use spaghetti (or balsa wood or toothpicks) and glue. Do a little research on the construction and engineering that make these bridges strong. There are lots of Web pages that will help. We would start here—http://webtech.kennesaw.edu/jcheek3/bridges.htm.

Buffalo Soldiers (1866–1955)

Nearly sixteen months after the end of the Civil War, Section 3 of an Act of Congress entitled "An Act to increase and fix the Military Peace Establishment of the United States" authorized the formation of two regiments of cavalry composed of "colored" men. The act was approved on 28 July 1866. On 21 September 1866, the 9th Cavalry Regiment was activated at Greenville, Louisiana, and the 10th Cavalry Regiment was activated at Fort Leavenworth, Kansas.—The Buffalo Soldiers, http://www.whc.net/buffalo/history.html

Words to Know

Act of Congress
Buffalo Soldiers
Cavalry
Cathy Williams
Colonel Benjamin Grierson
Colonel Edward Hatch

Emanuel Stance
Frontier
Homestead
Private
Regiments
Segregation

Related Jumpstarts

Cattle Drives
Go West, Young Man
Jackie Robinson Breaks Baseball's Color Barrier
Riding in the Back of the Bus
Rough Riders

You Are There

It is 1872. You are 11 years old and you live in the American West with your mother, brothers, and sisters. Your dad is a private in the 9th Cavalry. You help your mother with the homestead so that you can all remain closer to where your father is stationed. He is very brave. He was one of the nine men who rode with Emanuel Stance on a mission to track down and rescue two white children kidnapped by Indians. You are very proud, but you really wish your dad could come home. Life is hard on the frontier.

Topics to Consider

African American Soldiers During the Civil War (North or South)	Children of the Buffalo Soldiers
Buffalo Soldiers and the Indian Wars	Emanuel Stance, Congressional Medalist
Buffalo Soldiers and the Western Frontier	The First Black Peacetime Soldiers
Buffalo Soldiers of the Twentieth Century	Medals of the 10th and 11th Cavalry
Cathy (or Cathay) Williams: Female Buffalo Soldier	What Did the Buffalo Soldiers Do?
	World War II and the Buffalo Soldier

Books

Search Words: African American Soldiers; Buffalo Soldiers; Williams, Cathy

Cox, Clinton. *The Forgotten Heroes: The Story of the Buffalo Soldiers.* New York: Scholastic, 1993.

Flanagan, Alice. *The Buffalo Soldiers.* (We the People). Minneapolis, MN: Compass Point, 2005.

Hooker, Forrestine C. *Child of the Fighting Tenth: On the Frontier with the Buffalo Soldiers.* New York: Oxford University Press, 2003.

Schubert, Frank, Ed. *Voices of the Buffalo Soldier: Records, Reports, and Recollections of Military Life and Service in the West.* Albuquerque: University of New Mexico Press, 2003.

Tucker, Phillip Thomas. *Cathy Williams: From Slave to Female Buffalo Soldier.* Mechanicsville, PA: Stackpole, 2002.

Internet

Buffalo Soldiers and the Indian Wars—http://www.buffalosoldier.net/home.htm.

Buffalo Soldiers on the Western Frontier—http://www.imh.org/imh/buf/buftoc.html.

Buffalo Soldiers: 9th and 10th Cavalry has history—http://www.whc.net/buffalo/history.html.

Cathy Williams: Valuable Documents of the First Female Buffalo Soldier—http://www.buffalosoldier.net/CathayWilliamsFemaleBuffaloSoldierWithDocuments.htm.

Awards of the Buffalo Soldiers of the 9th and 10th Cavalry—http://www.buffalosoldiers.com/MOH.htm.

Vision Quest offers general background and specific information about the Buffalo Soldiers—http://www.vq.com/overview_buffalosoldierhistory.htm.

For the Teacher

Buffalo Soldiers of the nineteenth and twentieth centuries, especially for grades 6–8—http://school.discovery.com/lessonplans/programs/rediscoveringamerica-buffalosoldiers/.

Life as a Buffalo Soldier

Read about the Buffalo Soldiers' life on the frontier, then create a diary of daily life. Include sketches or illustrations of the sites you might see. Write about your comrades and the people you might meet on the trail. Don't forget to include a map. Ask permission to use this project as your report.

Business of Doing Good

Research has shown that people who volunteer often live longer.—Allen Klein, manager of rock and roll performers

Words to Know

Community Service
Give Back Volunteering,
Helping Hand

Service Learning
Volunteerism

Related Jumpstarts

History of Main Street

I Want That! Needs vs. Wants

Marketing to Kids

Peer Pressure

Who Runs Our Town?

You Are There

Throughout our lives many of us volunteer in our community, at church, at work, or in other groups we work or play with. During the summer some families travel to remote areas of the world to work on Habitats for Humanities or other projects. Some spend Thanksgiving or Christmas serving food to the homeless. A number of people have projects they sponsor throughout their lives. They may go to the Animal Shelter and walk the dogs or read to the elderly at nursing homes. Some volunteer in hospitals. Many care deeply about the environment and work on tree planting and other projects. Volunteering is a way to reach out to others. It is a way of saying, "I appreciate the life I have and I'd like to help others because I am so lucky." Helping others makes us feel valued. Many children throughout our country and the world are involved in volunteering—giving back—from an early age. You can be one of them. It is never too early to start.

Topics to Consider

The AIDS Walk, Run for Cancer, Etc.	Our Toys for Tots Project
Feeding the Homeless on Thanksgiving	Taking Pride in America My Way
Habitats for Humanities	Tutoring in Younger Grades
A Journal of My Giving to Others	Ways Kids Can Give Back
My Summer Helping at the Shelter	What Is Volunteering and Community Service?
Our Family Volunteers	Working at the Shelter

Books

Search Words: Community Service; Service Learning; Student Volunteers; Volunteerism

Burchard, Brendan. *The Student Leadership Guide.* 2d ed. Missoula, MT: UMontana, 2003.

Erlbach, Arlene. *The Kids' Volunteering Book.* Minneapolis, MN: Lerner, 1998.

Hurd, Michael. *Grow Up, America.* Washington, DC: Living Resources, 2000.

Kuitenbrouwer, Peter. *7 Secrets of Highly Successful Kids.* (Millennium Generation). Toronto: Lobster, 2001.

Lewis, Barbara A. *The Kid's Guide to Service Projects: Over 500 Service Ideas for Young People Who Want to Make a Difference.* Minneapolis, MN: Free Spiri, 1995.

Partners for Livable Communities. *The Livable City: Revitalizing Urban Communities.* Blacklick, OH: McGraw-Hill, 2000.

Ryan, Bernard. *Protecting the Environment.* (Community Service for Teens: Opportunities to Volunteer). Chicago: Ferguson, 1998.

Wandberg, Robert. *Volunteering: Giving Back.* (Life Skills). Mankato, MN: Capstone, 2002.

Internet

Youth Services America—for youthful volunteers—http://www.ysa.org/index.cfm.

Earn the President's Volunteer Service Award—http://www.nodogroup.com/polf/PSSA/kids.htm.

Y Earth Service Organization. Find the one closest to you and learn more about what service you can do locally—http://www.yesc.org/.

Join the "do something" generation. Ideas for kids—http://www.dosomething.org/.

Good Character.com has many suggestions and links to ways young kids can get involved—http://www.goodcharacter.com/SERVICE/webresources.html.

Zoom into Action by PBS—http://pbskids.org/zoom/grownups/action/resources.html.

Volunteer ideas for kids—http://www.timeforkids.com/TFK/pollzone/story/0,6271,249855,00.html.

Volunteer for Kids from HUD—http://www.hud.gov/kids/people.html.

For the Teacher

Background information about Service Learning. Find a project for your students and teach them the importance of working for others—http://www.goodcharacter.com/SERVICE/primer-1.html. Don't forget the reflection piece. It is the most important.

Become a Star

Do something good AND "Become a Star with Disney" by entering their contest —http://disney.go.com/allstars/index.html. You will find ideas for team and single person entries along with suggestions and past winning entries. Looks like fun for you and your friends. Get ideas here—http://www.idealist.org/kt/volunteercenter.html.

Cattle Drives (1850–1880)

Cattle drives to northern and western markets, and later to railroad-loading facilities, started in earnest in 1866, when an estimated 260,000 head of cattle crossed the Red River from Texas. The drives were conducted for only about 20 years, becoming unnecessary with the advent of the railroads and refrigeration in the 1880s.—Texas Almanac 2006–2007

Words to Know

Barbed Wire	Market
Branding	Quarantines
Cattle Drive	Stampede
Chuck Wagon	Trail Boss
Cook	Wranglers
Drovers	

Related Jumpstarts

Buffalo Soldiers
Coming to America
Custer's Last Stand
Go West, Young Man
Going to Market: From Seed to Sold
Gold Rush
Lewis & Clark Expedition
Oklahoma Land Rush

You Are There

Imagine yourself, 12 to 14 days on the trail; the trail boss, the cook, 11 other crew members and you, driving 2,000 to 3,000 head of cattle from Texas to Kansas. You will travel 10 to 15 miles a day for up to three months. You will sleep rough, manage delays caused by flood-swollen rivers, and during droughts, your thirsty animals will become crazed at the smell of water. You will deal with Indian threats and Texas fever. You will control stampedes caused by lightning or any number of sights, smells, and noises. You will become tired, dirty, and irritable. But in the end it will be worth your hard work. Because when you arrive in Kansas, you and your trail companions will be paid your wages of $60 per month. What a wild time! Yippee!

Topics to Consider

Barbed Wire Fences	End of the Cattle Drive
Cattle Branding	Hardship on the Cattle Drive
Cattle Drive Trails and Settlers	The Making of the Chisholm Trail
Charles Goodnight	On the Trail
Controlling a Stampede	The Round-Up
The Cook's Life on the Trail	Songs of the Cowboy on the Trail
Cowboy's Life on the Trail	Texas Longhorn or Texas Fever

Books

Search Words: Cattle Drives; Cowboys; West—U.S.

Bial, Raymond. *Cow Towns*. (American Community). New York: Children's Press, 2004.

Freedman, Russell. *Cowboys of the Wild West*. New York: Clarion, 1985.

Oatman, Eric. *Cowboys on the Western Trail: The Cattle Drive Adventures of Josh McNabb and Davy Bartlett*. (I Am American). Washington, DC: National Geographic, 2004.

Sanford, William R. *The Chisholm Trail in American History*. (In American History). Berkeley Heights, NJ: Enslow, 2000.

Savage, Jeff. *Cowboys and Cow Towns of the Wild West*. (Trailblazers of the Wild West). Springfield, NJ: Enslow, 1995.

Stanley, Jeffrey. *Cowboys and Longhorns*. New York: Crown, 2003.

Internet

Texas Almanac gives an overview of cattle drives; good for a background search—http://www.texasalmanac.com/history/highlights/cattle/.

Cattle men and drives, firsthand tales, and more—http://www.skyways.org/orgs/fordco/rath2/11.html.

Texas Longhorn Cattle Drives by One Sky Ranch has brief information and pictures—http://www.oneskyranch.com/drives.htm.

Missouri Beef History from 1839 to 1904. Information about the pre-Civil War cattle drives is interesting; also includes facts about Texas Fever and treatments—http://ag.missouristate.edu/mobeef.htm.

History of Cowboys and Cattle Drives, a true Texan tale told firsthand—http://www.forttumbleweed.com/cattledrives.html.

History of Barbed Wire includes essays—http://www.barbwiremuseum.com/barbedwirehistory.htm.

For the Teacher

Up the Trail without a Lasso is a social studies mapping lesson on the cattle trails, railroads, and grazing lands of the early cattle industry—http://www.nps.gov/grko/lessonUpthetrail.htm.

Hitting the Trail

- Today, many ranches in the West allow tenderfoot cowboys to experience cattle drives. There are several advertised on the Internet. See *Cattle Drives in Colorado*—http://www.hiddentrails.com/usa/cd/co.htm.

- Have a popcorn and soda movie night at your house. Invite your friends for a sleepover and enjoy *City Slickers* and *City Slickers II*. (Don't forget about *Red River* with John Wayne.)

Photograph (retouched) by the author, 2005.

Changing Family (1950–2000)

The family. We were a strange little band of characters trudging through life sharing diseases and toothpaste, coveting one another's desserts, hiding shampoo, borrowing money, locking each other out of our rooms, inflicting pain and kissing to heal it in the same instant, loving, laughing, defending, and trying to figure out the common thread that bound us all together.—Erma Bombeck, *Family: The Ties That Bind—and Gag,* 1987

Words to Know

Adoption　　　　　　Heritage
Blended Families　　　Media
Coping Techniques　　Multiracial Families
Divorce　　　　　　　Nuclear Family
Dysfunctional　　　　Stepfamilies

Related Jumpstarts

Cultures and Cuisines

Fighting Prejudice

I Want That! Needs vs. Wants

Marketing to Kids

Peer Pressure

Religions of the World

You Are There

As a child in the 1950s, you watch the *Adventures of Ozzie and Harriet* on television. Harriet is always dressed beautifully as she cooks and cleans the house and is almost always right. Meanwhile Ozzie, the father, is bumbling and confused, but he is still the undisputed master of the house. The boys get into the kinds of trouble that kids do, but the problem is always solved by the end of the show. Lesson learned. Ten years later, as a child in the 1960s, you watch *My Three Sons.* There is no mother; instead, it is a single-parent household! But still, there is someone to take care of the three boys in the form of Bub, their grandpa. A few years later, a single mother takes the stage in *The Lucy Show.* Do any of these examples sound like your family?

Topics to Consider

Changing Family in the History of Television	Media and Prejudice
Compare Television Families to Real Families in America	Mothers at Work—Children at Day Care
	My Nuclear Family
Explore the Reasons for the Changing Family	Rights and Responsibilities of Family Members
Importance of the Family Today	Television's Portrayal of Ethnic Groups

Books

Search Words: Adoption; Family Relationships; Stepfamilies

Bingham, Jane. *Why Do Families Break Up?* (Exploring Tough Issues). Chicago: Raintree, 2004.

Kuklin, Susan. *Families*. New York: Hyperion, 2006.

McGregor, Cynthia. *Jigsaw Puzzle Family: The Stepkids' Guide to Fitting It Together.* (Rebuilding Books, for Divorce and Beyond). Atascadero, CA: Impact, 2005.

Nemiroff, Mark A., and Jane Annunziata. *All about Adoption: How Families Are Made and How Kids Feel about It.* Washington, DC: American Psychological Association, 2003.

Internet

The Adventures of Ozzie and Harriet showed the idealized American family in the 1950s—http://www.museum.tv/archives/etv/A/htmlA/adventuresof/adventuresof.htm.

My Three Sons explored single parenthood for the first time in the 1960s—http://www.museum.tv/archives/etv/M/htmlM/mythreesons/mythreesons.htm.

The Lucy Show depicted single parenthood with a mother as the head of household in the 1960s—http://www.timvp.com/lucyshow.html.

The Brady Bunch introduced blended families in the 1970s, and reruns are still being shown—http://www.bradyworld.com/cover/history.htm.

Trends in the American family, with statistics, from the Population Resource Center—http://www.prcdc.org/summaries/family/family.html.

The U.S. Department of State has several articles on the changing American family—http://usinfo.state.gov/journals/itsv/0101/ijse/toc.htm.

For the Teacher

Working with Parents: A Survival Guide for New Teachers from the U.S. Department of Education offers tips on hitting it off with parents—http://www.ed.gov/teachers/become/about/survivalguide/parent.html.

Your Family

Explore your family through pictures. Create a scrapbook of a special family event, like a wedding. Include aunts and uncles. You can use PBS's scrapbook template to help—http://www.pbs.org/americanfamily/.

23

Charles Lindbergh: Spirit of St. Louis (1927)

There, under my left wing, only five or six miles distant, a coastline parallels my course. . . . But I'm in the mid-Atlantic, nearly a thousand miles from land! Half-formed thoughts rush through my mind. Are the compasses completely wrong? Am I hopelessly lost? Is it the coast of Labrador or Greenland that I see? Have I been flying north instead of east?—Charles Lindbergh, The Spirit of St. Louis

Words to Know

Aviator
Barnstorming
Center of Gravity
Cruising Speed
Daredevil
Fuselage
Monoplane

Navigation
Parachuting
Periscope
Runway
Transatlantic
Wingspan
Wingwalking

Related Jumpstarts

The American Industrial Revolution

Doughboys, Flying Aces, and Hello Girls

Man on the Moon

You Are There

You and your family are at Roosevelt Field in New York. You got up early this morning to see the famous pilot and barnstormer, "Lucky" Lindbergh, take off on a flight to Paris. Just imagine, flying an airplane all the way across the Atlantic Ocean, 3,635 miles! And he's going to do it all by himself. You look at the airplane, just 27 feet long with a single engine. What will he do if the engine breaks down? What will he do if he gets too tired to fly? Even though he set records flying here from California, at 110 miles per hour it will take him about 30 hours to cover the distance. As the airplane takes off, rising just barely high enough to miss the telephone wires, you and the rest of the crowd cheer.

Topics to Consider

Amelia Earhart	Principles of Flight
Anne Morrow Lindbergh	Right to Privacy
Daredevil Flying in the 1920s	*Spirit of St. Louis*
Early Airmail Service (1920s)	Training to Become an Aviator
Growth of the Airline Industry	Transatlantic Flight
Kidnapping of His Son	Was Lindbergh a Hero?
Lindbergh's Early Life	World War I Fighter Planes

 From *99 Jumpstarts for Kids' Social Studies Reports: Research Help for Grades 3–8* by Peggy J. Whitley and Susan Williams Goodwin. Westport, CT: Libraries Unlimited. Copyright © 2007.

Books

Search Words: Air Pilots; Lindbergh, Charles A.; Transatlantic Flights

Hansen, Ole Steen. *Amazing Flights: The Golden Age.* (Story of Flight). New York: Crabtree, 2003.

Hixson, Walter L. *Charles A. Lindbergh, Lone Eagle.* (Library of American Biography). New York: Pearson Longman, 2007.

Lindbergh, Charles A. *The Spirit of St. Louis.* New York: Scribner, 1953.

Meachum, Virginia. *Charles Lindbergh: American Hero of Flight.* (People to Know). Berkeley Heights, NJ: Enslow, 2002.

Monroe, Judy. *The Lindbergh Baby Kidnapping Trial: A Headline Court Case.* (Headline Court Cases). Berkeley Heights, NJ: Enslow, 2000.

Pisano, Dominic. *Charles Lindbergh and the Spirit of St. Louis.* Washington, DC: Smithsonian Air and Space Museum, 2002.

Wagner, Heather Lehr. *Charles Lindbergh.* (Famous Flyers). Philadelphia: Chelsea House, 2003.

Internet

A PBS site on Charles Lindbergh tells you about his plane, *The Spirit of St. Louis*, and the kidnapping of his son—http://www.pbs.org/wgbh/amex/Lindbergh/.

Explore Lindbergh's career as an aviation pioneer, including parachuting, barnstorming, and airmail delivery—http://www.charlesLindbergh.com/.

Worldbook tells you about the principles of flight, building an airplane, and two heroes of aviation, Lindbergh and Amelia Earhart—http://www.worldbookonline.com/wb/Article?id=ar009700&st=Earhart+Lindbergh.

Learn all about the kidnapping of Charles Lindbergh Jr., including a comic strip about the case, from *The Huntertown County Democrat*—http://www.nj.com/Lindbergh/.

The Smithsonian Institution's *Milestones of Flight* gives details and a picture of *The Spirit of St. Louis*—http://www.nasm.si.edu/exhibitions/gal100/stlouis.html.

The Museum of Unnatural Mystery explores Amelia Earhart's life and disappearance—http://www.unmuseum.org/earhart.htm.

For the Teacher

The Library of Congress Community offers lesson plans for exploring *From Fantasy to Flight*, including Lindbergh, Earhart, and the Wright Brothers—http://memory.loc.gov/learn/community/cc_flight.php.

A Taste of Hitory

Build a model of *The Spirit of St. Louis*. It will help you to understand how the airplane was designed. You can find model kits, or download this pattern to make it out of cardstock—http://nmwg.cap.gov/santafe/Activities/Spirit.htm. Or use an experimental plane design—http://www.ag.ohio-state.edu/~flight/.

24

Child Labor

Tragically, more than 200 million children today have no hope of benefiting from the dynamic worldwide economy because they are locked in a degrading, dead-end subculture of child labor. Many of these children, who are between the ages of five and 14 work under exploitive conditions including abduction by armed bands to serve as soldiers; being trafficked into commercial sexual exploitation; and being exposed to extreme workplace hazards and disease.—Steven Law, deputy secretary of the U.S. Department of Labor

Words to Know

Child Labor
Civil Rights
Exploitation
Hazardous
Human
Indenture

Industrialization
International Labor Organization (ILO)
Outsourcing
Reform Movements
Rights Regulate

Related Jumpstarts

American Sweatshops
I Want That! Needs vs. Wants
King Cotton
Poverty in America
Supply and Demand

You Are There

Your teacher has asked that each student find something he or she can learn about and become involved in, something that could result in helping to change the world. You recently read an article that stated that over 246 million children between the ages of 5 and 17 are working. Most come from very poor families, and large numbers of them work in commercial agriculture, fishing, manufacturing, mining, and domestic service. Some even work in illegal activities like the drug trade or serving as soldiers. You have been wondering what you can do to help change this. It seems a good way for you to become a thoughtful citizen of the world. Write about it. Find pictures that illustrate your points. Think about the law. What can you do?

Topics to Consider

Child Labor during the Industrial Revolution	Indentured Servants
Child Labor in Mexico (or Vietnam, or Kenya, or China)	Orphans (The Orphan Trains)
	Story of a Particular Child—
Child Labor in the U.S. from 1900 to 1940	Research This First
Child Miners (or Farm Workers, or Servants)	Sweatshops in New York
The Hazards of Child Labor (Health, Accidents, etc.)	Treatment of Children at Work
History of Child Labor Laws in U.S.	Victorian Working Children

Books

Search Words: Child Labor; Labor Statistics (use Juvenile)

Bartoletti, Susan Campbell. *Kids on Strike!* Boston: Houghton Mifflin, 2003.

Freedman, Russell. *Kids at Work: Lewis Hine and His Campaign against Child Labor.* New York: Clarion Books, 1998.

Kielburger, Craig. *Free the Children! A Young Man's Personal Crusade.* New York: HarperCollins, 1998.

Parker, David L. *Stolen Dreams: Portraits of Working Children.* Minneapolis, MN: Lerner, 1998.

Roberts-Davis, Tanya, ed. *We Need to Go to School: Voices of the Rugmark Children.* Toronto: Douglas & McIntyre, 2001.

Internet

Child Labor 1908–1912. Photographs by Lewis W. Hines covering children in a variety of jobs—http://www.historyplace.com/unitedstates/childlabor/.

Free the Children Web site. Learn more about an organization that is helping children worldwide. View the videos—http://www.freethechildren.com/index.php.

History of Child Labor in the United States—an excellent place to start. Includes a time line and laws—http://www.continuetolearn.uiowa.edu/laborctr/child_labor/about/us_history.html.

Child Labor in Factories during the Industrial Revolution—excellent information—http://nhs.needham.k12.ma.us//cur/Baker_00/2002_p7/ak_p7/childlabor.html.

Ending Child Labor—information about child labor today. By Steven Law, from the U.S. Department of Labor—http://usinfo.state.gov/journals/ites/0505/ijee/law.htm.

ILO World Day Against Child Labor—activities, statistics, and other information from the world organization—http://www.ilo.org/public/english/standards/ipec/wdacl/2006/index.htm.

Library of Congress *Child Labor in America* has an excellent collection of primary sources and links—http://memory.loc.gov/learn/lessons/98/labor/resource.html#Child%20Labor%20in%20History.

For the Teacher

Use the Library of Congress *Lesson Plans on Child Labor in America* for a complete primary source experience—http://memory.loc.gov/learn/lessons/98/labor/plan.html.

For the Student

Take a little time learning about child labor around the world. Study the videos of children from India, Indonesia, Mexico, and Kenya at work. Try the scavenger hunt and the quiz—http://teacher.scholastic.com/scholasticnews/indepth/child_labor/child_labor/.

Civil War Spies

In the Civil War both Union and Confederacy extensively engaged in clandestine activities. They acquired intelligence from clandestine agents, military scouts, captured documents, intercepted mail, decoded telegrams, newspapers, and interrogations of prisoners and deserters.—Central Intelligence Agency, https://www.cia.gov/cia/ciakids/history/american_history.shtml

Words to Know

Clandestine
Contraband
Crazy Bet
Espionage
Hot Air Balloons
Intelligence
Interrogation

Morse Code
Reconnaissance
Special Agent
Telegraph
Turncoat
Undercover

Related Jumpstarts

Buffalo Soldiers
Missouri Compromise
Underground Railroad
Women at War

You Are There

You are a slave to a Southern general. He and the other high-ranking soldiers usually act as if you are not even there. They are so used to slaves waiting on them that they don't even see you. Once that bothered you, but now you are happy that they don't notice you. While you serve their dinner and wait on them, filling their plates and glasses, you listen carefully to their talk about the war. They are going to send a small battalion to the east to fool the Union. They hope the Union officers will follow—or not pay attention to the fact that the rest of the Confederates will go another direction to attack from behind. You hear names of towns and generals, and you memorize them. Later, when the officers leave or go to sleep, you will slip out into the night and pass on the information you have learned. The master thinks he has control of you. Little does he know that you are really in control of his destiny!

Topics to Consider

Allan Pinkerton	Secret Service for the Union
Elizabeth Van Lew, "Crazy Bet"	Signal Bureau of the Confederacy
Freedom of the Press	Slaves Spying for the North
Harriet Tubman	What Life Was Like for a Spy
Hot Air Balloons for Reconnaissance	Women Spies for the Confederacy
How Intelligence Changed War	Women Spies for the Union
Mary Bowser, Former Slave	

Books

Search Words: Spies—United States; United States—History—Civil War—Secret Service

Historical Times Encyclopedia of the Civil War. New York: Harper & Row, 1986.

Nofi, Albert A. *Spies in the Civil War.* (Untold History of the Civil War). Philadelphia: Chelsea House, 2000.

Phillips, Larissa. *Women Civil War Spies of the Confederacy.* (American Women at War). New York: Rosen, 2004.

Poleskie, Stephen. *The Balloonist: The Story of T.S.C. Lowe, Inventor, Scientist, Magician and Father of the U.S. Air Force.* Savannah, GA: Frederic C. Bell, 2006.

Sakaney, Lois. *Women Civil War Spies of the Union.* (American Women at War). New York: Rosen, 2004.

Internet

Women spies on both sides of the Mason Dixon line are reviewed in this site from About.com—http://womenshistory.about.com/library/misc/cw/bl_cw_spies_union.htm.

CJ's Civil War site gives the biographies of Civil War spies, including blacks and women—http://www.wtv-zone.com/civilwar/spy.html.

Professor T. S. C. Lowe made reconnaissance balloons for the Union army. Here is his description—http://www.civilwarhome.com/balloons.htm.

Civil War Spies—http://www.civilwarhome.com/spies.htm.

History of American Intelligence from the Central Intelligence Agency (CIA)—https://www.cia.gov/cia/ciakids/history/american_history.shtml.

Balloons in the Civil War, from the American Centennial of Flight—http://www.centennialofflight.gov/essay/Lighter_than_air/Civil_War_balloons/LTA5.htm.

The story of Mary Bowser, a slave who worked in the Confederate White House and spied for the Union—http://www.npr.org/programs/morning/features/2002/apr/served/.

For the Teacher

Ladies, Contraband and Spies: Women in the Civil War by the Library of Congress American Memories uses primary sources to explore the roles of women in the Civil War. Lesson plans and resources—http://memory.loc.gov/learn/lessons/01/spies/index.html.

Communicate in Code

Many spies use a code to communicate. It helps if the enemy doesn't know the code in case they intercept the message, but even a simple code can help. Try communicating with a friend in code. Some suggestions—http://ww.nationalgeographic.com/ngkids/trythis/secretcodes/.

26

Cold War (1949–1989)

With the end of the Second World War, two hostile alliances emerged—one led by the United States and the other influenced by the Soviet Union. These nations emerged out of the holocaust of war, determined never to be taken by surprise as they were in 1941. The best way they knew how to protect themselves was to build alliances that served as a protective shield around them.—Korean War Veterans' Memorial 2002, http://www.nps.gov/kwvm/war/coldwar.htm

Words to Know

Atomic Bomb	Iron Curtain
Berlin Airlift	Joseph Stalin
Blacklist	MAD (Mutually Assured Destruction)
Capitalism	McCarthyism
Cold War	Nikita Khruschev
Communism	Socialism
Fallout Shelter	Truman Doctrine

Related Jumpstarts

9/11
Becoming a Citizen
Donkeys and Elephants
Fighting Prejudice
The First Amendment

You Are There

Duck and cover. As a child in the 1950s, you are worried about war with the Soviet Union. At school, you have bomb drills. When the warning bell rings, the whole class files out into the hall, the lights are turned off, and you sit on the floor with your head between your knees and your arms over your head. At home, you have a fallout shelter in your basement. It has thick walls and shelves stocked with food and water. If an atomic bomb is dropped near you, your whole family plans to go into the fallout shelter, close the door, and wait until the radiation levels go down so it is safe to go outside. You have never had to use your fallout shelter. You don't know of anyone who was in a bombing zone. But still you worry.

Topics to Consider

Atomic Bomb	First Amendment Rights
Berlin Wall	Hollywood and McCarthy
The Cold War	Korean War
Communism vs. Capitalism	McCarthyism
Cuban Missile Crisis	NATO (North American Treaty Organization)
Edgar R. Murrow and McCarthy	Soviet Union
Fallout Shelters	Two Chinas

Books

Search Words: Berlin Wall; Cold War; Communism; World Politics

Brooks, Phillip. *The McCarthy Hearings.* (20th Century Perspectives). Chicago: Heinemann, 2005.

Hatt, Christine. *The End of the Cold War.* (Cold War). Milwaukee, WI: World Almanac, 2002.

Keeley, Jennifer. *Containing the Communists: America's Foreign Entanglements.* (American War Library. Cold War Series). San Diego: Lucent, 2003.

Tracy, Kathleen. *The Fall of the Berlin Wall.* (Monumental Milestones). Hockessin, DE: Mitchell Lane, 2005.

Whiting, Jim. *The Cuban Missile Crisis: The Cold War Goes Hot.* (Monumental Milestones). Hockessin, DE: Mitchell Lane, 2006.

Internet

CNN has an interactive roadmap to the Cold War, including espionage tools, the space race, and the Internet—http://www.cnn.com/SPECIALS/cold.war/.

The Cold War Museum has online exhibits, including stories and pictures, and a time line—http://www.coldwar.org/.

HistoryWiz has a *Cold War Multimedia Exhibit*—http://www.historywiz.com/coldwar.htm.

PBS explains McCarthyismand the House Committee on Un-American Activities—http://www.pbs.org/wnet/americanmasters/database/mccarthyism.html.

Cold War Culture from CBS includes fallout shelters, the Cuban Missile Crisis, and nuclear warfare, in the form of radio and television shows—http://archives.cbc.ca/IDD-1-71-274/conflict_war/cold_war/.

The Hollywood blacklist examined: *A Different Look at the 1947 HUAC Hearings*—http://www.moderntimes.com/palace/blacklist.htm.

For the Teacher

The CBC Archives offers activities at different grade levels, including *Civil Defense or Nuclear Disarmament* and *What Was the Cold War About?*—http://archives.cbc.ca/ACT-1-71-274/conflict_war/cold_war/educational_activities/.

Prepare for the Worst

If you needed to stock a fallout shelter, what would be important? Try to plan for a stay of two weeks. Include food and water, a battery operated radio, and, of course, something to do. For more ideas—http://members.aol.com/rafleet/fallout.htm.

27

Colonial Williamsburg (1699)

The creation of an American identity began in the early 1600s, when the first English settlers landed in Virginia. The evolution of a separate American identity took place in towns like Williamsburg under British rule during the colonial era, and it spread as a unifying national force with the onset of the Revolution.—American Park Network, *Colonial Williamsburg History*

Words to Know

Blacksmith
Bray School
Carriage
Colonial Life
Ducking Stool
House of Burgesses
Loyalist

Middle Plantation
Pillory Post
Stamp Act
Tory
Tradesmen
Virginia Gazette

Related Jumpstarts

13 Colonies

Abigail Adams

Aboard the *Mayflower*

Coming to America

Pilgrim Harvest

Salem Witch Trials

You Are There

It is 1699. You and your family live in the newly named town of Williamsburg, which had been called Middle Plantation. You attend a one-room schoolhouse, learning reading, writing, and arithmetic. You use a horn book for your textbook. You memorize verses from the Bible. You use a quill pen to write on birch bark. You never misbehave because you do not want to sit in the corner wearing a dunce hat. When school is over, you have several chores to do. You feed the animals, bring in wood for the fire, and help your mother hang clothes on the outside clothesline. But plenty of time remains for fun with friends. You have fun trundling the hoop, stilt walking, jumping rope, lawn bowling, and leapfrogging.

Topics to Consider

African American Experience in Williamsburg	Life in Jamestown, Virginia, or Another Colonial Town
Colonial America Food (or Clothing)	
Forming a Government in Williamsburg	Making a Living in Williamsburg
George Washington Slept Here	A Newspaper for Williamsburg
Going to School in Colonial America	The People of Williamsburg, 1699
The History of the Dudley Digges House	Williamsburg Becomes the Capital

 From *99 Jumpstarts for Kids' Social Studies Reports: Research Help for Grades 3–8* by Peggy J. Whitley and Susan Williams Goodwin. Westport, CT: Libraries Unlimited. Copyright © 2007.

Books

Search Words: Colonial America; Colonial Williamsburg; Williamsburg

Alter, Judy. *Williamsburg.* (We the People). Minneapolis, MN: Compass Point, 2003.

Burgan, Michael. *The Stamp Act of 1765.* (We the People). Minneapolis: Compass Point, 2005.

Coleman, Wim, and Pat Perrin. *Colonial Williamsburg.* (Virtual Field Trips). Berkeley Heights, NJ: Myreportlinks.com, 2005.

Cooke, Jacob Ernest, and Milton M. Klein, eds. *North America in Colonial Times: An Encyclopedia for Students.* (4 vols.). New York: Scribner's, 1998.

Kent, Zachary. *Williamsburg.* (Cornerstones of Freedom). Chicago: Children's Press, 1992.

Wood, Peter H. *Strange New Land: Africans in Colonial America.* New York: Oxford University Press, 2003.

Internet

History of Colonial Wlliamsburg has modern-day pictures, but covers the history of this city completely. Look all through this site (don't miss the photographs and video clips) for your topic—http://www.history.org/Foundation/cwhistory.cfm.

American Park Network has excellent and easy to understand information about the formation of Williamsburg and its history—http://www.americanparknetwork.com/parkinfo/cw/history/.

Colonial America Food Timeline and Description—http://www.foodtimeline.org/foodcolonial.html.

Colonial Kids by Thinkquest—http://library.thinkquest.org/J002611F/index.htm.

Law in Colonial America has information about morals, ethics, laws, and punishment—http://www.uncp.edu/home/canada/work/allam/16071783/law.htm.

Mrs. Ann Wager was the teacher and founder of Bray School for African American students in Williamsburg—http://research.history.org/Historical_Research/Research_Themes/ThemeReligion/Wager.cfm and http://www.williamsburgpostcards.com/other/other178.htm (This Old House).

For the Teacher

Discovery School has several excellent lesson plans for different grade levels —http://school.discovery.com/lessonplans/programs/revwar4/.

Try an Internet Quiz

Have fun researching the Internet to answer questions about life in colonial times—http://www.kn.pacbell.com/wired/fil/pages/huntcolonialer2.html.

Columbus Discovers America (1492)

In fourteen hundred ninety-two
Columbus sailed the ocean blue.
He had three ships and left from Spain;
He sailed through sunshine, wind and rain.
He sailed by night; he sailed by day;
He used the stars to find his way.

—Traditional rhyme

Words to Know

Arakawa Indians	Mutiny
Cabin Boy	Native Americans
Caribbean	Navigation
Exploration	Sea Monsters
Horizon	Spices
Indigenous	Trade Routes

Related Jumpstarts

Aboard the *Mayflower*

The Fountain of Youth

Indian Tribes in Your State

Life in the Middle Ages

Mayan Mathematicians

Mesa Verde Cliff Dwellings

You Are There

You have been chosen to be a cabin boy for Christopher Columbus. From the time you were little, you have wanted to go to sea. You want to know what is beyond the horizon. Is the world flat, as most people believe? When the ship gets to the horizon, will it fall off the edge? And when you get far from land, is it true that the water is filled with dragons and sea monsters? You have always wondered, and now you will learn for yourself! But as the journey goes on, you begin to think this trip wasn't such a good idea. It has been so long since anyone has seen land! Some of the crew are threatening to mutiny if Columbus doesn't turn around and return to Spain. The admiral said, "Just three more days and we'll turn back if we don't see land." But what is this? A bird? A bird! Land must be just over the horizon!

Topics to Consider

Arakawa Indians	Fifteenth-Century Ships
Clothing of the Time	Foods of the New Eorld
Columbus as a Boy	Life Aboard the *Santa Maria*
Columbus Day Celebrations	Marco Polo
Compare the Four Voyages	Navigation
Discovering the World Is Round	Other Early Explorers

Books

Search Words: America, Discovery and Exploration; Columbus, Christopher; Explorers

Doak, Robin S. *Christopher Columbus: Explorer of the New World.* (Signature Lives). Minneapolis, MN: Compass Point, 2005.

Kneib, Martha. *Christopher Columbus: Master Italian Navigator in the Court of Spain.* (Library of Explorers and Exploration). New York: Rosen, 2003.

Sundel, Al. *Christopher Columbus and the Age of Exploration in World History.* (In World History). Berkeley Heights, NJ: Enslow, 2002.

Internet

Social Studies for Kids tells you about Columbus's life and has a time line—http://www.socialstudiesforkids.com/subjects/columbus.htm.

Parts of the *Journal of Christopher Columbus,* in which he describes his first exchanges with the natives—http://www.fordham.edu/halsall/source/columbus1.html.

The Columbus Navigation Homepage explains how Columbus found his way across the uncharted Atlantic Ocean—http://www.columbusnavigation.com/.

Learn about the foods Columbus and his sailors ate and how they prepared them—http://www.castellobanfi.com/features/story_3.html.

Hero History tells you about Columbus's life, his four voyages, and the new trade route he established—http://www.imahero.com/../../herohistory/christopher_herohistory.htm.

The Florida Museum of Natural History explores the possibilities about what really happened and where Columbus really went—http://www.flmnh.ufl.edu/caribarch/columbus.htm.

The European Voyages of Exploration discusses the reasons for Columbus's journeys and the impact they had on future explorations—http://www.ucalgary.ca/applied_history/tutor/eurvoya/columbus.html.

For the Teacher

Beyond Columbus; Teaching the Lessons of 1492 offers several ideas for a Columbus Day study, from Education World—http://www.education-world.com/a_curr/curr167.shtml.

A Taste of History

Live and work on the *Santa Maria*. A replica of Columbus's ship lies on the Scioto River in Columbus, Ohio, and offers an opportunity to live the life of a fifteenth-century sailor for a night. If you want to make it back, you'd better follow the first mate's orders! For more details—http://www.santamaria.org/overnight_program.php.

Coming to America

"Keep your ancient lands, your storied pomp," cries she
With silent lips. "Give me your tired, your poor,
Your huddled masses yearning to breathe free,
The wretched refuse of your teeming shore;
Send these, the homeless, tempest-tost to me,
I lift my lamp beside the golden door."

—Emma Lazarus, "The New Colossus," 1883

Words to Know

Emigration	Melting Pot
Immigration	Pogroms
Inspector	Tuberculosis
Language Barrier	

Related Jumpstarts

Aboard the *Mayflower*
America's Melting Pot
Becoming a State
Border Patrol
Columbus Discovers America
Cultures and Cuisines
Where Cities Bloom

You Are There

You stand at the rail of the ship that has brought you from Europe. You are steaming into New York Harbor. The Statue of Liberty greets you, welcoming you to America! But that is not where you get off the ship. You journey on to Ellis Island. You're almost in America, but not quite. First you have to pass through all the government inspectors. The officials want to make sure you are not sick. As your family comes into a great hall, you stay close to your mother, carrying everything you own in a small pillowcase. The hall is huge and frightening. Nobody around you speaks your language. You don't know what they are saying as they question you again and again. Finally they give you a card that says "Admitted." You made it! You are one of the lucky ones. You will become an American!

Topics to Consider

Angel Island	Compare Immigration Today to 100
Arriving at Ellis Island	Years Ago
Africans	Mail Order Brides
Asians	People Who Were Misnamed
Irish	Statue of Liberty
Italians	Tell Your Family's Immigration Story
Mexicans	Why Did They Come?
Russians	

From *99 Jumpstarts for Kids' Social Studies Reports: Research Help for Grades 3–8* by Peggy J. Whitley and Susan Williams Goodwin. Westport, CT: Libraries Unlimited. Copyright © 2007.

Books

Search Words: Emigration and Immigration; Immigrants, United States

American Immigrant Cultures: Builders of Nations. (2 vols.). Edited by David Levinson and Melvin Ember. New York: Macmillan Reference, 1997.

Collier, Chris, and James Lincoln Collier. *A Century of Immigration: 1820–1924.* (Drama of American History). New York: Marshall Cavendish, 2000.

Gale Encyclopedia of Multicultural America: Primary Documents. (2 vols.). Detroit: Gale, 1999.

Ingram, W. Scott. *Japanese Immigrants.* (Immigration to the United States). New York: Facts on File, 2005.

Worth, Richard. *Mexican Immigrants.* (Immigration to the United States). New York: Facts on File, 2005.

Internet

Take an interactive tour of Ellis Island courtesy of Scholastic—http://teacher.scholastic. com/activities/immigration/tour/index.htm.

The National Park Service tells you all about the Statue of Liberty—http://www. nps.gov/stli/.

The History Channel exhibit on Ellis Island tells you what it was like and has statistics and a chronology—http://www.historychannel.com/exhibits/ellisisle/reborn.html.

Students have built a ThinkQuest site on immigration that includes different nationalities, a time line, and even comics—http://library.thinkquest.org/20619/index.html .

An introduction to immigration from the Library of Congress, including primary source documents—http://memory.loc.gov/ammem/ndlpedu/features/immig/immigration_ set1.html.

Asian immigrants processed into the country through Angel Island in San Francisco— http://www.angelisland.org/immigr02.html.

For the Teacher

Several challenging ideas for incorporating the Internet into lessons on Ellis Island and beyond, from the University of South Carolina—http://www.libsci.sc.edu/ miller/EllisIsland.htm.

A Taste of History

Today, immigrants no longer enter the United States through Ellis Island or Angel Island. They may come by air, sea, or land. See if you can find someone who immigrated. Maybe it is someone in your class, or one of your relatives. Interview that person. Plan the questions you want to ask ahead of time. Some suggestions are: Why did you come? How did you get here? What differences have you found between the United States and your native country? What do you miss most? What do you like most here? Get more ideas at http://www.campsilos.org/excursions/grout/one/ act10.htm.

Cultures and Cuisines

American food began to distinguish itself from its European and British origins at the end of the 18th century, as the young nation developed its own cultural, political, and domestic traditions. Soon, American cookbooks would reflect the use of bountiful native ingredients, such as corn, squash, and cranberries.—Carl A. Koch Library, Cornell University 2002, http://rmc.library.cornell.edu/food/american_taste.htm

Words to Know

Chinatown
Chopsticks
Cookery
Cuisine
Culture
Ethnic
Heritage
Immigrants
Melting Pot
Pot Luck
Seasonings
Spices
Vegetarianism

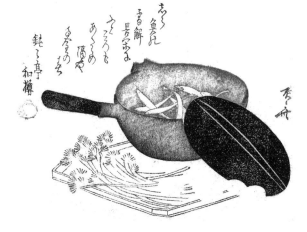

Related Jumpstarts

America's Melting Pot

Becoming a Citizen

Colonial Williamsburg

Coming to America

Pilgrim Harvest

You Are There

When you and your family boarded the ship for America, you brought enough food with you to last for the journey. Now that you have arrived in your new land, you go out to buy food for your family. But what different foods they have! As you walk through the streets of the city, you find the Italian part of town, where people eat towering mounds of spaghetti! You walk through the Irish part of town, where everyone is boiling potatoes and corned beef. You pass through Chinatown, the Asian area, watching people scoop rice and seaweed into their mouths with chopsticks. Doesn't anyone here have food like you had back home? How will this new food taste? Why are there so many types of food? Learn more.

Topics to Consider

Ceremonial Meals	History of the Turkey in America
Corn and How It Is Used in Different Cultures	Pioneer Cooking
	Thanksgiving
Food and Festivals	Vegetarianism
Food from Your Heritage	Who Brought Pizza to America? Tacos?
Foods Native to the Americas	Why Is Food Important in Your Culture?

Books

Search Words: Cookery, American; Dinners and Dining, United States; Food Habits, United States

Ancona, George. *Mi comida = My Foods.* New York: Children's Press, 2005.

Gunderson, Mary. *Cowboy Cooking.* (Exploring History Through Simple Recipes). Mankato, MN: Blue Earth, 2000.

Gunderson, Mary. *Southern Plantation Cooking.* (Exploring History Through Simple Recipes). Mankato, MN: Blue Earth, 2000.

Ichord, Loretta Frances. *Skillet Bread, Sourdough and Vinegar Pie: Cooking in Pioneer Days.* Brookfield, CN: Millbrook Press, 2003.

Parnam, Vanessa Roberts. *The African-American Child's Heritage Cookbook.* So. Pasadena, CA: Sandcastle, 1993.

Internet

The American Memories Site of the Library of Congress offers recipes from various American immigrant groups in the *Great American Potluck*—http://memory.loc.gov/learn/features/immig/ckbk/table_of_contents.html.

Menus and recipes of Africa from the University of Pennsylvania—http://www.africa.upenn.edu/Cookbook/about_cb_wh.html.

Not by Bread Alone, America's Culinary Heritage, from Cornell University, has the early history of American food—http://rmc.library.cornell.edu/food/.

Compare agriculture, the growing of food, from 1845 and today, from Harvest of History, the Farmers' Museum of Cooperstown, New York—http://www.harvestofhistory.org/.

Thanksgiving Day History—http://www.thanksgivingworld.com/thanksgiving-history.html.

For the Teacher

National Geographic has a lesson plan for cultures and cuisines—http://www.nationalgeographic.com/xpeditions/lessons/10/g68/fastfood.html. After exploring the cuisine of a particular country, students design a fast-food restaurant for that culture.

A Taste of History

Have a cultural feast! Host a party and ask everyone to bring one dish of food from their cultural heritage. If they would rather, they can bring something from a culture they admire. At the party, encourage everyone to be open-minded and try every dish. Maybe you could have prizes for the people who try everything. Yahoo has a guide to cooking of the world—http://dir.yahoo.com/Society_and_Culture/Food_and_Drink/Countries_and_Cultures/. It's full of information but you may need adult assistance.

Custer's Last Stand (1876)

The Battle of the Little Bighorn was the most successful action fought by the American Indians against the United States Army in the West. It was part of the Spring Campaign of 1876, an effort by the United States Government to force the Sioux and Cheyenne tribes onto their Reservations. The Indians' defeat of the finest cavalry unit in the United States Army had the same shocking effect then as the Challenger *explosion had on the nation in 1986. It simply was not supposed to happen.—Little Bighorn Association, http://www.lbha.org/*

Words to Know

Crazy Horse   Massacre
Indian Encampment   Renegade
Lieutenant Colonel George Custer   Scout
Little Bighorn   Sioux Indians
Major Marcus Reno   Sitting Bull

Related Jumpstarts

Buffalo Soldiers

Cattle Drives

Gold Rush

Indian Tribes in Your State

Mesa Verde Cliff Dwellings

Trail of Tears

You Are There

Your father is a lieutenant in the 7th Cavalry. Your mother, brothers, sisters, and you are in Kansas, waiting to hear if he survived the massacre. "There are not enough Indians in the world to defeat the Seventh Cavalry," stated Colonel Custer. The 7th Cavalry had 647 men, so no one considered that Custer might be wrong. Custer graduated last in his class at West Point. Ten years ago, he was court-martialed with seven charges against him. Next, he got into trouble for using poor judgment by sending men into danger unnecessarily. But Custer was brave, if foolish, and he worked hard. So he was asked to take charge of a group of soldiers to trap the Sioux and Cheyenne Indians and return them to the reservation. They met the Indians at Little Bighorn. It was a massacre, and Custer and many of his men were killed.

Topics to Consider

Benteen and the Buffalo Soldiers	The Lakota Indians
Causes of the Battle of Little Bighorn	Leaving the Reservation (Sioux)
Courts-Martial after the Battle at Little Bighorn	Life in the American West
	Living on the Great Sioux Reservation
Custer Biography	The Myth: Was Custer Right or Wrong?
Crazy Horse	Should Custer Have Led the 7th?
Describing the Battle of Little Bighorn	Sitting Bull
Finding Artifacts: After the Battle	

Books

Search Words: American Indian Battles; Battle of Little Bighorn; Custer's Last Stand; Lakota Indians; Names of People; Sitting Bull

Iannone, Catherine. *Sitting Bull: Lakota Leader.* (Book Report Biography). New York: Franklin Watts, 1998.

Link, Theodore. *George Armstrong Custer: General in the U.S. Cavalry.* (Primary Sources of Famous People in American History). New York: Rosen, 2004.

Russell, Jerry L. *1876 Facts about Custer & the Battle of the Little Big-Horn.* (Facts About). Reading, MA: Perseus, 1999.

Stein, R. Conrad. *The Battle of the Little Bighorn.* (Cornerstones of Freedom). New York: Children's Press, 1997.

Theunissen, Steve. *The Battle of the Little Bighorn.* (The American West). Broomall, PA: Mason Crest, 2003.

Internet

Eyewitness to History describes the battle—http://www.eyewitnesstohistory.com/custer.htm.

We Caught 'em Napping. Print if you have trouble reading because of the background. Be sure to look at the picture gallery—http://www.mohicanpress.com/battles/ba04001.html.

Custer's Last Stand and Beyond—http://www.sonofthesouth.net/union-generals/custer/custers-last-stand.htm.

BBC's *Custer and the Battle at Little Bighorn*—http://www.bbc.co.uk/history/war/custer_battle_01.shtml.

Archeology at Battle of Little Bighorn shows methods of finding artifacts and truth about the battle—http://www.cr.nps.gov/mwac/libi/index.html.

One of the best sites for information is Garryowen.com. Listen to the song that Custer's troop played—http://www.garryowen.com/.

For the Teacher

Suite 101 always does a good job of gathering resources for teachers. Battle of Little Big Horn plan—http://www.suite101.com/lesson.cfm/17638/1152/1.

A Taste of History

Research, then draw the battle or create a board with plastic soldiers and Indians. Fill in as much information as you can. Play *Garryowen* to get into the mood—http://www.garryowen.com/.

Dealing with Disaster

The key principle should be to give all adults able and willing to work access to training and a guaranteed job in the clean-up and rebuilding process. By doing so we will give them a stake in their future and the skills and opportunities they need to rebuild their lives for the long run.—Thomas A. Kochan, following Hurricane Katrina

Words to Know

Assessment
Disaster Plan
FEMA (Federal Emergency
    Management Agency)
Flooding
Home Land Security

NOAA (National Oceanographic and
    Atmospheric Administration)
Patrol
Recovery
Security

Related Jumpstarts

Border Patrol
Great Chicago Fire
Poverty in America
Trail of Tears
Yellow Fever Attacks Philadelphia

You Are There

Where do you live? What kind of potential disasters are there for your home and town? Flooding? Fire? Hurricane winds? Tornados? Ice storms? Blizzards? We live in Houston. Nearly every year we have to deal with the results of flooding; because there is too much rain or because a hurricane arrives. Sometimes we drive through deep water to get to the doctor or to the grocery store. Schools close. Often we go without lights for long periods of time. Even so, there are worse disasters. New Orleans and the Mississippi and Louisiana shore had worse when Hurricane Katrina came through and devastated the area. California and Colorado have terrible fires that move at alarming rates. Whole towns in Oklahoma, Kansas, and northern Texas are leveled by tornados in their rush across the sky. What is being done to help cope with the results of disasters? What is FEMA? Who are the local agencies involved in clean-up? The Red Cross? The Salvation Army? Find out the preventive measures the people in your area have for dealing with disaster.

Topics to Consider

After the Flood	Our School Security Plan
All about FEMA	The Red Cross or the Salvation Army
Dealing with Disaster, a Personal Story	The Tornado That Whizzed Through Our Town
Flooding Near Our Town—A City Plan	What If a Hurricane Come?
How to Assess the Damage	What If the Fire Reaches Our Town?
NOAA: Weather Watchers	What Is Home Land Security?

Books

Search Words: Hurricanes; Natural Disasters; Tornadoes

Boskey, Madeline. *Natural Disasters: A Chapter Book.* (True Tales). New York: Children's Press, 2003.

Ceban, Bonnie J. *Tornadoes: Disaster & Survival.* (Deadly Disasters). Berkeley Heights, NJ: Enslow, 2005.

Haulley, Fletcher. *The Department of Homeland Security.* (This Is Your Government). New York: Rosen, 2005.

Miller, Debra. *Hurricane Katrina: Devastation on the Gulf Coast.* (Lucent Overview). San Diego: Lucent, 2006.

O'Connor, Rebecca K., ed. *How Should the World Respond to Natural Disasters?* Farmington Hills, MI: Greenhaven, 2006.

Parry, Ann. *Red Cross.* (Humanitarian Organizations). Philadelphia: Chelsea, 2005.

Internet

FEMA for Kids has good background information—http://www.fema.gov/kids/dizarea.htm.

The Disaster Center has information about disasters at a glance—http://www.disastercenter.com/.

NOAA, weather watchers, warnings, and forecasts—http://www.noaa.gov/wx.html.

Flood Smart and *Flood Safety* are both government pages on how to deal with flooding conditions—http://floodsmart.gov and http://floodsafety.gov.

The Red Cross—http://redcross.org or The Salvation Army—http://www.salvationarmyusa.org/.

FEMA's *Are You Ready?* Three-step plan—http://www.fema.gov/areyouready/.

Homeland Security for Kids (Nevada) has great links—http://homelandsecurity.nv.gov/kids.htm.

Food safety in case of a disaster and power outages—http://www.foodsafety.gov/.

US Search and Rescue for Kids has excellent links to information for preparing for all types of disasters—http://www.ussartf.org/childrens_education_games.htm.

The Forces of Nature is an excellent site—http://library.thinkquest.org/C003603/english/index.shtml.

For the Teacher

Natural Disasters: Same Forces, Different Impacts. Select the grade level—by National Geographic—http://www.nationalgeographic.com/xpeditions/lessons/15/g68/.

Ready for Disaster

Ready Kids—http://www.ready.gov/kids/home.html—is a great place for you to learn the skills that make you ready for every disaster. The more you know, the safer you are and the less you worry. When you have completed your plan, show your parents the helpful adult information—http://www.ready.gov.

Declaration of Independence (1776)

We hold these truths to be self-evident, that all men are created equal, that they are endowed by their Creator with certain unalienable Rights, that among these are Life, Liberty and the pursuit of Happiness.—Declaration of Independence

Words to Know

American Revolution
Declaration of Independence
Edmund J. Randolph
George Mason

Independence Hall
James McClurg
Loyalist
Preamble

Related Jumpstarts

13 Colonies
Abigail Adams
Aboard the *Mayflower*
Right to Vote
Writing theConstitution

You Are There

It is 1776 and you live in Philadelphia with your family. Everyone seems to be talking about the rules the British monarchy has made for the colonies. The British government has raised taxes. People are getting mad. They don't want to pay taxes to a country far away. They want to make their own rules. They are talking about writing a document that declares their intention of being free from England. They will make their own government. Recently, a group of men representing all 13 colonies met to begin writing what will become the Declaration of Independence. Thomas Jefferson has been asked to write the first draft. You wander down to Chestnut Street between 5th and 6th Streets with friends so you can hear the daily news. Everyone wants to know what is happening. When will the signing take place?

Topics to Consider

America's Founding Fathers (Franklin, Jefferson, Washington, and Others)	Life, Liberty, and the Pursuit of Happiness
Any Related topic Leading up to the Declaration. For a List Go to http://www.ushistory.org/declaration/related/ index.htm	The Preamble—What Is It? What Does It Mean?
	Signing His John Hancock
Biography of a Signer	Spy Letters of the American Revolution
The Continental Congress	Thomas Jefferson
History of Graff House	What about George, James, and
Life in Philadelphia in 1776	Edmund? (the Nonsigners)
	Why Separate from England?

From *99 Jumpstarts for Kids' Social Studies Reports: Research Help for Grades 3–8* by Peggy J. Whitley and Susan Williams Goodwin. Westport, CT: Libraries Unlimited. Copyright © 2007.

Books

Search Words: American Revolution; Continental Congress; Declaration of Independence; Independence Day; Jefferson, Thomas (or Other Signer)

Brenner, Barbara. *If You Were There in 1776.* (If You Were There). New York; Simon & Schuster, 1994.

Fradin, Dennis. *The Signers: The 56 Stories Behind the Declaration of Independence.* New York: Walker, 2002.

Fritz, Jean. *Will You Sign Here, John Hancock?* New York: Putnam, 1996 (reissue).

Quiri, Patricia Ryon. *The Declaration of Independence.* (True Books: Government). NewYork: Children's Press, 1999.

Stein, Conrad. *The Declaration of Independence.* (Cornerstone of Freedom). New York: Children's Press, 1995.

Volo, Dorothy Denneen, and James M. Volo. *Daily Life during the American Revolution.* Westport, CT: Greenwood, 2003.

Internet

Start with this video—http://www.earlyamerica.com/independence.htm.

U.S.History.org has basic information, the text, and links to all background topics needed for a good report—http://www.ushistory.org/declaration/document/index.htm.

Colonial Hall and the Signers: John Hancock—http://www.colonialhall.com/hancock/hancock.php.

Spy Letters of the American Revolution—http://www.si.umich.edu/spies/.

American History Revolution—http://www.kidinfo.com/American_History/American_Revolution.html.

KidPort—http://www.kidport.com/RefLib/UsaHistory/AmericanRevolution/AmerRevolution.htm.

Life During the 18th Century—pick a topic—http://www.history.org/Almanack/life/life.cfm.

Archiving Early American History. Excellent information—http://www.history.org/Almanack/life/life.cfm.

For the Teacher

We the People Learning Page from Library of Congress has excellent information for both teachers and students—http://memory.loc.gov/learn/community/cc_wethepeople.php.

Writing the Declaration

Play some of the games and learn more about the Declaration—http://www.quia.com/jg/79190.html. Find two or three friends and write your own Declaration of Independence.

If you wanted to declare freedom to create your own classroom government, what would your declaration include? Don't forget to write an introduction, or preamble.

Donkeys and Elephants: A Two-Party System

[C]artoonist Thomas Nast is credited with making the donkey the recognized symbol of the Democratic Party. It first appeared in a cartoon in Harper's Weekly in 1870, and was supposed to represent an anti-Civil War faction. But the public was immediately taken by it and by 1880 it had already become the unofficial symbol of the party. ...(he) was also responsible for the Republican Party elephant. In a cartoon that appeared in Harper's Weekly in 1874, Nast drew a donkey clothed in lion's skin, scaring away all the animals at the zoo. One of those animals, the elephant, was labeled "The Republican Vote." That's all it took for the elephant to become associated with the Republican Party.—InfoPlease Daily Almanac, http://www.infoplease.com/askeds/4-18-00askeds.html

Words to Know

Conservative	Political Symbols
Electoral College	Politics
Federalist	Legislative Branch
Platform	Liberal
Political Parties	Whigs

Related Jumpstarts

Political Cartoons

Right to Vote

Who Runs Our Town?

You Are There

As one of the 5,000 delegates chosen to represent your political party from your state, you arrive at the convention center ready to celebrate your candidate for president of the United States. For four days, you and all the other delegates from all 50 states and 6 territories will discuss the candidate, the party platform, and the election campaign. Everyone agrees that your candidate is the best, and you're all having a wonderful time. The news media are there, too, to report on the issues, so smile! You may be on television.

Topics to Consider

Democrats	Political Debates
Electoral College	Political Symbols
Federalists and Anti-Federalists	Republicans
Political Cartoons	Thomas Nast
Political Conventions	A Two-Party System

Books

Search Words: Political Parties, United States; Third Parties (United States Politics)

Fish, Bruce, and Betty Durost Fish. *The History of the Democratic Party*. (Your Government: How It Works). Philadelphia: Chelsea, 2000.

Landau, Elaine. *Friendly Foes: A Look at Political Parties*. (How Government Works). Minneapolis, MN: Lerner, 2004.

Lutz, Norma Jean. *The History of Third Parties*. (Your Government: How It Works). Philadelphia: Chelsea, 2000.

Payan, Gregory. *The Federalists and Anti-federalists: How and Why Political Parties Were Formed in Young America*. (Life in the New American Nation). New York: Rosen, 2004.

Understanding Government: The Legislative Branch (videorecording). Thousand Oaks, CA: Goldhill, 2000.

Internet

The *American Memories* site of the Library of Congress explains the two-party system—http://memory.loc.gov/learn/features/election/partysys.html.

How did Republicans pick the elephant and Democrats the donkey? C-Span explains—http://www.c-span.org/questions/week174.htm .

Congress for Kids explains political parties—http://congressforkids.net/Elections_politicalparties.htm.

Republican National Committee home page—http://www.rnc.org/.

Democratic Party home page—http://www.democrats.org/.

The origin of the Electoral College, from Election Atlas—http://uselectionatlas.org/INFORMATION/INFORMATION/electcollege_history.php.

The History Learning site explains one-party, two-party and multiparty political systems—http://www.historylearningsite.co.uk/party_systems.htm.

For the Teacher

The *Federal Register* has extensive information on the Electoral College, including historic election results and lesson plans—http://www.archives.gov/federal-register/electoral-college/index.html.

Join the Party!

Get involved in a political campaign! If you have a candidate whom you feel would be good for your community, go to campaign headquarters and learn all about the issues. Volunteer to pass out flyers and put up signs supporting your candidate. You may have to get one of your parents involved, too. To find out who your representatives are and where they are getting their money, go to http://www.opensecrets.org/states/index.asp.

Doughboys, Flying Aces, and Hello Girls (1914–1918)

In winter I get up at night,
and have to scratch by candle-light;
In summer, quite the other way;
I have to scratch the livelong day.
A soldier boy should never swear
When coots are in his underwear,
Or underneath his helmet label—

At least, as far he is able.
The trench is so full of a number of coots,
I'm actually growing quite fond of the brutes.

— Franklin P. Adams.
"A Cootie's Garden of Verses,"
The Stars and Stripes, April 26, 1918

Words to Know

Aces
Doughboys
Foxholes
General John J. Pershing
Great

Hello Girls
Musketry
Signal Corp Operators
Switchboard
War Trenches

Related Jumpstarts

Prohibition and Gangsters
Rosie the Riveter
Rough Riders
Women at War
Women on the Home Front

You Are There

Dear Mom and Dad, we landed in France though I can't say where. We have been here for a week and I haven't been in the trenches yet. I'm a musketry instructor, so am having a good time of it. I've been chumming around with a boy from Kansas who is like me, about 19 years old. He has been in France for 16 months. He belongs to the cyclist corps, has seen considerable roughing but very little fighting. I miss your cooking. Thanks for the warm sox you sent—put brownies in your next care box. Tell Greg to stay in school. I will fight for the country. He should get an education. Your loving son, John.

Topics to Consider

Doughboys of WWI	A Hero of WWI—(Any Person)
Eddie Rickenbacher, Flying Ace	In the Trenches with the Doughboys
Fighting in the Trenches	Pershing's Doughboys
Flying Aces of WWI	Stars and Stripes Newspaper of WWI
General John J. Pershing	Tomb of the Unknown Soldier
Hello Girls—The Signal Corp Operators	WWI Overview

Books

Search Words: Doughboys; Flying Aces; Hello Girls; World War I—Juvenile

American Doughboys: Heroes of World War I (videorecording). Los Angeles: OnDeck, 2004.

Bosco, Peter. *World War I.* (America at War). New York: Facts on File, 2003.

Greenwald, Maurine Weiner. *Women, War, and Work: The Impact of World War I on Women Workers in the United States.* Ithaca, NY: Cornell University Press, 1990.

McGowen, Tom. *World War I.* (First Book). Danbury, CT: Franklin Watts, 1993.

Mead, Gary. *Doughboys: America and the First World War.* Woodstock, NY: Overlook, 2000.

Wucovits, John F. *Flying Aces.* (American War Library). Farmington Hills, MI: Lucent, 2002.

Internet

This World War I site is a good starting-place, with many links—http://www. uen.org/themepark/liberty/wwi.shtml.

Biographies and Diaries from Doughboys, Aces, and Hello Girls of World War I. Photos and links to these heroes—http://www.worldwar1.com/dbc/biograph.htm.

Eddie Rickenbacker, top ace of WWI—http://www.acepilots.com/wwi/us_ rickenbacker.html.

WWI—Trenches is worth taking time to navigate—http://www.worldwar1.com/.

Tomb of the Unknown Soldier, Arlington Cemetery, and fact sheets—http://www.mdw. army.mil/.

Use search for your particular topic or browse—http://www.eyewitnesstohistory.com/ w1frm.htm.

Hello Girls—http://www.worldwar1.com/dbc/hello.htm or http://www.jung-soul.com/ Hello-Girls.html.

Legendary Aces & Aircraft of WWI includes people and planes—http://www. acepilots.com/wwi/main.html.

Aces of WWI, includes biography and victories—http://www.wwiaviation.com/ aces/aces.html.

World War I links by subject—http://www.teacheroz.com/wwi.htm.

Stars and Stripes Newspaper of World War I—This paper from American Memory, Library of Congress, was written for and by the soldiers—http://rs6.loc.gov/ammem/ sgphtml/sashtml/sashome.html.

For the Teacher

World War I, 14 lessons—http://collections.ic.gc.ca/history_units/Mindy-ww1/ ww1_01.htm.

Tracking Sergeant Barr

Enjoy the diary, photographs, and letters of Sergeant Weldon M. Barr, U.S. Army. Use a world map and follow Sergeant Barr from Franklin, Pennsylvania, through his discharge in Fort Dix. Don't forget to read the introductory paragraph if you are to track his entire journey—http://www.sheilascorner. com/waropening.shtml.

Dust Bowl (1930)

And then the dispossessed were drawn west—from Kansas, Oklahoma, Texas, New Mexico; from Nevada and Arkansas, families, tribes, dusted out, tractored out. Car-loads, caravans, homeless and hungry; twenty thousand and fifty thousand and a hundred thousand and two hundred thousand. They streamed over the mountains, hungry and restless—restless as ants, scurrying to find work to do—to lift, to push, to pull, to pick, to cut—anything, any burden to bear, for food. The kids are hungry. We got no place to live. Like ants scurrying for work, for food, and most of all for land.—John Steinbeck, Grapes of Wrath

Words to Know

Black Blizzards   Hoovervilles or Shanty Towns
Caravans   Migrant Workers
Depression   New Deal
Drought   Okies
Dust Bowl   Soil Erosion
Farm Security Administration (FSA) Camps

Related Jumpstarts

American Sweatshops   Banking   Child Labor
Going to Market: From Seed to Sale   Great Depression   King Cotton
Oklahoma Land Rush   Poverty in America   Supply and Demand
Telling America's Story with Photographs

You Are There

It is 1936. You are 10 years old. Your family has owned a small farm in Oklahoma since the 1889 Land Rush when Oklahoma was still a territory. For the past two years your farm has been drying up. First came the record-breaking heavy rains, blizzards, tornadoes, and floods. Then the drought. Now the wheat your family grows has been carried away by the dust storms. Even the dirt has blown away. Broke, your family packs everything they can into their old Ford truck and head to California. Neighbors and school friends are part of the caravan as you travel west. Promises of work make everyone hopeful. It is a long journey. Will you get to the land of plenty?

Topics to Consider

Causes of the Dust Bowl	Migrant Workers in California
Farming in the 1930s	President Roosevelt and the Dust Bowl
Government Programs for Migrants	Schools for the Dust Bowl Children
The Great Depression	Stories from Dust Bowl Migrants
Hoovervilles and the Dust Bowl	What Farmers Learned from the Dust Bowl
Journal of the Trip West	What Was the Dust Bowl?
Life in a FSA Camp	

    From *99 Jumpstarts for Kids' Social Studies Reports: Research Help for Grades 3–8* by Peggy J. Whitley and Susan Williams Goodwin. Westport, CT: Libraries Unlimited. Copyright © 2007.

Books

Search Words: Droughts (use Juvenile); Dust Bowl

Janke, Katelan. *Survival in the Storm: The Dust Bowl Diary of Grace Edwards.* (Dear America). New York: Scholastic, 2002. (fiction)

Levey, Richard H. *Dust Bowl: The 1930's Black Blizzards.* (X-treme Disasters That Changed America). New York: Bearport, 2005.

McArthur, Debra. *The Dust Bowl and the Depression in American History.* (In American History). Berkeley Heights, NJ: Enslow, 2002.

Stanley, Jerry. *Children of the Dust Bowl: The True Story of the School at Weedpatch Camp.* New York: Crown, 1992.

Steinbeck, John. *Harvest Gypsies.* Berkeley, CA: Heyday, 2002.

Internet

The Dust Bowl Timeline from PBS. Audios, transcripts, and other information about this horrible period in American history—http://www.pbs.org/wgbh/amex/dustbowl/timeline/index.html.

University of South Dakota has an excellent site. Includes information about causes. Take time for the videos and link to *Wind Erosion* from Kansas State University—http://www.usd.edu/anth/epa/dust.html.

1930 Dust Bowl, excerpts from *The Dust Bowl, Men, Dirt and Depression,* by Paul Bonnifield—http://www.ptsi.net/user/museum/dustbowl.html.

The Migrant Experience from American Memory—http://memory.loc.gov/ammem/afctshtml/tsme.html.

The Dust Bowl from Humanities-Interactive has pictures with descriptions, essays, and activities—http://www.humanities-interactive.org/texas/dustbowl/.

EH.net Encyclopedia article, "What Was the Dustbowl?" Be sure to click through to the photographs—http://www.eh.net/encyclopedia/article/Cunfer.DustBowl.

Farming in the Thirties—http://www.livinghistoryfarm.org/farminginthe30s/farminginthe1930s.html.

For the Teacher

American Memory Collection Connection—*Voices from the Dust Bowl.* Excellent background—http://memory.loc.gov/ammem/ndlpedu/collections/vdb/history.html.

A Dust Bowl Photo Essay

This is a wonderful topic for a project like collecting photographs and creating a photo essay. Write a description of each. Document people, places, and the land. Start (but don't end) your selection at http://history1900s.about.com/library/photos/blyindexdepression.htm.

37

Election of Abraham Lincoln (1861)

I do solemnly swear (or affirm) that I will faithfully execute the office of President of the United States, and will to the best of my ability, preserve, protect and defend the Constitution of the United States.—Oath of the President

Words to Know

Election
Emancipation Proclamation
Inauguration
Lincoln-Douglass Debates
Majority

Martial Law
National Republican Party
Secession
Slavery
Voting

Related Jumpstarts

Civil War Spies

Donkeys and Elephants

Fighting Prejudice

The President Has Been Shot!

Telling America's Story with Photographs

Women at War

You Are There

Abraham Lincoln has been elected president of the United States. Even though Lincoln won the majority of votes in every state east of the Rocky Mountains except New Jersey, he will not have an easy time running the country. Slavery and other issues threaten to divide the country. However, Monday, March 4, 1861, was a big day for Abraham Lincoln and for America—and especially for you and your family. You will be going into Washington to watch the new president take the oath of office. You and your family stand in the huge crowd. Lincoln leaves the Willard Hotel, which is near the White House, in a horse-drawn carriage bound for the Capitol. Here he comes—he will pass very close to where you are standing. Lincoln gives a stirring address, calling for compromise. One month later war comes.

Topics to Consider

Abe Lincoln and the Civil War	Inauguration of Abraham Lincoln
Abraham Lincoln, President	Inauguration Speeches: 1861 and 1865
Abraham Lincoln Presidential Library	Lincoln and the Emancipation Proclamation
Becoming a President	On the Campaign Trail
History of the Lincoln Penny	Young Abe Lincoln

From *99 Jumpstarts for Kids' Social Studies Reports: Research Help for Grades 3–8* by Peggy J. Whitley and Susan Williams Goodwin. Westport, CT: Libraries Unlimited. Copyright © 2007.

Books

Search Words: Lincoln, Abraham (add Juvenile to limit)

Harness, Cheryl. *Abe Lincoln Goes to Washington 1837–1863.* Washington, DC: National Geographic, 2003. (See also *Young Abe Lincoln: The Frontier Days 1809–1837.*)

Lincoln, Abraham. *Abraham Lincoln the Writer: A Treasury of His Greatest Speeches and Letters.* Edited by Harold Holzer. Honesdale, PA: Boyds Mills, 2000.

Marrin, Albert. *Commander in Chief: Abraham Lincoln and the Civil War.* New York: Dutton, 2003.

Olson, Steven P. *Lincoln's Gettysburg Address.* (Great Historical Debates and Speeches). New York: Rosen Central Primary Source, 2005.

Schoen, Douglas. *On the Campaign Trail: The Long Road of Presidential Politics, 1860–2004.* New York: Regan, 2004.

Internet

American Presidents.org has good information including on the campaign trail. Take your time, this is one of the best—http://www.americanpresident.org/history/abrahamlincoln/biography/.

Electing Lincoln—http://www.durand.k12.wi.us/hs/history/ElectingLincoln/ElectingLincoln.htm.

Mr. Lincoln's Whitehouse is a good starting point—http://www.mrlincolnswhitehouse.org/.

Speech by Lincoln at inauguration, 1861—http://illinoisissues.uis.edu/features/2005jan/oath.html and http://www.bartleby.com/124/pres31.html; 1865 inaugural speech— http://www.bartleby.com/124/pres32.html.

The White House Web site for presidents—http://www.whitehouse.gov/history/presidents/al16.html.

The inauguration of Lincoln—http://www.americaslibrary.gov/cgi-bin/page.cgi/jb/civil/lincoln2_1.

Abraham Lincoln Research has much information from a past history teacher. He will also answer any questions you have on Lincoln—http://members.aol.com/RVSNorton/Lincoln2.html.

History of the penny—http://www.pennies.org/history/intro.html.

The Presidential Library—http://www.alplm.org/.

For the Teacher

Have your students publish their art and writings about Lincoln. Or send them to Berwick Academy and they will publish them on their own site—http://www.berwickacademy.org/lincoln/lincoln.htm.

Hitting the Campaign Trail

It would be fun to follow Abraham Lincoln on the campaign trail when he ran for president of the United States. No Air Force One jet was available. How did Lincoln get from place to place? No television or radio was available. How did the crowds know he was coming to their town? Make a chart or a map, gather pictures, or even run a mock campaign.

Fighting Prejudice

We are each burdened with prejudice; against the poor or the rich, the smart or the slow, the gaunt or the obese. It is natural to develop prejudices. It is noble to rise above them.—Author unknown, http://www.quotegarden.com/prejudice.html

Words to Know

Bias   Race
Bigotry   Respect
Discrimination   Skinheads
Diversity   Stereotypes
Ethno-violence   Tolerance
Individuality

Related Jumpstarts

Buffalo Soldiers

Peer Pressure

Religions of the World

Underground Railroad

You Are There

You and your family have recently arrived in America. You come from Pakistan, where life was very hard. You are Muslim. Except for your brothers and you, there is not another Pakistani in your entire school. You look different because your skin is dark. You speak differently because you learned English in Pakistan from a British teacher. You have a heavy accent and you don't know American slang that the students often use. A couple of the students tease you because you are different. You go home and cry. You love school, but sometimes you beg your mother to let you stay home. One day, a pretty girl in your class asks you to sit with her at lunch. She asks you about Pakistan. She wants to learn about your native country. She actually wants to get to know you better. She believes that you are lucky to be different from the other children. Finally there is someone who likes you because you are you. Will this be what it takes to help you feel that you are becoming an American? Will others accept you? Will they see what makes you special? Yes, they will.

Topics to Consider

Advantages of Diversity	Ghettos
Affirmative Action	Glass Ceiling
Any Famous Civil Rights Leader	Melatonin, or Why Some Skin Is Darker
Are Girls Smarter Than Boys?	Than Others
Comparative Religion	Racial Prejudice
Genetics and Race	What Causes Prejudice?

From *99 Jumpstarts for Kids' Social Studies Reports: Research Help for Grades 3–8* by Peggy J. Whitley and Susan Williams Goodwin. Westport, CT: Libraries Unlimited. Copyright © 2007.

Books

Search Words: Prejudices; Racism; Toleration (use Juvenile to limit)

Davidson, Tish. *Prejudice.* (Life Balance). New York: Franklin Watts, 2003.

Gay, Kathlyn. *Cultural Diversity: Conflicts and Challenges: The Ultimate Teen Guide.* (It Happened to Me). Lanham, MD: Scarecrow Press, 2003.

Lamachia, John. *So What Is Tolerance Anyway?* (Students' Guide to American Civics). New York: Rosen, 2002.

Lester, Julius. *Let's Talk about Race.* New York: HarperCollins, 2005.

Levy, Debbie. *Bigotry.* (Lucent Overview). San Diego: Lucent, 2002.

Popcorn Park Puppets. *Groark Learns about Prejudice* (videorecording). (Getting Along with Groark). San Francisco: Live Wire Media, n.d.

Internet

KidsHealth defines diversity, prejudice, and respect for others—http://kidshealth.org/kid/grow/tough_topics/diversity.html.

The Prejudice Institute has a study on prejudice in children, considering when and how they learn prejudice. The Fact Sheets also discuss ethno-violence and skinheads—http://www.prejudiceinstitute.org/childrenandprejudice.html.

The American Psychological Association lists 10 things you can do about prejudice—http://www.apa.org/pi/oema/racism/q17.html.

What is prejudice? And more specifically, what is racial prejudice? Gender prejudice? Religious prejudice? Explore these ideas with Kids' Health—http://www.cyh.com/HealthTopics/HealthTopicDetailsKids.aspx?p=335&np=286&id=2348.

The Two Towns of Jasper, by PBS, shows what happens when prejudice gets out of hand—http://www.pbs.org/pov/pov2002/twotownsofjasper/.

Thinkquest's site, *Why Is My Loyalty Questioned?*, explores the prejudice against Japanese Americans during World War II—http://library.thinkquest.org/CR0210341/.

For the Teacher

The Anti-Defamation League discusses the ways children learn to be prejudiced and what you can do to help them learn to embrace differences—http://www.adl.org/ctboh/default.asp. PBS also has four lesson plans on combating prejudice—http://www.pbs.org/pov/pov2002/twotownsofjasper/classroom.html.

Do Your Part

Take the first step in trying to rid yourself of prejudice. Try to go seven days and seven nights without saying anything bad about *anybody*. The Scary Guy will inspire you to get started—http://www.thescaryguy.com/

From *99 Jumpstarts for Kids' Social Studies Reports: Research Help for Grades 3–8* by Peggy J. Whitley and Susan Williams Goodwin. Westport, CT: Libraries Unlimited. Copyright © 2007.

The First Amendment

Congress shall make no law respecting an establishment of religion, or prohibiting the free exercise thereof; or abridging the freedom of speech, or of the press; or the right of the people peaceably to assemble, and to petition the Government for a redress of grievances.—U.S. Constitution—First Amendment

Words to Know

Amendment	Freedom of Assembly
Bill of Rights	Freedom of Press
Constitution	Freedom of Religion
Establishment	Freedom of Speech
Freedom	Freedom to Petition the Government

Related Jumpstarts

Becoming a Citizen

Jury System

Political Cartoons

Right to Vote

Writing the Constitution

You Are There

A constitution is a written document establishing the laws and principles by which an organization is governed. The U.S. Constitution is the document that describes the government of the United States. It spells out the power and duties of its citizens and leaders. When the original constitution caused people to complain, the Bill of Rights was added (1791). The First Amendment was one of these additions. It protects the rights of citizens to have their own religion, say or print what they want, get together for any reason, and even ask the government to consider their issues. These are rights that make us free. The First Amendment has been challenged many times. Learn more about those challenges and what the courts decided. Remember, this document was written 200 years ago—and is still argued about today.

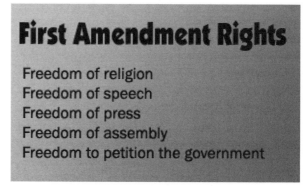

First Amendment Rights

Freedom of religion
Freedom of speech
Freedom of press
Freedom of assembly
Freedom to petition the government

From *99 Jumpstarts for Kids' Social Studies Reports: Research Help for Grades 3–8* by Peggy J. Whitley and Susan Williams Goodwin. Westport, CT: Libraries Unlimited. Copyright © 2007.

Topics to Consider

Any Recent Decision about the First Amendment	Five Freedoms
The Bill of Rights	History of the First Amendment
Describe Each Freedom in One Paper	Right to School Prayer
Explain the Amendment in Your Own Simple Terms	Select One of the "Rights"
	Time Line of Court Decisions

Books

Search Words: Bill of Rights; First Amendment; U.S. Constitution—Juvenile

Abrams, Floyd. *Speaking Freely: Trials of the First Amendment.* New York: Viking, 2005.

Day, Nancy. *Censorship or Freedom of Expression?* Minneapolis, MN: Lerner, 2001.

Farish, Leah. *The First Amendment: Freedom of Speech, Religion, and the Press.* (Constitution). Springfield, NJ: Enslow, 1998.

Gold, Susan Dudley. Engel v. Vitale: *Prayer in the Schools.* New York: Marshall Cavendish, 2006.

Horn, Geoffrey M. *The Bill of Rights and Other Amendments.* (Library of American Government). Milwaukee, WI: World Almanac, 2004.

McGlone, Catherine. New York Times v. Sullivan *and the Freedom of the Press Debate: Debating Supreme Court Decisions.* Berkeley Heights, NJ: Enslow, 2005.

Internet

Ben's Guide to the US for Kids—Easy to understand guide. Choose your grade level, then historical documents—http://bensguide.gpo.gov/index.html.

Cornell Law School has an explanation of the First Amendment for older students, with decisions and materials—http://www.law.cornell.edu/wex/index.php/First_amendment#federal_material.

First Amendment Schools—good information and activities—http://www.firstamendmentschools.org/.

Charters of Freedom has information from the Declaration of Independence through the Amendments. Find out what led up to the writing of the First Amendment at this excellent Web page—http://www.archives.gov/national-archives-experience/charters/charters.html.

The Bill of Rights with the amendments—http://usinfo.state.gov/usa/infousa/facts/funddocs/billeng.htm.

For the Teacher

Education World Lesson Plans has an excellent plan to help your class and school become a First Amendment School—http://www.educationwold.com/a_admin/admin/admin298.shtml

Mock Trial

One of the most satisfying things you will do in school is to argue for (or against) a principle. Get a few friends together and argue for and against one of the First Amendment freedoms. The most obvious one for schools is whether school prayer should be allowed. Look at both sides of the issue. Do your homework. Get a moderator. Ask your teacher if you can do this for the class. Get started with a guide to mock trials—http://www.19thcircuitcourt.state.il.us/bkshelf/resource/mt_conduct.htm.

Flower Children (1964–1972)

If you're going to San Francisco
Be sure to wear some flowers in your hair
If you're going to San Francisco
You're gonna meet some gentle people there.

—John Phillips. "San Francisco," 1967

Words to Know

Afro (Hairstyle)   Neo-hippie
Baby Boomers   Psychedelic
Civil Disobedience   Sit-ins
Counterculture   Students for a Democratic Society (SDS)
Haight Ashbury   Summer of Love
Hippies   Vietnam War
National Guard   Woodstock Festival
Make Peace, Not War

Related Jumpstarts

Fighting Prejudice
Lives and Times of My Grandparents
Marketing to Kids
Peer Pressure
The President Has Been Shot!
Religions of the World

You Are There

It is 1965. You are tired of hearing about war. It seems like there is just one war after another. Why, you think, can't people just love one another and be friends? What are wars really about? Your friends feel the same way. You decide to show how you feel by having a sit-in on the courthouse steps. You and your friends bring signs saying, "Peace Now." Sometimes you walk around with your sign and chant slogans like, "Bring our troops home." Sometimes you just sit on the steps. You are in the way if someone wants to go into the courthouse, and that is just fine with you. You want people to notice your protest. The police come and ask you to move, but all of you stay where you are. You have a wreath of flowers in your hair. You take one out and give it to a policeman.

Topics to Consider

Back-to-Nature Lifestyle	Peace Movement
Civil Disobedience	Rock and Roll Music
Hippies and Flower Children	Sit-ins
Flower Children and the Civil Rights Movement	Students and Cultural Change
	Vietnam War
Living in Communes	Woodstock Festival

Books

Search Words: Nineteen Sixties; United States History 1961–1969; Vietnam War 1961–1975

Feinstein, Stephen. *The 1960's from the Vietnam Era to Flower Power.* (Decades of the 20th Century). Berkeley Heights, NJ: Enslow, 2000.

Grant, R. G. *The Sixties.* (Look at Life In). Austin, TX: Raintree Steck, 2000.

Gresko, Jessica A. *The 1960's.* (American History by Decade). San Diego: Kidhaven Press, 2004.

Hurley, Jennifer A. *The 1960's.* (Opposing Viewpoints Digests). San Diego: Kidhaven Press, 2000.

Mason, Andres. *The Vietnam War: A Primary Source History.* (In Their Own Words). Milwaukee, WI: Gareth Stephens, 2006.

Pendergast, Sara, and Tom Pendergast, eds. *Bowling, Beatniks and Bell-bottoms: Pop Culture of 20th Century America.* (Vol. 4, *1960s and 1970s*). Detroit: UXL, 2002.

Schnyert, Mark. *Women of the Vietnam War.* (Women in History). Detroit: Lucent, 2005.

Internet

Answers.com describes the hippie movement of the 1960s and the neo-hippie movement of the twenty-first century—http://www.answers.com/topic/hippie.

American Cultural History of the 1960s from Kingwood College Library includes fashions, fads, music, and historical events—http://kclibrary.nhmccd.edu/decade60.html.

Woodstock memories and photographs—http://www.woodstock69.com/.

The antiwar movement in the United States—http://www.english.uiuc.edu/maps/vietnam/antiwar.html.

Protest music of the Vietnam era; includes some audio files—http://www.jwsrockgarden.com/jw02vvaw.htm.

For the Teacher

Your students will consider the emotions of the sixties in this primary document exploration and assignment from History Matters—http://historymatters.gmu.edu/d/5803/.

Share the Peace

Flower children got the name because some of them would give flowers to people passing them on the street. People have different reactions to receiving an unexpected gift. Try it and see. Get some flowers from the grocery store or your garden and pass them out in a safe place such as school, a scout meeting, or church. If anyone asks you why you're doing this, just smile and say, "Peace." Get the definition of flower child—http://www.bartleby.com/61/2/F0200200.html.

The Fountain of Youth (1513)

Don Juan Ponce de Leon arrived in America with Columbus on his second voyage, 1493. Leon and his fellows, not Columbus, completed Spain's claim to the New World. . . . Historians do not unanimously honor at full value the beautifully romantic story that Ponce was seeking to find the fountain of youth. Yet it was not incredible to men of that day—when the very existence of a New World was hardly believable to those who had not seen it with their own eyes—that those who had touched these shores should believe in greater magic in this strange realm.—http://www.2000orlando-florida. com/Orlando/fountain-of-youth.htm

Words to Know

Bimini

Calusa Indians

Columbus

Conquistador

Explorer

Hernando De Soto

Juan Ponce de León

St. Augustine

Related Jumpstarts

Columbus Discovers America

Lewis & Clark Expedition

Mesa Verde Cliff Dwellings

Indian Tribes in Your State

Mayan Mathematicians

Rough Riders

You Are There

You are a young solder who has sailed from Spain to Puerto Rico with Ponce de León. In 1513 you arrive in Florida a little south of the St. Johns River. Ponce de León plants a cross with a royal banner there, claiming the land for King Ferdinand of Spain. He calls this new land Terra de Pascua Florida, which means Land of Easter Flowers. You have traveled with Ponce de León on the *Santiago* and will continue as he travels around the land of Florida, using instruments to draw maps and searching for gold. Ponce de León has been told of a magical fountain or spring that keeps people forever young. He has searched, but has not found it. Now Ponce de León has decided to return to Puerto Rico in the *Santiago*. He orders his men to continue the search in the *Santa Maria* for this wonderful fountain of rejuvenating water, which he had failed to find. Will you go, too?

Topics to Consider

Columbus and Ponce de León	Legend of the Fountain of Youth
The Explorations of Ponce de León	Life Aboard the Santiago
Florida and the Conquistadors	Ponce de León Claims the New Continent for Spain
Fountain of Youth History	
Hernando de Soto, Explorer	Spanish Explorers in the New World
Juan Ponce de León, Explorer	St. Augustine, America's Oldest City

From *99 Jumpstarts for Kids' Social Studies Reports: Research Help for Grades 3–8* by Peggy J. Whitley and Susan Williams Goodwin. Westport, CT: Libraries Unlimited. Copyright © 2007.

Books

Search Words: Conquistadors; Explorers—Spain; Fountain of Youth; Ponce de Leon

Davenport, John. *Ponce de Leon and His Lands of Discovery.* (Explorers of New Lands). Philadelphia: Chelsea House, 2006.

Dolan, Sean. *Juan Ponce De Leon.* (Hispanics of Achievement). Philadelphia: Chelsea House, 1995.

Fuson, Robert Henderson. *Juan Ponce de Leon and the Spanish Discovery of Puerto Rico and Florida.* Blacksburg, VA: McDonald & Woodward, 2000.

Smith, Tom. *Discovery of the Americas, 1492–1800.* (Discovery & Exploration). New York: Facts on File, 2005.

Thompson, William. *The Spanish Exploration of Florida: The Adventures of the Spanish Conquistadors.* (Exploration & Discovery). Broomall, PA: Mason Crest, 2002.

Worth, Richard. *Ponce de Leon and the Age of Spanish Exploration in World History.* (In World History). Berkeley Heights, NJ: Enslow, 2003.

Internet

Fountain of Youth, St. Augustine, Florida—history—http://www.fountainofyouth florida.com/.

Florida of the Conquistadors—http://www.floridahistory.org/floridians/conquis.htm.

Catholic Encyclopedia's Ponce de Leon—http://www.newadvent.org/cathen/12228a.htm.

Ponce de Leon at A&E, good resources—http://www.aetv.com/class/bioproject/ponce_bio.html.

The *Floripedia* has several entries that will be helpful—http://fcit.usf.edu/florida/docs/d/deleon.htm.

History of St. Augustine, America's oldest city—http://www.augustine.com/history/index.html and http://www.staugustinelinks.com/st-augustine-history.asp.

Florida of the Conquistadors—finding Florida—http://www.floridahistory.org/floridians/conquis.htm.

Columbus and Ponce de Leon information—http://www.uflib.ufl.edu/digital/collections/flap/Education/Explorer/SPANISHEXPLORERS.pdf.

For the Teacher

Lesson plan especially for fourth-grade teachers—http://www.valdosta.edu/~elrodden/intro.html. Or use this excellent site for more history of Florida for students—http://www.uflib.ufl.edu/digital/collections/flap/Education/Explorer/SPANISHEXPLORERS.pdf.

Mapping the Spanish Explorers

Start with a time line of the Spanish explorers in Florida and create a map depicting the locations of their arrivals. Be sure to label the explorer and the years—http://www.mce.k12tn.net/explorers/explorers_timeline.htm. Other maps—http://fcit.usf.edu/FLORIDA/maps/1500/1500.htm.

Go West, Young Man (1830–1890)

I am tired of fighting. Our chiefs are killed. Looking Glass is dead. Toohulhulsote is dead. The old men are all dead. It is the young men who say yes or no. He who led the young men is dead. It is cold and we have no blankets. The little children are freezing to death. My people, some of them, have run away to the hills and have no blankets, no food. No one knows where they are–perhaps freezing to death. I want to have time to look for my children and see how many I can find. Maybe I shall find them among the dead. Hear me, my chiefs. I am tired. My heart is sick and sad. From where the sun now stands, I will fight no more forever.—Surrender speech by Chief Joseph of the Nez Perce Tribe

Words to Know

Annexation	Gold Rush
Chinese in the West	Lawmen
Comstock	Lode Outlaws
The Donner Party	Pony Express
Exploration	Settlements
Homestead Act	Stagecoach
Indian Tribes	

Related Jumpstarts

Atchison, Topeka, and Santa Fe Railroad	Banking	Becoming a State
Cattle Drives	Custer's Last Stand	Gold Rush
Lewis & Clark Expedition	Seward's Folly	

You Are There

It is 1873. You are 14 years old. You and your dad moved West in 1865 and discovered gold. You live in Virginia City, Nevada. The boisterous town is booming. Miners are becoming millionaires overnight. You know John Mackay, Jim Fair, James Flood, and William O'Brien, owners of the Consolidated Virginia Mine. You and your dad plan to open a new bank in town. You will build a beautiful home and have furniture sent from the East. Your mom and two sisters are finally joining you in Virginia City. Wow! This is the life!

Topics to Consider

Billy the Kid, Wyatt Earp, or Other Biographies	Life on the Reservation
Boom Towns (Virginia City)	Mountain Men of the Western Frontier
Chief Joseph, Sacagawea, Another Indian or Tribe	Pony Express
The Cowboy and the Rancher	The U.S. Government and the Indian
The Gold Rush (Comstock Lode)	Wells Fargo Overland Line
Lewis and Clark (or Other Explorers and Trails)	Women of the West

Books

Search Words: Explorers—West (U.S.); Frontier and Pioneer Life; Old West

Doeden, Matt. *John Sutter and the California Gold Rush.* (Graphic History). Mankato, MN: Graphic Library, 2005.

Epstein, Dwayne. *Lawmen of the Old West.* (History Makers). Detroit: Lucent, 2005.

Freedman, Russell. *Cowboys of the Wild West.* New York: Clarion Books, 1985.

Furbee, Mary Rodd. *Outrageous Women of the American Frontier.* New York: Wiley, 2002.

Jones, Charlotte Foltz. *Westward Ho!: Eleven Explorers of the West.* New York: Holiday House, 2005.

Sanford, William R. *The Chisholm Trail in American History.* (In American History). Berkeley Heights, NJ: Enslow, 2000.

Wittmann, Kelly. *Explorers of the American West.* (Exploration and Discovery). Broomall, PA: Mason Crest, 2005.

Internet

Use this Lewis-Clark site first for background information, drawings, and maps—http://lewis-clark.org/.

PBS has one of the best sites on the Web. Find a topic, read background information, see maps, media, and more. Rent the video at your local video store—http://www.pbs.org/weta/thewest/.

Old West Legends: Gunfighters, Lawmen and Frontiersmen has many short essays with multiple links. If you are writing a biography, try http://www.legendsofamerica.com/WE-Gunfighters.html.

Eyewitness to History, *The Old West* index page—http://www.eyewitnesstohistory.com/owfrm.htm.

Western Outlaw Lawman has links to information on the gravesites (with biographical information) of famous people of the Old West—http://www.westernoutlaw.com/gravesites/index.html. (Enjoy the stories, too.)

The American West site is nicely divided by subject headings and links to follow. Take a little time to browse—http://www.americanwest.com/.

Virginia City, first Western industrial city—http://www.virginiacity-nv.com/our%20history/ourhistory.htm.

For the Teacher

ProTeacher has a collection of Old West plans for grades 4 to 6—http://www.proteacher.com/090023.shtml.

Exploring the Past

Explore the past with Lewis and Clark. Create a map of the route they took. Find the largest paper you can for this project. Make a map legend with symbols showing the terrain. Where were they by land? Where by water? What wildlife might they have encountered? Who did they meet? Where did they stay? List their supplies. PBS has an excellent site to help you get started. It contains a list of supplies, a map, and a list of members of the exploration party and more. Don't forget Sacagawea—http://www.pbs.org/lewisandclark/inside/index.html.

Going to Market: From Seed to Sale

To market, to market, to buy a fat pig,
Home again, home again, jiggety jig.
To market, to market, to buy a fat hog,
Home again, home again, jiggety jog.

To market, to market, to buy a plum bun,
Home again, home again, market is done

—Nursery rhyme, author unknown

Words to Know

Entrepreneur   Selling
Farmer's Market   Truck Farming
Market Stand

Related Jumpstarts

I Want That! Needs vs. Wants

Marketing to Kids

Supply and Demand

You Are There

You are very lucky. You have a stay-at-home mom, one with lots of energy. She loves to garden and has a large vegetable garden that grows beans, tomatoes, zucchini, onions, okra, and lettuce. Just this spring she decided to sell her vegetables at the local Farmer's Market on Saturday mornings. You and your sister have been appointed as helpers. That means you will help prepare the ground, fertilize, plant the seeds, water, and weed while the vegetables grow. Then each Saturday in summer you will work with mom at the market. You will get up very early to pick the vegetables that are just ripe and put them in baskets to take to market. You even get to help make the signs for your family business. This is hard work. But mom is sharing the profits with you and your sister as you enter this new endeavor. You are beginning your life as an entrepreneur. Congratulations!

Topics to Consider

Dr. Leonard Pike and the Sweet 1015 Onion Story	Starting from Seed
From Seed to Market	Sunkist from Tree to Market
Growing Tomatoes to Sell	Truck Farming
Running a Successful Fruit Stand	The Vegetable Stand on the Corner
	A Visit to the Farmer's Market
Development of a New Vegetable Grown Close to Where You Live, Like the Vidalia or the 1015 Onion	

Books

Search Words: Business for Kids; Farmers Market; Gardening; Seed to Market

Bernstein, Daryl. *Better Than a Lemonade Stand: Small Business Ideas for Kids.* Hillsboro, OR: Beyond Words, 1992.

Chasek, Ruth. *Essential Gardening for Teens.* (Outdoor Life). New York: Children's Press, 2000.

Corum, Vance, Marcie Rosenzweig, and Eric Gibson. *The New Farmer's Market: Farm-fresh Ideas for Producers, Managers, and Communities.* Auburn, CA: New World, 2005.

Erlbach, Arlene. *The Kids' Business Book.* Minneapolis, MN: Lerner, 1998.

Lee, Andrew W. *Backyard Market Gardening: The Entrepreneur's Guide to Selling What You Grow.* Burlington, VT: Good Earth, 1993.

Orloff, Judith, and Darrell Mullis. *The Accounting Book: Basic Accounting Fresh from the Lemonade Stand.* Naperville, IL: Sourcebooks, 1998.

Parks, Carmen. *Farmers Market.* Orlando, FL: Harcourt, 2002.

Rendon, Marcie R., and Cheryl Walsh Bellville *Farmer's Market: Families Working Together.* Minneapolis, MN: Carolrhoda, 2001.

Snyder, Inez. *Oranges.* (Harvesttime). New York: Children's Press, 2004. (Good book if you can find it.)

Internet

Dallas Farmer's Market with history—http://www.dallasfarmersmarket.org/

Farming Now and Then—http://www.campsilos.org/mod4/students/life.shtml.

Growing vegetables for the market stand—http://www.farm-garden.com/growing-vegetables.

The Market Stand—learn how—http://www.greensgrow.org/pages_04/market.html.

Pick Your Own: Where You Can Find a Pick-Your-Own Farm Near You,—http://www.pickyourown.org/.

Gardening with Children—http://www.coopext.colostate.edu/4DMG/Children/children.htm.

Hints to Run a Successful Lemonade (or Other) Stand—http://www.sunkist.com/takeastand/success/.

Dr. Leonard Pike and the 1015 Onion—http://www.sweetonionsource.com/varieties/texassweets.html.

For the Teacher

The National First Ladies Library has an extensive resource for classroom exploration of first ladies and related diplomats—http://www.firstladies.org/curriculum/choose.aspx .

Take a Stand

Sunkist wants kids to *Take a Stand* by running a successful lemonade stand for their favorite charity. This could really be fun. Find out more—http://www.sunkist.com/takeastand/. There are several books you can read about starting a lemonade stand or another business.

Gold Rush (1850–1890)

I wanted the gold, and I sought it,
I scrabbled and mucked like a slave.
Was it famine or scurvy—I fought it;
I hurled my youth into a grave.
I wanted the gold, and I got it—

Came out with a fortune last fall,—
Yet somehow life's not what I thought it,
And somehow the gold isn't all.

—Robert Service, The Spell of the Yukon

Words to Know

Forty-niners
The Elephant
John Sutter
Klondike
The Long Tom Tailings

Narrow Gauge Railroad
Panning for Gold
Prospectors
Stampeders Yukon

Related Jumpstarts

Atchison, Topeka, and Santa Fe Railroad
Banking
Becoming a State
Go West, Young Man
Indians in Your State
Seward's Folly
Where Cities Bloom

You Are There

The discovery of gold in California attracted miners from diverse backgrounds, all with the goal of striking it rich. Among them were the members of your family. Your family traveled from China. You live in Nevada City, in the Chinese Quarter, where the stores carry your traditional food and clothing, you go to temple, and you gather with friends for Chinese New Year celebrations. Your father works hard as a laborer in the gold mine. Your mother and aunt have opened a small herbal shop in town. Your older brothers and sisters are from China, but you were born here. You are a first-generation American.

Topics to Consider

Boomtowns	Leadville, Silver Plume, or Aspen
California Gold Rush (or Another State)	Million Dollar Highway
Chinese (and others) and the Gold Rush	Prospecting for Gold—Tools of the Trade
Daily Life for the Gold (or Silver) Miner	Seeing the Elephant
Durango and Silverton Narrow Gauge Railroad	Silver Mining
Ghost Towns Today	Supplies for the Gold Miner
History of Sutter's Mill	The Unsinkable Molly Brown
James Marshall, John Sutter, or Sam Brannan	Woman in the Gold Rush
The Klondike	Zebulon Pike and Pikes Peak

Books

Search Words: Gold Rush; Million Dollar Highway; (Names of People); (Names of Places); Silver Mining; Sutter's Mill; Westward Expansion and Gold

Emert, Phyllis Raybin. *All That Glitters: Men and Women of the Gold and Silver Rushes.* (Perspectives on History). Auburn, MA: History Compass, 1995.

Engstrand, Iris Wilson. *John Sutter: Sutter's Fort and the California Gold Rush.* (Library of American Lives and Times). New York: Rosen, 2004.

Simon, Charnon. *Molly Brown: Sharing Her Good Fortune.* (Community Builders). New York: Children's Press, 2000.

Thompson, Linda. *The California Gold Rush.* (Expansion of America). Vero Beach, FL: Rourke, 2005.

Internet

The American Experience: Gold Fever in the Klondike—http://www.pbs.org/wgbh/amex/gold/.

Overland Gold—links to the Gold Rush—http://www.over-land.com/trgold.html.

Gold Rush from PBS: the California Gold Rush—http://www.pbs.org/goldrush/discovery.html.

Women in the Gold Rush and many firsthand accounts—http://www.goldrush.com/~joann/.

Durango and Silverton Narrow Gauge Railroad—http://www.durangosilvertonrailroad.com/history.html.

Alaska's Gold has daily life, discovery, travel, and the law—http://www.library.state.ak.us/goldrush/.

All About the Gold Rush from Idaho State University—http://www.isu.edu/~trinmich/allabout.html.

Land of Glittering Dreams has a collection of letters and photos—http://www.glittering.com/home.html.

Zebulon Pike and Pikes Peak, a landmark for prospectors—http://www.pikes-peak.com/Page/69.aspx.

The California Gold Rush has all kinds of information about ways to mine gold and more—http://www.kidport.com/RefLib/UsaHistory/CalGoldRush/CalGoldRush.htm.

John Sutter's Report on finding gold in California—http://www.sfmuseum.org/hist2/gold.html.

Gold Rush towns today and yesterday—http://henkbinnendijk.tripod.com/goldrush/index.html.

For the Teacher

The Gold Rush Teacher's Guide has activities, tests, links and more. Planning a film? Try Video 101—http://www.isu.edu/~trinmich/teacher.html.

Hitting the Trail

Write a journal about your life as a forty-niner. Write about the traffic jam on the trail. Be sure to write about supplies and the price of the items you have to purchase. Start at http://www.isu.edu/~trinmich/funfacts.html.

Great Chicago Fire (1871)

Late one night, when we were all in bed,
Mrs. O'Leary lit a lantern in the shed.
Her cow kicked it over,
Then winked her eye and said,
"There'll be a hot time in the old town tonight!"

—Popular song lyric

Words to Know

Burnt	District Disaster
Chicago Tribune	Horse-Drawn Fire Wagons
Common Council	Lantern
Conflagration	Mrs. O'Leary's Cow
Destruction	Refugees

Related Jumpstarts

9/11

Brooklyn Bridge

Dealing with Disaster

History of Main Street

Who Runs Our Town?

Yellow Fever Attacks Philadelphia

You Are There

Chicago, 1871. It is hot and dry. There has been only one inch of rain during the past three months. The buildings are mostly made of wood, and small fires have broken out. The *Chicago Tribune* has warned about the danger of the city going up in smoke. The city's 185 firefighters have requested better equipment and more help, but it hasn't arrived. The firefighters are exhausted and still the city burns. Another fire breaks out nearby while you are asleep. Your parents awaken you, and you run for your lives. You can't take anything with you. Seventy-three miles of streets burn. What a disaster! What can you do? Now it is time to rebuild.

Topics to Consider

Causes of the Great Chicago Fire	Other Great Disasters (Texas City Explosion; San Francisco Earthquake; Hawaii Tsunami; New York on 9/11/01)
Chicago Tribune Reports the Fire	
Did the Cow Do It?	
The Few Buildings Left Standing After the Fire	
Follow the History of Mrs. O'Leary's House to Its End	Personal Accounts of the Great Fire
History of the Palmer House	Rebuilding Chicago after the Fire

From *99 Jumpstarts for Kids' Social Studies Reports: Research Help for Grades 3–8* by Peggy J. Whitley and Susan Williams Goodwin. Westport, CT: Libraries Unlimited. Copyright © 2007.

Books

Search Words: Fires—Chicago; Great Chicago Fire

Bates, Richard F., and Thomas Schwartz. *The Great Chicago Fire and the Myth of Mrs. O'Leary's Cow.* Jefferson, NC: MacFarland, 2005.

Lowe, David. *The Great Chicago Fire: In Eyewitness Accounts and 70 Contemporary Photographs and Illustrations.* New York: Dover, 1979.

Marx, Christy. *The Great Chicago Fire of 1871.* (Tragic Fires Throughout History). New York: Rosen Central, 2004.

Murphy, Jim. *The Great Fire* (sound recording). Northport, ME: Audio Bookshelf, 2003.

Murphy, Jim. *The Great Fire.* New York: Scholastic, 1995.

Stein, Conrad. *The Great Chicago Fire.* (Cornerstones of Freedom). New York: Children's Press, 2005.

Internet

Did the Cow Do It? Background about Mrs. O'Leary's cow—http://www.thechicagofire.com/index.php.

Chicago Historical Society has collected essays, photographs, newspaper articles, videos, and much more at this site. Don't miss it—http://www.chicagohs.org/fire/intro/detail.html#fanning.

Chicago Tribune Newpaper Reports—http://www.chicagohs.org/fire/conflag/tribune.html. (Find out about the warnings the *Tribune* made before the fire—http://www.prairieghosts.com/great_fire.html.)

Palmer House Hotel—http://en.wikipedia.org/wiki/Palmer_House.

About.com has a good collection of articles written in 1871 and links to sites of interest—http://chicago.about.com/cs/history/a/13_history_fire.htm.

American Experience has an excellent film—http://www.pbs.org/wgbh/amex/chicago/maps/.

For the Teacher

Education World's lesson plans on the Great Chicago Fire focus on problem solving. Did the cow really do it?—http://www.education-world.com/a_lesson/dailylp/dailylp/dailylp013.shtml.

Did the Cow Do It?

Some people believe that Mrs. O'Leary's cow did start the Great Chicago Fire. Some believe it is a myth. Make up your own mind. Become a detective. Do some research and draw your own conclusions. Make a list defending your decision. Two good places to start are http://www.thechicagofire.com/index.php and http://www.chicagohs.org/fire/oleary/index.html.

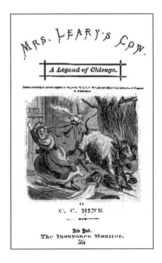

The Great Depression (1929–1939)

Once I built a railroad,
I made it run, made it race against time.
Once I built a railroad; now it's done.
Brother, can you spare a dime?
Once I built a tower, up to the sun,
brick, and rivet, and lime;

Once I built a tower, now it's done.
Brother, can you spare a dime?

—Lyrics by Yip Harburg, 1931
(Song can be heard at http://scars.
    tv/av/jk-material-listing.htm.)

Words to Know

Black Tuesday	Recession
Breadlines	Soup Kitchen
Deflation	Stock Market Crash
Depression	Unemployment
New Deal Programs	

Related Jumpstarts

Child Labor

Dust Bowl

Poverty in America

You Are There

Brother, can you spare a dime? It is 1931 and you are 16 years old. For the past two years you have lived the life of a hobo. Your younger brother is traveling with you. Lately you are living in the woods of East Texas with four other hobos your own age. You traveled there from St. Louis in a boxcar on the Southern Pacific Railroad. You have been in Texas for a month. You have created a very nice home for yourselves in the woods. You keep it neat and clean. There is a lady nearby who sometimes gives you a sandwich. You and your friends find a little work. Occasionally, you have to beg for food or money. You don't like that. Your brother cries at night because he is homesick. You are homesick, too, but you are strong. You stay away from home. You don't want to be a burden to your family. Life is very hard.

Topics to Consider

Black Thursday	New Deal Programs
Causes of the Great Depression	Prices During the 1930s
The Great Depression	Riding the Rails—Hobos in the 1930s
The Great Depression and Children	Roosevelt's New Deal Programs
Interview (Oral History)	Soup Kitchens and Bread Lines
Life During the 1930s	The Stock Market Crash of 1929

From *99 Jumpstarts for Kids' Social Studies Reports: Research Help for Grades 3–8* by Peggy J. Whitley and Susan Williams Goodwin. Westport, CT: Libraries Unlimited. Copyright © 2007.

Books

Search Words: Great Depression; New Deal; Nineteen-Thirties—Juvenile

Cooper, Michael. *Dust to Eat: Drought and Depression in the 1930's.* New York: Clarion, 2004.

Feinstein, Steven. *The 1930s: From the Great Depression to the Wizard of Oz.* (Decades of the 20th Century). Berkeley Heights, NJ: Enslow, 2001.

Gow, Mary. *The Stock Market Crash of 1929: Dawn of the Depression.* (American Disasters). Berkeley Heights, NJ: Enslow, 2003.

Graves, Kerry A. *Going to School During the Great Depression.* (Going to School in History). Mankata, MN: Blue Earth, 2002.

Hanes, Sharon M. *Great Depression and the New Deal: Biographies.* (Great Depression and New Deal Reference Library). Detroit: UXL, 2003.

Ruth, Amy. *Growing Up in the Great Depression, 1929 to 1941.* (Our America). Minneapolis: Lerner, 2003.

Stein, R. Conrad. *The Great Depression.* (Cornerstones of Freedom). Danbury, CT: Children's Press, 1993.

Internet

University of Virginia's Crossroads site has everything you need—http://xroads.virginia.edu/~1930s/front.html.

Use Kingwood College Library's decade for background—http://kclibrary.nhmccd.edu/decade30.html.

We Made Do is an award-winning oral history project—http://www.mcsc.k12.in.us/mhs/social/madedo/.

Riding the Rails includes time line, stories, and maps—http://www.pbs.org/wgbh/amex/rails/index.html.

Dear Mrs. Roosevelt and how the Depression affected children—http://newdeal.feri.org/eleanor/index.htm.

Causes of the Great Depression—http://www.socialstudieshelp.com/Lesson_83_Notes.htm.

The New Deal Network features documents from Roosevelt's administration—http://newdeal.feri.org/.

Encarta's Great Depression—http://encarta.msn.com/related_761562953_1/Great_Depression.html.

For the Teacher

Twelve lesson plans for the Great Depression, crossing curriculum areas. Excellent links—http://www.todaysteacher.com/TheGreatDepressionWebQuest/Introduction.htm and http://www.educationworld.com/a_lesson/lesson/lesson147.shtml.

The Teenage Hobo

During the Depression more than 250,000 teenagers were hobos. Read their stories —http://www.pbs.org/wgbh/amex/rails/sfeature/tales.html. Do some research about these young homeless teens. Write a story about being a hobo during this period. Describe your "camp." Why did you leave home? Where have you traveled? How? Describe your companions. Relate one or two experiences. Make your story as real as possible.

History of Main Street

When you're alone and life is making you lonely
You can always go—downtown
When you've got worries, all the noise and the hurry
Seems to help, I know—downtown
Just listen to the music of the traffic in the city
Linger on the sidewalk where the neon signs
  are pretty
How can you lose?

The lights are much brighter there
You can forget all your troubles, forget all your cares
So go downtown, things'll be great when you're
Downtown—no finer place, for sure
Downtown—everything's waiting for you

—Petulla Clark, "Downtown"

Words to Know

Campaign	Population
City Planner	Preservation
Committee	Revitalize
Economic	Revitalization
Gentrification	Suburban Sprawl
Historical Landmark	

Related Jumpstarts

Coming to America	Oldest Person in Town	Place Names
Route 66	Wal-Mart Comes to Our Town	Where Cities Bloom
Who Runs Our Town?		

You Are There

You are 13 years old. You and your family live in a small town in Texas. Your grandparents live there, too. When your mom was a young girl, she went downtown every Saturday with her $3 allowance. She would spend the day with her girlfriends. They would go to the dime store (gone now) and to the movie theater (gone, too). Later they would treat themselves to an ice cream soda at the local drugstore. Today there are only a few stores left on Main Street. The new stores are at the end of town where Wal-Mart is located. What happened? Why have the stores closed? What is the town doing about it? You hear there is a committee that meets to find ways to preserve the beautiful old buildings. You hope they can. You love your town.

Topics to Consider

10 Fun Things to Do on Main Street	The History of Main Street
A Campaign for Main Street Renewal	Interviews with People on Main Street
Chinatown (or Another Ethnic Area)	Making Downtown Come Alive
History of an Historic Landmark	My Town
The History of "_____" (One of the Oldest Shops in Your Town)	My Town, a Digital Story
	Why Are Main Streets Important?

From 99 Jumpstarts for Kids' Social Studies Reports: Research Help for Grades 3–8 by Peggy J. Whitley and Susan Williams Goodwin. Westport, CT: Libraries Unlimited. Copyright © 2007.

Books

Search Words: Cities and Towns; Main Street

Dave, Shilpa, Leilani Nishime, and Tasha Oren. *East Main Street: Asian American Popular Culture.* New York: New York University Press, 2005.

Geisert, Bonnie, and Arthur Geisert. *Mountain Town.* (Small Town U.S.A.). Boston: Houghton Mifflin, 2000. (Good series.)

Goist, Park Dixon. *From Main Street to State Street: Town, City, and Community in America.* Port Washington, NY: Kennikat Press, 1977.

Goodall, John. *The Story of a Main Street.* New York: Margaret K. McElderry, 1987.

Gratz, Roberta Brandes, and Norman Mintz. *Cities Back from the Edge: New Life for Downtown.* Hoboken, NJ: Wiley, 2000.

Stokes, Samuel N., A. Elizabeth Watson, and Shelley Smith Mastran. *Saving America's Countryside: A Guide to Rural Conservation.* (National Trust for Historic Preservation). Baltimore: Johns Hopkins University Press, 1997.

Internet

Mainstreet Projects by the National Trust for Preservations—http://www.mainstreet.org/.

Why Are Main Streets Important?—http://www.mainstreet.org/content.aspx?page=1927.

Conway, S.C., makes downtown come alive—http://www.conwaymainstreet.com/making_alive.cfm.

Downtown History—examples—http://www.downtowncr.org/gettoknowus_downtownhistory.asp and http://www.humblearea.com/history/.

Walk through a Historic Building—http://www.cr.nps.gov/hps/tps/walkthrough/.

Texas Mainstreet Project (find your state's)—http://www.thc.state.tx.us/mainstreet/msdefault.html.

Main Street America from PBS has information about towns that have revitalized and about city planners—http://www.pbs4549.org/mainst/mainedu.htm.

For the Teacher

View this 30-second Google video with your class—http://video.google.com/videoplay?docid=-940900417095611288. Arkansas Preservation Organization has provided excellent lesson plans and projects—http://www.arkansaspreservation.org/preservation-services/youth-education/.

Rating Places to Live

Find *Places Rated Almanac* at your local library. Find five places you would like to live and create a chart comparing them. Analyze your chart. What do you think makes a town a good place for kids to live?

I Am the Pharaoh (3100 BC–AD 395)

The word "pharaoh" comes from the Bible. It was first used by Joseph and Moses. We use it to refer to the Egyptian kings prior to the eighteenth dynasty. The pharaohs began ruling Egypt in 3000 BC, when Upper and Lower Egypt were united. They considered themselves to be living gods who ruled with absolute power. . . . The pharaoh was the head of state and the divine representative of the gods on earth.—Mysteries of Egypt, http://www.civilization.ca/civil/egypt/egypt_e.html

Words to Know

Cleopatra	New Kingdom
Djoser	Obelisk
Dynasty	Old Kingdom
Egypt	Pharaoh
Hatshepsut	Pyramid
Khnum	Ramses
Mastabas	Sphinx
Middle Kingdom	Tutankhamen ("King Tut")
Mummy	

Related Jumpstarts

All Roads Lead to Rome	Ancient Greece	Life along the Nile
Mayan Mathematicians	Mesa Verde Cliff Dwellings	Religions of the World

You Are There

You are Pharaoh Menes and the year is 3100 BC. You have united the Upper and Lower regions of Egypt. You then divide the country into 40 regions (like states) with a governor for each. You are the head of government and you represent the gods. You have total power over the people. Farmers give three-fifths of their crops to you in taxes. Everyone spends a few months every year working on your pyramid. You start a period in Egyptian history that will last over 3,000 years. Because of you, Egypt will become one of the richest and most powerful nations in the world.

Topics to Consider

Building the First Pyramid with King Djoser	The Life of Tutankhamen, Boy King
Cleopatra or Hatshepsut, Female Pharaohs	Preparing the Pharaoh for Burial
I Am the Pharaoh	The Valley of the Kings
Inside the Tomb of King Tut	Women in Ancient Egypt
Khnum Builds the Great Pyramid of Giza	Writing in Hieroglyphics

Books

Search Words: Egypt—Kings and Rulers; Hatshepsut (or other); Pharaohs; Pyramids

Giblin, James Cross. *Secrets of the Sphinx*. New York: Scholastic Press, 2004.

Macaulay, David. *Pyramid*. Boston: Houghton Mifflin, 1975.

Morley, Jacqueline, Mark Bergin, and John James. *An Egyptian Pyramid*. (Inside Story). New York: Peter Bedrick Books, 1991.

Roberts, Russell. *Rulers of Ancient Egypt*. (History Makers). San Diego: Lucent, 1999.

Thomas, Susanna. *Hatshepsut: The First Woman Pharaoh*. (Leaders of Ancient Egypt). New York: Rosen, 2003.

Internet

Mysteries of the Nile includes sphinx, excavation, and pyramids—http://www.pbs.org/wgbh/nova/egypt/.

 Tour Egypt takes you on a virtual tour of the pyramids, throughout Egypt—http://www.touregypt.net/featurestories/pyramids.htm.

A well-researched site on Egyptian kings. For older students, very interesting. Search the whole site—http://interoz.com/egypt/kings.htm.

The *Pharaoh's Court History Section* is background information for a game. Search *Pharaoh's Court* for economics of life in Egypt—http://pharaoh.heavengames.com/egypt/history/index.shtml.

Community High School created this site—http://www.communityhigh.org/old/pyramids/burial.html.

The Secret of the Pharaohs includes how mummies are made—http://www.pbs.org/wnet/pharaohs/.

For the Teacher

Ancient Egypt Lesson Plans—http://falcon.jmu.edu/~ramseyil/egypt.htm—resources for older students; http://www.geocities.com/Athens/Atrium/5924/ancientegyptlessonplans.htm—for younger students.

A Taste of History

⅄ Build your own Pharaoh death mask—http://www.clevelandart.org/kids/egypt/index.html. Be sure to enjoy the rest of this great Web site, especially for kids.

⅄ Mummify a chicken—ask your mommy to help make this mummy—http://www.geocities. com/Athens/Atrium/5924/ancientegyptlessonplans.htm.

I Want That! Needs vs. Wants

[T]here is a basic hierarchy of needs. Only when the most fundamental needs are met do we seek the next level. First are physiological needs such as oxygen, food and water. Next comes Safety, then Love and Belonging. The last of these "deficit needs" is esteem. Only when all these needs are met do we seek self-actualization.—Abraham Maslow (1908–1970), *Motivation and Personality*

Words to Know

Abraham Maslow's Hierarchy of Needs   Luxuries
Budgeting   Materialism
Fads   Necessities

Related Jumpstarts

American Sweatshops   Banking   Business of Doing Good
Child Labor   Great Depression   Peer Pressure
Poverty in America   Supply and Demand

You Are There

You're at the mall, looking at back-to-school clothes. Your mom already bought your things, and now for the last hour, it's been your brother's turn. You're incredibly bored. Then someone walks by with a pretzel. You know those pretzels, the fresh-baked kind, dripping with butter and covered with coarse salt. Mmmh! That looks good! "Mom," you say. "I'm hungry."

You're out hiking with your scout troop. The sun is bright and there isn't much wind. It's been at least two hours. You notice your friend open his canteen and take a long drink of water. You didn't bring your own canteen, even though the leader suggested it. You thought it would be too dorky. But now, watching your friend swallowing the water, you can almost taste it. You ask your friend for a drink. "No way," he says. "That would be gross!" And so you stumble along, hot, tired and incredibly thirsty.

Which is a want? Which is a need?

Topics to Consider

Advertising and the Creating of Desire	How Needs Have Changed in the Past 100
Basic Necessities—What Are They?	Years
Compare Your Needs with Your Dad's	Poverty and Meeting Real Needs
Creating a Budget	Ways to Get What You Want
Difference Between Need and Want	What Does It Take to Plan Ahead?
Fads That I NEED!	What Is Materialism?

Books

Search Words: Acquisitiveness; Child Consumers; Finance, Juvenile; Materialism

Kasser, Tim. *The High Price of Materialism*. Cambridge, MA: MIT, 2002.

Schor, Juliet B. *Born to Buy: The Commercialized Child and the New Consumer Culture*. New York: Scribner's, 2004.

Madame Blueberry (videorecording). (VeggieTales Classics). Burbank, CA: Warner Home Video, 2003.

McGillian, Jamie Kyle. *The Kid's Money Book: Earning, Saving, Spending, Investing, Donating*. New York: Sterling, 2003.

Internet

Social Studies for Kids explains the difference between needs and wants—http://www.socialstudiesforkids.com/articles/economics/wantsandneeds1.htm.

It All Adds Up has games to test your budgeting and investing savvy—http://www.italladdsup.org/.

PBS compares needs and wants in *It's My Life*—http://pbskids.org/itsmylife/money/managing/article2.html.

Explore needs and wants through games, courtesy of the Smith Family of Australia—http://www.smithfamily.com.au/documents/Kids_Helping_Kids03_Unit2_C8278.pdf.

The U.S. Mint explains a four-bank system for savings—http://www.themint.org/young/index.php.

Kids' Money discusses ways to earn money, allowances, financial tips, and much more—http://www.kidsmoney.org/.

Maslow's Hierarchy of Needs is illustrated—http://www.mcps.k12.md.us/schools/senecavalleyhs/childdev/maslow.htm.

For the Teacher

Social studies lesson plans for grades 4–5 include a plan for colonizing Mars. Students will use various skills to determine what they really need—http://www.lessonplanspage.com/SS45.htm—or check the lesson plans for all grades—http://www.lessonplanspage.com/SS.htm.

A Taste of History

Go on a backpacking trip. As you plan your trip, make a list of everything you'll need. Remember, everything you bring will be carried on your back, so you'd better be really sure you will need it! You can find out how to get started—http://www.backpacking.net/beginner.html.

50

Indian Tribes in Your State

Their parties usually voyaged from place to place along the coast in their canoes or dug-outs, which were made from large trees, the bark left on. One side of the log was hewed flat and the log was then dug out, the ends bluntly pointed, leaving a triangular place or deck at each end. The women and children and household goods occupied the "hold," while the father of the family stood on the stern and poled the boat along, keeping not far away from the shore.—Charles A. Hammond, "The Carancahua Tribe of Indians," *Archaelogical and Ethnological Papers of the Peabody Museum* 1, no. 2 (1891).

Words to Know

Amerindians	Native Americans
Archaeology	Paleoindians
Coming of Age	Pow Wow
Culture	Puberty
Hunter-gatherers	Shaman
Indigenous	Sovereignty
Initiation	Rites Spirits
Kennewick Man	Vision Quest

Related Jumpstarts

Lewis & Clark Expedition

Mayan Mathematicians

Mesa Verde Cliff Dwellings

Trail of Tears

You Are There

You are reaching puberty, the time when your body starts to become like that of an adult. It is time for you to be initiated into adulthood in your tribe. When the time comes, you go away to the lodge with other boys and the men of the tribe. For several days, you stay in the lodge while the shaman performs ceremonies and chants. He is in contact with the spirits, and from them he receives your new name. When you leave the lodge, you are no longer a boy. You have now become a man and are expected to hunt with the men and take on adult responsibilities.

Topics to Consider

Compare Native Languages	Kennewick Man
How Did the First Amerindians Arrive?	Lodging and Clothing of Your Local Tribe
Indians in _____	Native Foods
Indian Reservations in Your State	Religion and Mythology
Indian Tribe That Originally Inhabited Your Area	Trading between Tribes

Books

Search Words: Indians of North America; Tribe Names

Murdock, David Hamilton. *North American Indian.* (DK Eyewitness). New York: DK Publishing, 2005.

Webster, M. L. *On the Trail Made of Dawn: Native American Creation Stories.* North Haven, CT: Linnet, 2001.

Wolfson, Evelyn. *From Abenaki to Zuni: A Dictionary of Native American Tribes.* New York: Walker, 1988.

Wood-Trost, Lucille. *Native Americans of the Plains.* (Indigenous Peoples of the Plains). San Diego: Lucent, 2000.

Internet

Native Web discusses some of the arts of the Native Americans, including beads, pottery, tools, stonework, and use of porcupine quills—http://www.nativetech.org/.

Resources of American Indians for Children and Teachers has an alphabetical list of tribes with links to fact sheets about their history, culture, and language—http://www.native-languages.org/kids.htm—and a listing by state—http://www.native-languages.org/states.htm. Excellent site.

Native American Tribes links to sites maintained by the tribes themselves—http://www.nativeculturelinks.com/nations.html.

500 Nations lists tribes by state—http://500nations.com/tribes/Tribes_State-by-State.asp.

The e-museum by the University of Minnesota explores the cultures of various Indian tribes, sometimes including daily life and history—http://www.mnsu.edu/emuseum/cultural/northamerica/.

Who were the first Americans, and where did they come from?—http://www.kidinfo.com/American_History/Native_Americans.html.

Edward S. Curtis's *The North American Indian* photographic images, from the Library of Congress—http://memory.loc.gov/ammem/award98/ienhtml/curthome.html.

Video clips of a Navajo coming-of-age ceremony—http://www.nativetelecom.org/realmedia/video/kinaalda/.

For the Teacher

The National Endowment for the Humanities Edusitement site has a lesson to help your students investigate and understand the variety of Native American cultures—http://edsitement.neh.gov/view_lesson_plan.asp?id=324.

Attend a Pow-Wow

A great way to get a taste of Native American culture is to attend a powwow. To learn all about them, including a calendar and map to help you find a powwow near you, check out http://www.powwows.com/.

51

Jackie Robinson Breaks Baseball's Color Barrier

Jackie Robinson was a pioneer in desegregating baseball. He broke through racial barriers to become one of the most historically-significant baseball players ever when he became the first African American to play baseball in the major leagues in the 20th Century.—http://www.whitehouse.gov/kids/dreamteam/jackierobinson.html

Words to Know

Athletic Scholarship
Barnstorming
Baseball Hall of Fame
Boycott
Branch Rickey
Civil Rights

Color Barrier
Desegregation
Negro Leagues
Petition
Values

Related Jumpstarts

Fighting Prejudice

Lives and Times of My Grandparents

Riding in the Back of the Bus

You Are There

It's April 15, 1947. You and your dad are at the Brooklyn Dodgers Stadium for the opening day game. It is a momentous occasion, because Jackie Robinson is playing first base. He is the first African American to play on an all-white major league team. You have read all about Mr. Robinson. He was the first person at UCLA to letter in four sports. What an athlete! You know that some of the Dodgers had signed petitions to have him removed from the team. But today the stands are filled. The fans love him. He bunts a single and then steals second base. The crowd roars. You and your family cheer loudly. Jackie Robinson has broken the color barrier. That same season, he leads the Dodgers to play against the New York Yankees at the World Series. What a day! And what a lucky kid you are to see history in the making.

Topics to Consider

Biography of Jackie Robinson	Jackie Robinson, Civil Rights Leader
Branch Rickey, Manager	Jackie Robinson's First Year with the Dodgers
Breaking the Color Barrier	Negro Leagues
History of the Brooklyn Dodgers	Nine Values of Jackie Robinson
Jackie Robinson at UCLA	Riding in the Back of the Bus (Jackie Robinson
Jackie Robinson, Athlete	Travels with the Team)

Books

Search Words: Negro Baseball Leagues; Robinson, Jackie

Frommer, Harvey. *Rickey and Robinson: The Men Who Broke Baseball's Color Barrier.* New York: Macmillan, 1982.

Patrick, Denise Lewis. *Jackie Robinson: Strong Inside and Out.* (Time Life Books). New York: Harper, 2005.

Robinson, Jackie. *I Never Had It Made: An Autobiography of Jackie Robinson.* New York: Harper, 2003. Originally published by Putnam, 1972.

Robinson, Sharon. *Jackie's Nine: Jackie Robinson's Values to Live By: Courage, Determination, Teamwork, Persistence, Integrity, Citizenship, Justice, Commitment, Excellence.* New York: Scholastic, 2001.

Robinson, Sharon. *Promises to Keep: How Jackie Robinson Changed America.* New York: Scholastic, 2004.

Internet

Major League Baseball's Jackie Robinson Day: The Nine Values of Robinson, videos, audios, don't miss this page—http://mlb.mlb.com/NASApp/mlb/mlb/events/jrd/index.jsp and http://mlb.mlb.com/NASApp/mlb/la/history/jackie_robinson_timeline/timeline_index.jsp.

Jackie Robinson's daughter speaks at the Library of Congress—http://www.loc.gov/locvideo/robinson/.

The *Houston Chronicle* collection of African American sports figures who "broke the color barrier"—http://www.chron.com/content/chronicle/sports/special/barriers/index.html.

American Memory at Library of Congress has time line (follow it for excellent information), essay, pictures, and more—http://memory.loc.gov/ammem/collections/robinson/.

Baseball Hall of Fame has information on both Robinson and Branch Rickey, who brought him to the Dodgers—http://www.baseballhalloffame.org/default.htm.

Government archives for Jackie Robinson as a civil rights leader, telegrams, letters, etc.—http://www.archives.gov/education/lessons/jackie-robinson/index.html.

For the Teacher

The Library of Congress three-hour research project into the life of Jackie Robinson—http://memory.loc.gov/learn/lessons/98/robinson/intro.htm.

Win $1,000

Enter the National Baseball League's Physical Fitness Event contest—http://mlb.mlb.com/NASApp/mlb/mlb/official_info/community/bb.jsp. Win a $1,000 grant for your school or sports group.

John Muir (1838–1914)

Everything is flowing—going somewhere, animals and so-called lifeless rocks as well as water. Thus the snow flows fast or slow in grand beauty-making glaciers and avalanches; the air in majestic floods carrying minerals, plant leaves, seeds, spores, with streams of music and fragrance; water streams carrying rocks. . . . While the stars go streaming through space pulsed on and on forever like blood . . . in Nature's warm heart.—John Muir

Words to Know

Conservation Programs
Environmentalist
Hetch Hetchy
John Muir
Naturalist

Preservationist
Sequoia
Valley Sierra Club
Yosemite

Related Jumpstarts

Fountain of Youth

King Cotton

Mighty Mississippi

Where Cities Bloom

You Are There

John Muir was born in the nineteenth century and died in 1912. Yet today he is remembered. Why? Streets, parks, and schools carry his name. Ecology and environmental projects go forward in his name. In 2006 California named him to its Hall of Fame. He has received honors from all over the world. Why? If you lived around Yosemite in 1869, you might have seen John Muir making his 1,000-mile walk from Kentucky to the Gulf of Mexico. Why? Later you would find him in California in the great sequoia forests. A few years later he started the Sierra Club. Why? Why is John Muir one of the great names in conservation? Why do presidents still give him accolades?

Topics to Consider

Conservation Programs Today	John Muir Gets Inducted into the California
Environmentalists—Who Are They?	Hall of Fame
The Giant Sequoia	John Muir Remembered Today
Hetch Hetchy Valley	John Muir Project Today
The History of the Sierra Club	Letters of John Muir
The Horse Journey by Grandson	Who Was John Muir?
Michael Muir	Writings of Muir (Select One to Review)

Books

Search Words: Environmentalists; Muir, John; Sierra Club

Armentrout, David. *John Muir: People Who Make a Difference.* Vero Beach, FL: Rourke, 2002.

Lasky, Katherine. *John Muir: America's First Environmentalist.* Cambridge, MA: Candlewick, 2006.

Locker, Thomas. *John Muir: America's Naturalist.* Golden, CO: Fulcrum: 2003.

Muir, John, Donnell Rubay. *Stickeen: John Muir and the Brave Little Dog.* Nevada City, NV: Dawn, 1998.

Muir, John. *The Wild Muir: Twenty-two of John's Greatest Adventures.* El Portal, CA: Yosemite, 1994.

Peterson, David. *National Parks.* (True Books). Chicago: Children's Press, 2000.

Warrick, Karen. *John Muir: Crusader for the Wilderness.* Berkeley Heights, NJ: Enslow, 2002.

Internet

Sierra Club John Muir exhibit with information—http://www.sierraclub.org/john_muir_exhibit/.

Ecology Hall of Fame tribute to John Muir—http://www.ecotopia.org/ehof/muir/bio.html.

My Hero Web site has an excellent biography—http://myhero.com/myhero/hero.asp?hero=j_muir.

A collection of links to the writings of Muir—wow!—http://www.yosemite.ca.us/john_muir_writings/.

The John Muir Project tells about logging in the sequoia forest—http://www.johnmuirproject.org/.

John Muir letters archived at Wisconsin Historical Society. See conservation letters, especially. This is a wonderful find—http://www.wisconsinhistory.org/turningpoints/search.asp?id=1224.

Follow the Horse Journey by grandson Michael Muir—http://www.es4pd.co.uk/HorseJourney/.

For the Teacher

The Sierra Club has lesson plans to use for all grade levels whether you plan a John Muir Day or not—http://www.sierraclub.org/john_muir_exhibit/frameindex.html?http://www.sierraclub.org/john_muir_exhibit/john_muir_day_study_guide/.

A Nature Journal of Your Own

Make your own nature journal over the course of a month or two. Don't try to do it all at once. Learn about journals—http://www.sierraclub.org/education/nature_journal.asp. A nature journal should express your inner thoughts about nature. Not only can you take pictures and describe what you see, you might also find poems or quotations you like about nature. A  nature journal can be private. You do not have to share it unless you want to. Keep your journal and go back a year or more later and see what you have written. What have you learned during the past year?

53

Jury System

I consider trial by jury as the only anchor ever yet imagined by man by which a government can be held to the principles of its constitution.—Thomas Jefferson, 1789

Words to Know

Accused
Constitutional Rights
Defendant
District Attorney
Grand Jury

Judge
Juror
Justice System
Testimony
Witness

Related Jumpstarts

Becoming a Citizen
Right to Vote
Salem Witch Trials
Who Runs Our Town?
Writing the Constitution

You Are There

John and Jacob got into a fight, and John was hurt. Now Jacob is on trial for causing bodily harm to the other. But the other one says it wasn't his fault. He was just protecting himself. As a registered voter in your community, you receive a notice in the mail that you have jury duty. Now you and 11 other people sit in the jury box, listening to each of the witnesses. Each tells what he or she thinks happened. They are eyewitnesses, but their testimony doesn't always agree. Finally, the lawyers summarize what the witnesses said, emphasizing their client's point of view. You and the other jurors are dismissed to a small room to discuss the trial and decide who was at fault. If you decide the defendant is guilty, Jacob goes to jail. If you decide he's innocent, he goes free. That's an important decision. You don't want a dangerous person to go unpunished, but neither do you want to send an innocent man to jail. Only the jury decides on the facts. The judge's duty is to uphold and make decisions on the law.

Topics to Consider

Ancient Greek Courts	Jury Trial vs. Trial by Judge
A Famous Trial	Rights of the Accused
Grand Jury	Supreme Court
How a Jury Trial Works	What Does a Judge Do?
How Juries Are Chosen	What Does a Juror Do?

Books

Search Words: Jury, United States; Justice, Administration of, United States

12 Angry Men (videorecording). Santa Monica, CA: MGM, 2001.

Berger, Leslie. *The Grand Jury.* (Crime, Justice and Punishment). Philadelphia: Chelsea House, 2000.

De Capua, Sarah. *Serving on a Jury.* (True Book). New York: Children's Press, 2002.

Egendorf, Laura K. *The Legal System: Opposing Viewpoints.* San Diego: Greenhaven Press, 2003.

Wolf, Robert V. *The Jury System.* (Crime, Justice and Punishment). Philadelphia: Chelsea House, 2002.

Internet

New Jersey Courts Online explains the jury system, including the difference between civil and criminal courts and between types of juries—http://www.judiciary.state.nj.us/juror.htm

Facts about federal courts—http://www.uscourts.gov/faq.html.

Factmonster explains the jury system to kids—http://www.factmonster.com/ce6/society/A0826802.html.

About the Supreme Court—http://www.supremecourtus.gov/about/about.html.

The Supreme Court Historical Society, including cases for and about students—http://www.supremecourthistory.org/.

The Plea, by PBS, tells about the court system—http://www.pbs.org/wgbh/pages/frontline/shows/plea/.

Greek Law Courts, by History for Kids—http://www.historyforkids.org/learn/greeks/government/courts.htm.

Criminal Law Procedure on Kids' Web explains what happens when you're arrested—http://www.metrokc.gov/kcsc/kids/incident.htm.

For the Teacher

The American Jury: Bulwark of Democracy has a detailed explanation of the jury system and suggestions for classroom projects—http://www.crfc.org/americanjury/.

We the Jury

When you have a disagreement, it will often be resolved by a parent or teacher. That's pretty much like having a judge decide. Next time there is a disagreement at home, ask your parents if you can have a trial. The judge's responsibility in a jury trial is to know the law. A jury of your peers, that is, your sisters and brothers or cousins, will decide on the facts of the case. State your case and let the jurors decide.

54

King Cotton (1790–1890)

From 1866 to 1872, inclusive, the port of New Orleans received 6,114,000 bales, or fully one-third of the entire production of the United States. Knowing these statistics, one can hardly wonder at the vast masses of bales on the levee at the landings of the steamers, nor at the numbers of the boats which daily arrive, their sides piled high with cotton.
—The Great South

Words to Know

Agrarian   Gullah
Antebellum   Indigo
Boll Weevil   Plantation
Cotton Gin   Sharecroppers
Eli Whitney   Slavery
Field Hand   Spirituals

Related Jumpstarts

Buffalo Soldiers

Colonial Williamsburg

Underground Railroad

Women at War

You Are There

In 1820 you are 12 years old. You are a slave on a Louisiana plantation. You have been planting and picking cotton for four long years and will probably continue until you are either sold or are too old to work. Life is hard, but you find ways to have fun. You feel pride in the amount of cotton you and your fellow slaves are able to grow and pick. You like the music the slaves sing. Some white masters will not allow the field hands to talk with each other while they work. There is a way, though. The slaves tell stories when they sing. The masters think the songs are spirituals. But really, the slaves are sending secret messages in the words of the songs. Your favorite song is "Steal away. Steal away home." What do you think the slaves mean when they sing this song?

Topics to Consider

Colonial Women	Eli Whitney and the Cotton Gin
Cotton: From Seed to Sale	Life on a Southern Plantation
Cotton and the Old South	Secrets Hidden in Slave Songs
Cotton Gin and Slavery	Sharecroppers in the South
Down on the Docks in 1830	Slavery and Cotton

Books

Search Words: Cotton; Cotton Gin; King Cotton; Plantation Life; Whitney, Eli

Eli Whitney (videorecording). (Inventors of the World). Wynnwood, PA: Schlessinger, 2001.

Erickson, Paul. *Daily Life on a Southern Plantation, 1853.* New York: Lodestar, 1998.

Kalman, Bobbie. *A Slave Family.* (Colonial People). New York: Crabtree, 2003.

Krebs, Laurie. *A Day in the Life of a Colonial Indigo Planter.* New York: PowerKids, 2004.

Nelson, Robin. *From Cotton to T-Shirts.* (Start to Finish). Minneapolis, MN: Lerner, 2003.

Owsley, Frank Lawrence. *King Cotton Diplomacy: Foreign Relations of the Confederate States of America.* Chicago: University of Chicago Press, 1959.

Patchett, Kaye. *Eli Whitney: Cotton Gin Genius.* (Giants of Science). San Diego: Black Birch, 2004.

Walker, Nickie. *Colonial Women.* (Colonial People). New York: Crabtree, 2003.

Internet

Life on a Southern Plantation—http://www.eyewitnesstohistory.com/plantation.htm.

Slave Life: Life on a Plantation has the autobiography of a slave working in the field—http://www.jmu.edu/madison/center/main_pages/madison_archives/era/african/life/hughes/.

The Economy of the South section has good information about life and the economics of cotton in the South—http://www.sagehistory.net/jeffersonjackson/topics/EconomicIssues.htm.

Eli Whitney Museum has information about changes created when the cotton gin was invented—http://www.eliwhitney.org/.

King Cotton in the Civil War—http://www.civilwarhome.com/kingcotton.htm.

Gullah Music—learn how the slaves sent secret codes—http://knowitall.org/gullahmusic/index.html. Turn on your sound and take time at this site. It is very neat.

For the Teacher

Slavery in America has many suggestions—http://www.slaveryinamerica.org/history/overview.htm. For younger students, we love the Gullah site—http://www.knowitall.org/gullahnet/. Go to *Know it All*, the home site, for more. See also http://www.picture-history.com/cotton-index-001.htm.

A Story in Painting

Read the *Great Migration* by Jacob Lawrence online or in a book at your library. Mr. Lawrence is the artist who told this story through his art. The *Great Migration* is the story of slaves finding freedom in the North—http://www.columbia.edu/itc/history/odonnell/w1010/edit/migration/migration.html. Draw your own story about King Cotton or plantation life after you research the topic. Make a series, as Jacob Lawrence did.

55

Lewis & Clark Expedition (1803–1806)

This little fleet altho' not quite so rispectable as those of Columbus and Captain Cook were still viewed by us with as much pleasure as those deservedly famed adventurers ever beheld theirs.—Meriwether Lewis, April 7, 1805

Words to Know

Botany	Flora
Cartography	Louisiana Purchase
Corps of Discovery	Meriwether Lewis
Expedition	Sacagawea (or Sacajawea)
Fauna	William Clark

Related Jumpstarts

Becoming a State

Columbus Discovers America

Go West, Young Man

Indian Tribes in Your State

Making Maps

Mighty Mississippi

Where Cities Bloom

You Are There

President Thomas Jefferson asked Meriwether Lewis and William Clark to explore the land to the west and find a water route from the Atlantic Ocean to the Pacific Ocean. You and about 40 other men load your canoes and head out into territory that no white man has ever explored before. After a year on the trail, you feel pretty confident about your ability to survive in this wild country, but still, every day you find new surprises. There are so many animals and plants that have never been seen before. You have all been collecting as many samples as you can. It's a lot to bring along with you, and Captains Lewis and Clark have decided to send some of them back to President Jefferson. As you watch the canoe with several men head home, you wonder if you will ever see them again. You wonder what is ahead.

Topics to Consider

Dangers on the Trail	Meriwether Lewis
Flora and Fauna on the Trail	Methods of Determining Where They Were
Food on the Trail	Sacagawea
Fur Trade	Smallpox and Other Illnesses on the Trail
Lewis and Clark	Supplies Needed for Exploring
Louisiana Purchase	United States Geological Survey
Mapping the Expedition	William Clark

Books

Search Words: Lewis and Clark Expedition (1804–1806); Sacagawea; West, U.S.—Discovery and Exploration

DeKeyser, Stacy. *Sacagawea*. (Watts Library). New York: Franklin Watts, 2004.

Fox, Michael D., and Suzanne G. Fox. *Meriwether Lewis and William Clark: The Corps of Discovery and the Exploration of the American Frontier*. (Library of American Lives and Times). New York: Rosen, 2005.

Fritz, Harry W. *The Lewis and Clark Expedition*. (Greenwood Guides to Historic Events). Westport, CT: Greenwood Press, 2004.

Isserman, Maurice. *Across America: The Lewis and Clark Expedition*. (Discovery and Exploration). New York: Facts on File, 2005.

Internet

Rivers, Edens and Empires: Lewis & Clark and the Revealing of America, by the Library of Congress. Includes a virtual tour—http://www.loc.gov/exhibits/lewisandclark/lewisandclark.html.

The USGS (United States Geological Survey) considers the Lewis & Clark expedition the first of its surveys—http://www.usgs.gov/features/lewisandclark.html.

PBS Special, *Lewis and Clark: The Journey of the Corps of Discovery*, includes interactive maps and story—http://www.pbs.org/lewisandclark/.

The National Geographic site, *Lewis and Clark*, has a section on Sacajawea, photographs of the trail today, and an online game—http://www.nationalgeographic.com/lewisandclark/.

This site by the Smithsonian Institution features cartography—http://www.edgate.com/lewisandclark/.

The *Journals of the Lewis and Clark Expedition* are available online, for older students—http://lewisandclarkjournals.unl.edu/.

For the Teacher

The National Endowment for the Humanities Edsitement site offers lesson plans on the Lewis & Clark expedition—http://edsitement.neh.gov/view_lesson_plan.asp?id=297.

Exploration

Go on an expedition of discovery of your own. Although there isn't much wilderness to explore, you can choose an area such as a local park or your own back yard. In your journal, record each of your discoveries. Illustrations are very important. Map out your area. Identify each animal and insect that you see, and note where you found them. Collect samples of as many of the plants as you can. Press them and glue or tape them in your journal. You can borrow books from the library to help you identify each of your plants and animals, or flora and fauna. The Online Herbarium Project tells you how to make a plant press—http://www.uen.org/utahlink/pond/buildpress.htm.

Life Along the Nile to 332 BC

Mortals extol (him), and the cycle of gods!
Awe is felt by the terrible ones;
His son is made Lord of all,
To enlighten all Egypt.

Shine forth, shine forth, O Nile! Shine forth!
Giving life to men by his oxen:
Giving life to his oxen by the pastures!
Shine forth in glory, O Nile.

—Hymn to the Nile, 2100 BC

Words to Know

Crocodile	New Kingdom
Giza	Nomadic
Hapy	Old Kingdom
Hieroglyphics	Rosetta Stone
Hippopotamus	Upper Egypt, Lower Egypt
Innundation	

Related Jumpstarts

All Roads Lead to Rome

Ancient Greece

I Am the Pharaoh

Mayan Mathematicians

You Are There

You live along the Nile, the longest river in the world. In the early morning, your mom sends you and your sister to carry water from the river. You carry a large pottery jar to the riverbank. When you get there, you see a hippopotamus mother swimming with her new baby. Farther down the river, a crocodile is asleep on the bank. You talk to your friends, fill the pottery jar, and hurry back home. Your father farms, and you help him. The black earth is very healthy, and crops grow fast. Your mother takes care of the household. She also makes pottery to sell or trade in the village. She has just finished a two-handed pottery saucepan. She will use it to cook your dinner in the clay oven. Life is good.

Topics to Consider

Children in Ancient Egypt	Government in Ancient Egypt
Compare Upper Egypt and Lower Egypt During Ancient Times	Hapy, the Nile God (or Osiris)
	People of the Nile
Daily Life in Ancient Egypt	The Pyramids or Colossus of Memnon
Education in Early Egypt	Rafting on the Nile (What Do You See?)
Farming Along the Nile (in Ancient Egypt)	Tutankhaman or Ramses III

Books

Search Words: Egypt; Egypt—Social Life and Customs; Nile River

Honan, Linda. *Spend the Day in Ancient Egypt: Projects and Activities That Bring the Past to Life.* New York: Wiley, 1999.

Jordan, Shirley. *Ancient Egypt: Moments in History.* (Cover to Cover). Logan, IA: Perfection Learning, 2000.

Koenig, Viviane. *The Ancient Egyptians: Life in the Nile Valley.* (Peuples du Passé). Brookfield, CT: Millbrook, 1992.

Landau, Elaine. *Exploring Ancient Egypt with Elaine Landau.* (Exploring Ancient Civilizations with Elaine Landau). Berkeley Heights, NJ: Enslow Elementary, 2005.

Time-Life Books. *What Life Was Like on the Banks of the Nile.* (What Life Was Like). Alexandria, VA: Time-Life Books, 1996.

Internet

The Nile and Ancient Egypt—http://nefertiti.iwebland.com/geography/nile.htm. (Use the index to find more information about life in ancient Egypt.)

History—The Nile, from BBC, has information on the source of the Nile, its people, and its gods, and is worth your time—http://www.bbc.co.uk/history/ancient/egyptians/nile_01.shtml.

A virtual tour of *Mysteries of the Nile* from PBS—http://www.pbs.org/wgbh/nova/egypt/.

Four essays about the Nile and ancient Egypt by University of Colorado at Denver students, DeNile Team. Very useful—http://carbon.cudenver.edu/stc-link/AE/.

Archived articles on ancient Egypt—*Tour Egypt*—http://www.touregypt.net/magazine/masterindex.htm.

Life in ancient Egypt—http://www2.sptimes.com/Egypt/EgyptCredit.4.2.html.

For the Teacher

PBS—*Egypt's Golden Empire* is an excellent resource for teachers, grades 6–8. Watch PBS video—http://www.pbs.org/empires/egypt/education_lesson1.html.

A Time Capsule

After reading about life in ancient Egypt, create two time capsules. The first will have items from your life today. In the second time capsule put items from life of children along the Nile. Share your selections with your friends. This would be a fun activity to do with your mother and grandmother. What would they put in a time capsule for the time when they were exactly your age?

57

Life in the Middle Ages (1066–1485)

We think of knights in shining armor, lavish banquets, wandering minstrels, kings, queens, bishops, monks, pilgrims, and glorious pageantry. In film and in literature, medieval life seems heroic, entertaining, and romantic. In reality, life in the Middle Ages, a period that extended from approximately the fifth century to the fifteenth century in Western Europe, was sometimes all these things, as well as harsh, uncertain, and often dangerous.—Middle Ages, Annenberg, Learner.org

Words to Know

Bailiff	Open Field Communal System
Enclosures	Peasant
Earl	Reeve
Feudal	System Serf
Herbs	Sheriff
Guild	Shire Court
Journeymen	Steward
Knight	Vassal
Lord	Villien
Manoral System	Waddle-and-Daub

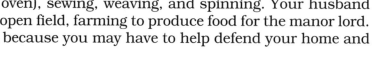

Related Jumpstarts

Aboard the *Mayflower*

Columbus Discovers America

Mayan Mathematicians

Mesa Verde Cliff Dwellings

Salem Witch Trials

You Are There

Imagine yourself as a peasant housewife in the year 1380. Your job is to take care of your family—a difficult task. You live in the small village and are ruled by the manor lord. You grow a garden behind your one-room, waddle-and-daub home. You must include herbs to keep your family healthy, because you are both doctor and nurse. You spend your time cleaning the dirt floors, cooking, baking bread (you have to walk to the edge of town to use the shared oven), sewing, weaving, and spinning. Your husband and children are working in the open field, farming to produce food for the manor lord. You must learn to use weapons because you may have to help defend your home and village.

Topics to Consider

Art and Music of the Middle Ages	Open Field System
Black Death in Medieval Times	The Manoral System
Everyday Life in the Middle Ages	Monk, Nun, Peasant, or Merchant
Feudal System	Peasant Women in the Village
The Justice System in Medieval England	Religion in the Middle Ages
Knighthood	Town Life in the Middle Ages
Lord of the Manor	Witchcraft During the Middle Ages

Books

Search Words: Knights and Knighthood; Medicine or Health; Medieval Civilization; Middle Ages; Other Words with Middle Ages

Barter, James. *Life in a Medieval Village.* (Way People Live). San Diego: Lucent, 2003.

Eastwood, Kay. *Women and Girls in the Middle Ages.* (Medieval World). New York: Crabtree, 2003.

MacDonald, Fiona. *The Plague and Medicine in the Middle Ages.* (World Almanac Library of the Middle Ages). Cleveland, OH: World Almanac, 2005.

Streissguth, Thomas. *The Greenhaven Encyclopedia of the Middle Ages.* San Diego, Greenhaven, 2003.

Internet

If you can't find your information in this collection of information about the Middle Ages—http://www.teacheroz.com/Middle_Ages.htm—you may need another subject.

Medieval England site contains links to personalities and events and other topics for study of this time period—http://www.historylearningsite.co.uk/Year%207.htm.

Britannia: Medieval Resource has great background information for most topics—http://www.britannia.com/history/h60.html.

What was it like to live in the Middle Ages? Find out about life, religion, health, entertainment, and more at this site created for kids—http://www.learner.org/exhibits/middleages/feudal.html.

For older students, this site links to *Middle Age Life.* Find a link to your information or to a specific town or event—http://www.trytel.com/~tristan/towns/towns.html.

For the Teacher

Middle Ages/Renaissance at ProTeacher.com has a long list of plans and activities for all ages—http://www.proteacher.com/090074.shtml.

Back in the Middle Ages

⌁ Learn more about technology in the Middle Ages by creating a time line of inventions used during that period. Share your discoveries with your class—http://scholar.chem.nyu.edu/tekpages/Timeline.html

⌁ Try your hand at creating a book with your own illuminated painting. The monks did this during the Middle Ages (for older students).—http://www.leavesofgold.org/learn/index.html.

58

Lives and Times of My Grandparents

Humankind has not woven the web of life.
We are but one thread within it.
Whatever we do to the web, we do to ourselves.
All things are bound together.
All things connect.

—Chief Seattle

Words to Know

Ancestors	Interview
Celebration	Marian McQuade
Cold War	Recall
Family	Reunion Recollect
Family Tree	Reminisce
Heritage	Scrapbook

Related Jumpstarts

Business of Doing Good	Changing Family	Coming to America
Doughboys, Flying Aces, and Hello Girls	History of Main Street	Man on the Moon
The President Has Been Shot!	Cold War	

You Are There

In 1978 the U.S. Congress passed legislation proclaiming the first Sunday after Labor Day National Grandparents Day. President Jimmy Carter signed it into law. There had long been a Father's Day and a Mother's Day, but no one remembered grandparents. At least not until Marian McQuade of West Virginia decided that someone should set aside a special day just for these parents' parents. The purpose is to honor grandparents, to give grandparents an opportunity to show love for their children's children, and to help children become aware of the strength, information, and guidance older people offer.

Topics to Consider

If your grandparents live nearby, be sure to visit with them and ask them about the past. What was school like when they were growing up? What did they do for entertainment? What are the wonderful things they remember? What about something that was sad or scary? What did they read? What music did they listen to? Have them show you vacation pictures. Family vacations are always memorable. Take notes—or record your conversation.

- Marian McQuade and the First Grandparents Day
- Me and My Granddad (or Grandma)
- My Family Tree
- National Grandparents Day
- What My Grandparents Did When They Were Young

Books

Search Words: American Holidays; Genealogy; Grandparenting; National Grandparents Day

> *Foster Grandparent Program: Operations Handbook.* Washington, DC: National Senior Service Corps, 2000.
>
> Hunter, Dette. *38 Ways to Entertain Your Grandparents.* Toronto: Annick, 2002.
>
> Kent, Susan. *Let's Talk About Living with a Grandparent.* (Let's Talk About). New York: Powerkids, 2000.
>
> Kettman, Susan M. *The 12 Rules of Grandparenting: A New Look at Traditional Roles and How to Break Them.* New York: Facts on File, 2000.
>
> Lakin, Patricia. *Grandparents Around the World.* (We All Share). Farmington Hills, MI: Blackbirch, 1999.
>
> Shepherdson, Nancy. *Ancestor Hunt: Finding Your Family Online.* Danbury, CT: Franklin Watts, 2003.
>
> Taylor, Maureen Alice. *Through the Eyes of Your Ancestors.* Boston: Houghton Mifflin, 1999.

Internet

Genealogy for Kids will get you started—http://genealogy.about.com/library/lessons/blintro1b.htm or http://www.kidsturncentral.com/topics/hobbies/kidsgenealogy.htm.

Select the decade your grandparents grew up in and share the cultural past with them—http://kclibrary.nhmccd.edu/decades.html.

National Grandparents Day—http://www.grandparents-day.com/history.htm.

Marian McQuade biography—http://www.americanprofile.com/issues/20040829/20040829_4148.asp.

History of National Grandparents Day has information about the holiday and about Mrs. McQuade—http://www.associatedcontent.com/article/21769/the_history_of_national_grandparents.html.

KidsHealth discusses living with grandparents—http://www.kidshealth.org/kid/feeling/home_family/grandparents.html.

If you don't have a grandparent, you might be able to get a foster grandparent. Learn all about the Foster Grandparents' Program at Senior Corps—http://www.seniorcorps.gov/about/programs/fg.asp.

For the Teacher

American Cultural History Decades (nineteenth and twentieth centuries)—http://kclibrary.nhmccd.edu/decades.html—at the authors' library site has great information for reports and projects on the past. Or, try these projects—http://www.educationworld.com/a_lesson/lesson/lesson136.shtml.

National Grandparents Day Contest

Follow the directions at http://www.grandparents-day.com/ and enter your artwork and photographs of you and your grandparents into the National Grandparents Day contest. You will be very happy to win the prizes and to see a picture of you and your grandparents online. Look at other winners and watch for the summer deadline.

Making Maps

The ideal geographer should be able to do two things: He should be able to read his newspaper with understanding, and he should be able to take his country walk - or maybe his town walk—with interest.—H. C. Darby, 1946

Words to Know

Cartography
GeoCaching
Geographic Information Systems
Global Positioning
Green mapping

Latitude
Location Tracking
Longitude
System Surveying

Related Jumpstarts

Columbus Discovers America

Fountain of Youth

Lewis & Clark Expedition

You Are There

Your dad just bought a new Mercedes with a GPS navigation system. How does it work? What will it do? Will it stop your dad's getting lost and not asking for directions? That would be nice! Your family also installed a wireless network so that you can all use your computers at the same time. Then, your mom buys you and your sister a Disney mobile phone. With this phone she can track you using GPS technology. And your dad is using a GPS receiver to participate in GeoCaching adventures with friends online. But you wonder: GPS, GIS, GeoCaching, Satellite surveillance, Wireless Area Networks, Radio Frequency Identification; these are all words you have heard in connection with mapping and tracking. My goodness, your head spins. What next? How do you feel about the new mapping devices?

Topics to Consider

Calendars and Mapping	Mapping the Moon
The Degree Confluence Project	Mapping with Aerial Photographs Nowhere to
Disney Mobile Phones for Moms	Hide: Location Tracking
Explorers and Maps	Satellites and Mapmaking
Exploring Google Earth	Visualizing Information
Green Maps—What Are They?	What Is Cartography?
History of Maps and Mapmaking	What Is G.I.S.? Or G.P.S.? Geocaching
Latitude and Longitude	What Is Surveying?

Books

Search Words: Cartography; GIS; GPS; Mapping; Surveying

Alter, Judy. *Exploring and Mapping the American West*. (Cornerstones of Freedom). New York: Children's Press, 2001.

Banquieri, Eduardo. *Secrets of the Earth*. (Our Planet). Philadelphia: Chelsea House, 2006.

Bramwell, Martyn. *How Maps Are Made*. (Maps and Mapmaking). Minneapolis: Lerner, 1998.

Chancellor, Deborah. *Maps and Mapping*. (Kingfisher Young Knowledge). New York: Kingfisher, 2004.

Map Skills for Children: Making and Reading Maps (videorecording). Wynnewood, PA: Schlessinger, 2004.

Olesky, Walter G. *Maps in History*. (Watts Library). New York: Franklin Watts, 2002.

Zelon, Helen. *The Endeavour SRTM: Mapping the Earth*. (Space Missions). New York: PowerKids, 2002.

Internet

Geography World is one of the best sites on the Web for mapping. It is well-organized and has all the information you need. Bookmark it—http://members.aol.com/bowermanb/101.html.

Google Earth is worth spending time with—http://earth.google.com/.

Green Maps describe the environment. Try the project, too—http://www.greenmap.com/home/home.html.

This site teaches about latitude and instruments used in mapping—http://www.ruf.rice.edu/~feegi/.

Use the map machine to see your home or school—http://plasma.nationalgeographic.com/mapmachine/.

Degree Confluence Project may be interesting for older students—http://confluence.org/index.php.

Mathematics of Cartography has excellent information about the history of mapmaking and a time line from ancient maps to the present—http://math.rice.edu/~lanius/pres/map/.

History of Maps is simple to use—http://academic.emporia.edu/aberjame/map/h_map/h_map.htm.

Good historic information with illustrations—http://www.antiquemapsandprints.com/a-map-history.htm.

Explorers and Maps—http://www.collectionscanada.ca/explorers/kids/h3-1211-e.html.

How Stuff Works is a good start point—http://people.howstuffworks.com/location-tracking.htm.

For the Teacher

We love this National Geographic site so much we are recommending it for both educators and students. It is filled with ideas and information—http://www.mywonderfulworld.org/educators_welcome.html.

A Taste of History

Visit *My Wonderful World* by National Geographic. Listen to the sounds, play the games, follow the links, take the tests, and discover your Global IQ. This is a great site for preteens and teens to learn and have fun—http://www.mywonderfulworld.org/kidsteens_welcome.html.

Making Money

Money is not the value for which Goods are exchanged, but the Value by which they are Exchanged: The use of Money is to buy Goods, and Silver while Money is of no other use.—John Law, *Money and Trade Considered With a Proposal for Supplying the Nation with Money,* 1705, http://www.yale.edu/lawweb/avalon/econ/mon.htm

Words to Know

Bartering Gold
Coin Blanks
Counterfeiting
Credit
Currency
Debit
Denomination
National Debt

Standard
Planchet
Strike
Trade
Treasury
Upsetting
U.S. Mint
Wampam

Related Jumpstarts

Banking
Marketing to Kids
Stocks and Bonds
Taxes
Writing the Constitution

You Are There

Watch as a sheet of metal shoots into the machine. The automatic presses come down—whomp—and cut the metal into coin blanks, or planchets. Next, the planchets zip into a giant washing machine to soften and polish them. They roll on over to the upsetting machine to get their smooth, beveled edges if they are nickels or pennies. Dimes, quarters, half dollars, and dollars get ridged edges. Finally, all shiny and upset, they wait for the final strike to stamp both the front and back at the same time. The United States Mint produces over 28 billion coins a year! That's 28,000,000,000. But don't worry; you don't have to count them. The Mint checks to see how many coins are in a roll or a bag by weighing it.

Topics to Consider

Ancient Money	History of the U.S. Mint
Bartering	How Coin Designs Are Chosen
Coin Collecting	Life without Money
Compare Making Coins to Making Paper Money	Loans
Counterfeiting	National Debt
Credit Cards	Report on the History of the Silver Dollar
Gold Standard	State Quarters
History of Money	Treasury Department

Books

Search Words: Money, Juvenile Literature; Money, United States History

Cooper, Jason. *Around the World with Money*. (Money Power). Vero Beach, FL: Rourke, 2003.

Cooper, Jason. *Money Through the Ages*. (Money Power). Vero Beach, FL: Rourke, 2003.

Cribb, Joe. *Money*. (DK Eyewitness). New York: DK Publishing, 2005.

Drobot, Eve. *Money, Money, Money: Where It Comes from, How to Save It, Spend It and Make It*. Toronto: Maple Tree, 2004.

Loewen, Nancy. *Cash, Credit Cards or Checks: A Book about Payment Methods*. (Money Matters). Minneapolis. MN: Picture Window, 2005.

Internet

The United States Bureau of Printing and Engraving tells about money facts and anti-counterfeiting efforts—http://www.moneyfactory.gov/.

The Federal Reserve Bank explains currency and checks and has a video clip, *The Life of a Dollar Bill*—http://www.federalreserveeducation.org/fed101/index.htm.

Learn about state quarters and Westward Journey nickels through the U.S. Mint's Web site—http://www.usmint.gov/mint_programs/.

The United States Mint has information about how coins are minted as well as cool games and coin collecting tips—http://www.usmint.gov/kids/flashIndex.cfm.

Maryland Public Television's Web page *Sense and Dollars* is designed to help middle and high school kids think about money. Includes interactive games and facts—http://senseanddollars.thinkport.org/.

The International Monetary Fund promotes international monetary cooperation. Learn about it—http://www.imf.org/external/np/exr/st/eng/index.htm.

For the Teacher

The United States Department of the Treasury Education page has history, facts, and a virtual tour of the Treasury—http://www.ustreas.gov/education/.

Dollars and Cents

What do Philadelphia, Denver, Washington, D.C., and Fort Worth, Texas, have in common? They are each the location of a United States Mint—http://www.ustreas.gov/education/faq/treasury/tours.shtml#q3. See also the Bureau of Printing and Engraving site—http://www.bep.treas.gov/locations/index.cfm/3.

Man on the Moon (1969–1972)

I slowly pivoted, trying to see everything, and was overwhelmed by the silent, majestic solitude. Not so much as a squirrel track to indicate any sort of life, not a green blade of grass to color the bland, stark beauty, not a cloud overhead, or the slightest hint of a brook or stream. But I felt comfortable, as if I belonged here from where I stood on the floor of this beautiful mountain-ringed valley that seemed frozen in time.—Eugene Cernan, *The Last Man on the Moon*

Words to Know

Apollo	Lunar Roving Vehicle (LVR)
Astronaut	Moon Rocks
Buzz Aldrin	Neil Armstrong
Columbia	Orbital Flight
Command Module	Orion
Cosmonaut	Space Shuttle
Eugene Cernan	Spacesuit
Hermetic Cabin	Suborbital Flight
John Glenn	Trajectory
Lunar	Velocity

Related Jumpstarts

Charles Lindbergh: *The Spirit of St. Louis*
Cold War
Flower Children
Lives and Times of My Grandparents

You Are There

You have been getting ready for this for a long time. In some ways, you have been getting ready since you were a child. You used to look up at the moon and wonder what it would be like up there. You built rockets and shot them up into the sky, imagining that they would reach the moon and leave your mark up there. But now you have prepared in more important ways. You have studied engineering, learned to fly airplanes, and kept yourself in top physical condition. You have worked hard for years for just one goal. You wanted to become an astronaut. Today, you are seated in the space shuttle, waiting for launch.

Topics to Consider

First Man on the Moon International Space Station	Soviet Union's Luna Series
Lunar Camera	Space Debris
Lunar Rover	Space Race with USSR
NASA in Houston	Sputnik
Preparing to Be an Astronaut	Will Man Walk on Mars?
Robot Reconnaissance	

Books

Search Words: Astronautics, History; Moon, Exploration; Space Race

Aaseng, Nathan. *The Space Race.* (World History Series). San Diego: Lucent, 2001.

Cernan, Eugene, and Don Davis. *The Last Man on the Moon: Astronaut Eugene Cernan and America's Race in Space.* New York: St. Martin's Press, 1999.

Dyson, Marianne J. *Home on the Moon.* Washington, DC: National Geographic, 2003.

Feinstein, Stephen. *The Moon.* (Solar System). Berkeley Heights, NJ: MyReportLinks.com, 2005.

Kerrod, Robin. *Dawn of the Space Age.* (History of Space Exploration). Milwaukee, WI: World Almanac, 2005.

Kerrod, Robin. *Space Shuttles.* (History of Space Exploration). Milwaukee, WI: World Almanac, 2005.

Internet

PBS explores moon journeys, including the last man on the moon, Eugene Cernan—http://www.pbs.org/wgbh/nova/tothemoon/.

The NASA Kids page explains simulators, men on Mars, and news in the world of space exploration, with Flash and videos—http://www.nasa.gov/audience/forkids/home/index.html.

The National Aeronautics and Space Administration (NASA) tells about moon exploration past and future, including moonquakes and meteoroids. Includes video and audio presentations—http://www.nasa.gov/mission_pages/exploration/main/index.html.

Exploring the Moon, from the Lunar and Planetary Institute, provides details about the Apollo missions to the moon—http://www.lpi.usra.edu/expmoon/lunar_missions.html.

Go along on a journey to the moon with a video from the Smithsonian Institution—http://www.smithsonianeducation.org/students/idealabs/walking_on_the_moon.html.

Dateline Moon explores the space race, the role of media, and the lunar camera—http://www.newseum.org/datelinemoon/.

For the Teacher

Sky Calls provides educational activities and breaking news about space and astronomy for grades 3–8. Subscribe, and you'll receive weekly updates and maybe even a phone call from space! Sponsored by NASA. Check it out—http://skycalls.org/. Show this wonderful digital story to your class for discussion—http://www.coe.uh.edu/digital-storytelling/civilization.htm.

Build a Crew Exploration Vehicle

Maybe someday you will be an astronaut and be able to travel into space. Meanwhile, try building a model spacecraft. You can get a plastic model at a hobby shop or try this paper model—http://www.esa.int/esaKIDSen/build.html.

Marketing to Kids

Children's identities shouldn't be defined by their consumer habits; yet that is the main way they see themselves reflected in the media—as consumers, and advertisers are targeting younger and younger children with this message. The marketing of merchandise based on the popular pre-school TV programs Barney *and* Teletubbies *marked the beginning of identifying toddlers as a consumer market. Reporting on this trend, the industry magazine* KidsScreen *noted that: "Agencies are cautiously eyeing the zero-to-three year-old demographic—a group that poses tremendous challenges and opportunities, because research has indicated that children are capable of understanding brands at very young ages."—Media Awareness*

Words to Know

Advertising
Brand Consciousness
Buying Power
Commercialism
Consumers
Disposable Income
Expenditures

Kidfluence
Manipulation
Marketing
Media
Sales Pitch
Tween

Related Jumpstarts

American Sweatshops
Banking
I Want That! Needs vs. Wants
Peer Pressure
Supply and Demand
Wal-Mart Comes to Our Town

You Are There

Imagine this: Your parents spend lots of money on you, buying you pretty much everything you want. You have an allowance. You have a bank account with money from birthdays and Christmas. Your grandparents give you money on special holidays. You and your friends are a real force in the marketplace. You understand that the 19.5 million tweens (kids ages 8–14) spend about $14 billion a year. It is no wonder that advertising focuses on you and your fellow tweens. From junk food to fast food to brand name toys and clothes, marketers are selling things you need—on television and on the Internet. It is paradise for a born-to-shop tween like you.

Topics to Consider

Are We a Junk Food Nation?	Peer Pressure and Marketing
Can Kids Understand Advertising vs. Truth?	Subliminal Advertising
Character Licensing	Television and Online Marketing for Kids
How Does Online Marketing Affect Me?	The Tween Market—Big Spenders
How Does Television Marketing Affect Me?	What Is Marketing Aimed at Kids?

Books

Search Words: Advertising and Children; Brand Name Marketing; Child Consumers (add Juvenile Literature to the terms); Marketing—Kids; Teenage Consumers

Day, Nancy. *Advertising: Information or Manipulation?* (Issues in Focus). Springfield, NJ: Enslow, 1999.

Frisch, Carlienne. *Hearing the Pitch: Evaluating All Kinds of Advertising.* (Life Skills Library). New York: Rosen, 1994.

Graydon, Shari. *Made You Look: How Advertising Works and Why You Should Know.* New York: Annick, 2003.

Linn, Susan E. *Consuming Kids: The Hostile Takeover of Childhood.* New York: New Press, 2004.

Schor, Juliet. *Born to Buy: The Commercialized Child and the New Consumer Culture.* New York: Scribner's, 2004.

Sutherland, Anne. *Kidfluence: The Marketer's Guide to Understanding and Reaching Generation Y—Kids, Tweens and Teens.* New York: McGraw-Hill, 2003.

Internet

Differences between Online and Television Marketing to Kids—Media Awareness—http://www.media-awareness.ca/english/resources/educational/handouts/internet/tv_versus_internet.cfm.

Marketing to Kids has good statistics about kids and spending. It includes a bibliography with online links—http://www.newdream.org/kids/facts.php.

Understanding the Kids' Market—http://www.kidsmarketing.com/index.php.

Three articles about tweens—http://www.toydirectory.com/monthly/online_archive.asp#tween.

Tween Loyalty—with statistics—http://www.ogilvy.com/uploads/koviewpoint/v8_tween_loyalty_0.pdf.

For the Teacher

Online Marketing to Kids: Strategies and Techniques has information, links, and activities for grades 6–9—http://www.media-awareness.ca/english/resources/educational/lessons/secondary/internet/online_kids_strategies.cfm.

The Marketing Campaign

Create a marketing campaign to sell several toys to your friends. What will make your friends want your toys? A fair price? A collection? Good condition? A test drive? Something they don't have? Think about the complete campaign. You might make an ad for the Sunday paper or send out coupons. And don't forget the Internet and television. Include a creative display of your sale items.

Mayan Mathematicians (AD 150–1500)

The Mayans of Guatemala and the surrounding regions had one of the most advanced civilizations of the ancient world. . . . Particularly skilled in mathematics and astronomy, Mayan scientists developed a calendar more precise than that used by NASA even today.—Court Services, District of Columbia, http://www.csosa.gov/eeo/Hispanic/guatemala.htm

Words to Know

Archeology
Artifacts
Calendar
Chichen Itza
Chicklet Tree
Codex
Dynasty

Frederick Catherwood
Hieroglyphs
John Lloyd Stevens
Pyramid
Quetzalcoatl
Tortillas
Yucatec

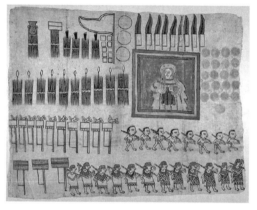

Related Jumpstarts

All Roads Lead to Rome
Ancient Greece
Indian Tribes in Your State
Life along the Nile
Mesa Verde Cliff Dwellings

You Are There

It is a day like any other day. Your brothers and father awaken with the dawn to eat a breakfast of toasted tortillas before walking out to the corn fields to work. Your sisters take the pots of dried corn that have been soaking in water all night, wash the corn, and grind it to make dough for fresh tortillas. They make a stew from beans and vegetables, seasoned with nice, hot chilies. Mother carries the new baby with her, keeping boards around her head to be sure she grows up with a flat, broad skull. A bead dangles between her eyes to encourage her eyes to cross. In the afternoon you and the other boys and men return from the field, tired and hungry, to find the fresh stew and corn tortillas ready. You eat and eat. After you finish, the girls eat what is left and set new corn aside to soak for tomorrow. Soon after dark, everyone is asleep.

Topics to Consider

Archeology	John Lloyd Stephens
Calendars of the Past	Mayan Architecture
Chichen Itza	Mayan Mathematics
Explore the Codex	Pyramids of Antiquity
Food of the Mayans	Rise and Fall of the Mayan Dynasty
Frederick Catherwood	

Books

Search Words: Indians of Central America; Mayas, History; Mayas, Social Life and Culture

Ackroyd, Peter. *Cities of Blood.* (Voyages through Time). London: DK Publishing, 2005.

Baquedano, Elizabeth. *Aztec, Inca and Maya* (DK Eyewitness). New York: DK Publishing, 2005.

George, Charles, and Linda George. *The Maya.* (Life during the Great Civilizations). San Diego: Blackbirch, 2004.

Meyer, Carolyn, and Charles Gallenkamp. *Mystery of the Ancient Maya.* New York: Atheneum, 1985.

Perl, Lila. *The Ancient Maya.* (People of the Ancient World). New York: Franklin Watts, 2005.

Trout, Lawana Hooper. *The Maya.* (Indians of North America). New York: Chelsea House, 1991.

Internet

Why Do Cities Fail? Explore the fall of the Mayan city of Copan—http://www.learner.org/exhibits/collapse/.

MayanKids has brief, easily understood information on all aspects of Mayan life, including the calendar, games, food, and music—http://www.mayankids.com/.

Pictures of Chichen Itza and other Mayan sites from Villanova University—http://facultysenate.villanova.edu/maya/itza.html.

The Mayan calendar explained in detail by Web Exhibits—http://webexhibits.org/calendars/calendar-mayan.html.

More about the Mayan calendar—http://www.mayacalendar.com/.

Mayan Culture and Architecture from the University of Guadalajara—http://mexico.udg.mx/historia/precolombinas/ingles/maya/index.html.

This PBS site has information on the explorers John Lloyd Stephens and Frederick Catherwood, maps, and hieroglyphs—http://www.pbs.org/wgbh/nova/maya/.

For the Teacher

PBS offers new insight into the collapse of the Mayan civilization. It includes math activities related to the calendar—http://www.pbs.org/wgbh/nova/teachers/programs/2804_maya.html.

Mayan Math

Go to http://www.hanksville.org/yucatan/mayamath.html to learn more about Mayan math. For a few days, do your math homework using this ancient system. Teach your teacher and your friends.

Mesa Verde Cliff Dwellings (600–1300)

We have lived upon this land from days' memory, deep into the time of legend. The story of my people and the story of this place are one single story. We are always joined together.—Pueblo elder

Words to Know

Anasazi	Kiva
Ancient Ones	Mesa
Basketmakers	Petroglyphs
Clan	Pit Houses
Cliff Dwellings	Pueblo Indians
Indigenous	Tribe
Kachina	

Related Jumpstarts

Go West, Young Man

Indian Tribes in Your State

You Are There

It is 1154. You are a Pueblo Indian, 13 years old. You live in a village above a cliff. Your village consists of pueblos. There is a large underground ceremonial structure known as a kiva. The council chamber, made up of the elders, meets in the kiva to discuss issues about survival. Your father helps other members of your community farm the land. They grow pumpkins, squash, melons, and corn. You help the men farm, and hunt deer and wild turkeys. Your mother weaves the beautiful blankets you sleep under and the clothes you wear. She and other women make baskets and pottery. Your sister is learning, too.

Topics to Consider

Agriculture of the Pueblo People	Daily Life of the Anasazi Indians
The Anasazi People	The Kiva
Anasazi Stages of Life	Mesa Verde Cliff Dwellings
Apartment Living in the Cliff Palace	Pueblo Indians and the Spanish
Art of the Pueblo Indian Women	Pueblo Village Government
Basketmakers in Mesa Verde	Religion of the Anasazi
Crafts of the Cliff Dwellers	The Taos Pueblo
Creation of Mesa Verde National Park, 1906	

Books

Search Words: Cliff Dwellings; Mesa Verde; Native Americans—Homes

Anderson, Dale. *The Anasazi Culture at Mesa Verde.* (Landmark Events in American History). Milwaukee, WI: World Almanac, 2003.

Folsom-Dickerson, W. E. S. *Cliff Dwellers.* San Antonio, TX: Naylor, 1968.

Goodman, Susan. *Stones, Bones, and Petroglyphs: Digging into Southwest Archaeology.* New York: Atheneum Books for Young Readers, 1998.

Kopper, Philip. *The Smithsonian Book of North American Indians.* Washington, DC: Smithsonian, 1986.

Quigley, Mary. *Mesa Verde.* (Excavating the Past). Chicago: Heinemann, 2005.

Radlauer, Ruth. *Mesa Verde National Park.* Chicago: Children's Press, 1989.

Internet

Anasazi: The Ancient Ones site covers everything about the ancient tribe to the present Pueblo Indians—http://www.cliffdwellingsmuseum.com/anasazi.htm.

Mesa Verde, Anasazi history—http://gorp.away.com/gorp/resource/us_national_park/co/his_mes.htm.

National Park Service has an excellent site containing history of Mesa Verde and information about the different dwellings—http://www.nps.gov/meve/park_info/park_history.htm.

Early History of the Mesa Verde Area—http://www.mesaverdefoundation.org/area-history-early.shtml.

Mesa Verde National Park and its history—http://www.design.upenn.edu/hspv/mesaverde/mesa_verde.htm.

Excavating Mug House—http://www.design.upenn.edu/hspv/mesaverde/site_mughouse.htm.

This article in the *Online Albuquerque Journal* has background information—http://www.abqjournal.com/venue/travel/tourism/heritage_mesaverde.htm.

The *Pueblo Indian History* is quite long, but thorough and worth reading for your own topic—http://www.puebloindian.com/pueblo_history_001.htm.

Pueblo Indians' Influence. Village planning—http://www.cabq.gov/aes/s3pueblo.html.

For the Teacher

Anasazi Indians site has much for teachers and students. Enjoy this fabulous Web site—http://www.scsc.k12.ar.us/2002Outwest/Ecology/Projects/JeffersE/Default.htm.

The Cliff Dwellings

Have a little fun. Just think about homes on the sides of mountains. Compare the cliff dwellers with city apartment houses. Find materials and build an example of each. Or create a chart with comparisons. Make your own adobe bricks for your cliff house—http://www.nps.gov/tuma/AdobeBricks.html.

The Mighty Mississippi

Here we all work 'long the Mississippi
Here we all work while the white folk play
Pullin' them boats from the dawn till sunset
Gettin' no rest till the judgment day

Ol' Man River, that Ol' Man River
He must know somepin', but he don't say nothin'
He just keeps rollin', he keeps on rollin' along

I gets weary and so sick of tryin'
I'm tired of livin', but I'm feared of dyin'
And Ol' Man River, he just keeps rollin' along.

—Oscar Hammerstein II, "Ol' Man River"

Words to Know

Floodplain   River Pilots
Mark Twain   Riverboat
Mississippi   River Steamboat
Paddle Wheel   Sternwheelers

Related Jumpstarts

Atchison, Topeka, and Santa Fe Railroad   Becoming a State
Go West, Young Man   Indian Tribes in Your State
Lewis & Clark Expedition   Life Along the Nile

You Are There

It is 1840, and you are 12 years old. You live in a small town in Missouri, along the banks of the Mississippi River. Your dad is a river boat pilot, and during the summer you are lucky enough to be able to travel along the river with him. At other times you roam the river banks in search of treasure. You take home a string of fish for your mom to cook for dinner. Your town is lively because river travel is the primary method of travel. All kinds of goods are delivered up and down the river. New people arrive in town everyday. Many are traveling west to make a new life. You listen to their tales of adventure. What a wonderful life!

Topics to Consider

Ancient Life along the Mississippi	Mississippi River Bridges
Commerce on the Mississippi	Music Along the Mississippi
Explorers on the Mississippi	Steamboats and River Pilots
Facts about the Mississippi Life in a	Transportation on the Mississippi
Nineteenth-Century River Town	When the River Was King
Mark Twain's Mississippi River	

From *99 Jumpstarts for Kids' Social Studies Reports: Research Help for Grades 3–8* by Peggy J. Whitley and Susan Williams Goodwin. Westport, CT: Libraries Unlimited. Copyright © 2007.

Books

Search Words: City and Town Life—Mississippi River; Exploration; Mississippi River

Bowden, Rob. *Settlements of the Mississippi River.* (Rivers through Time). Chicago: Heinemann, 2004.

Fischer, Laura. *Life in a Mississippi River Town.* (Picture the Past). Chicago: Heinemann, 2003.

Harmon, Daniel E. *LaSalle and the Exploration of the Mississippi.* (Explorers of New Worlds). Philadelphia: Chelsea House, 2001.

Pollard, Michael. *The Mississippi.* (Great Rivers). New York: Benchmark, 1997.

Stein, R. Conrad. *The Story of Mississippi Steamboats.* (Cornerstones of Freedom). Chicago: Children's Press, 1987.

Vieira, Linda. *The Mighty Mississippi: The Life and Times of America's Greatest River.* New York: Walker, 2005.

Internet

PBS *River of Song* project has clips and information about music genres up and down the Mississippi River. Choose a part of the Mississippi—http://www.pbs.org/riverofsong/project/.

Mark Twain's Mississippi. Don't miss the audios, videos, and photographs—http://dig.lib.niu.edu/twain/.

Nile of the New World has information about the Lower Mississippi Delta. Find topics to write about (perhaps the Civil War along the Mississippi)—http://www.cr.nps.gov/delta/.

Ancient Life Along the Mississippi—http://www.cr.nps.gov/archeology/feature/riverlif.htm.

The Mighty Mississippi—use the links at this excellent site. Find out about steamboats and river pilots—http://cgee.hamline.edu/rivers/Resources/river_profiles/mississippi.html.

Old Man River museum exhibit has good information and photographs. Find your topic and follow the links—http://hoover.archives.gov/exhibits/Mississippi/index.html.

History of River Transportation—http://cgee.hamline.edu/rivers/Resources/Voices/transportation1.htm.

For the Teacher

Discovery School has excellent lesson plans for several grade levels and crossing disciplines—http://school.discovery.com/lessonplans/programs/mississippi/.

Steamboat News

Create your own newspaper of happenings along the Mississippi. Have a few friends contribute articles. Use newsprint. Choose a time period (like 1840) and write articles about the river pilots, passengers on the steamboats, a list of arrivals, recipes (get vintage ones from http://theoldentimes.com/ms_river_news.html.) Don't forget a few pictures to make your paper interesting. You may want to publish helpful hints for travelers on the Mississippi.

Missouri Compromise (1820)

And be it further enacted, *That in all territory ceded by France to the United States under the name of Louisiana which lies north of 36 degrees and thirty minutes north latitude, not included within the limits of the state contemplated by this act, slavery and involuntary servitude, otherwise than in the punishment of crimes, whereof these parties shall have been duly convicted, shall be and is hereby forever prohibited: Provided always that any person escaping into the same, from whom labor or service is lawfully claimed, in any state or territory of the United States, such fugitive may be lawfully reclaimed and conveyed to the person claiming his or her labor or service as aforesaid.*—Missouri Compromise, March 6, 1820, 16th Cong., 1st Sess., Ch, 22, § 8.

Words to Know

Abolitionist
Anti-slavery
Compromise of 1820
Compromise of 1850
Dred Scott
Fifth Amendment

Fugitive Slave Act
Nullification Crisis
Pro-slavery
Secession
Slave Catchers

Related Jumpstarts

Becoming a State
Civil War Spies
King Cotton
Underground Railroad
Writing the Constitution

Effects of the Fugitive-Slave-Law.

You Are There

Some of the people in Missouri own slaves now, in 1818. Some of them don't. But when it was time to petition Congress to let Missouri become a state, they asked to be a slave state. You can't believe what a ruckus that has caused! The House of Representatives says Missouri can be a state only if it's a free state. The Senate says Congress doesn't have a right to say any such thing. For a while, it looked like Missouri wasn't going to become a state at all. Then Henry Clay came up with a compromise solution. He set a dividing line between slave states and free states in the Louisiana Territory. He may have just prevented the Union from dissolving . . . yet.

Topics to Consider

Abolitionists	Fugitive Slave Act
American Colonization Society	Henry Clay Biography
Amistad (Slave Ship)	Kansas-Nebraska Act
Balance of Power in Congress	Missouri Comprise—What Is it?
Compromise of 1850 (Pearce Act)	Should Missouri Be a Slave State? (You Are There)
Dred Scott Case	Slave Auction

Books

Search Words: Dred Scott Trial; Slavery, Law and Legislation; United States—Politics and Government—1815–1861

Burgan, Michael. *The Missouri Compromise.* (We the People). Minneapolis, MN: Compass Point, 2006.

January, Brendan. *The Dred Scott Decision.* (Cornerstones of Freedom). New York: Children's Press, 1998.

Ray, Delia. *A Nation Torn: The Story of How the Civil War Began.* (Young Readers History of the Civil War). New York: Lodestar, 1990.

Swain, Gwyneth. *Dred and Harriet Scott: A Family's Struggle for Freedom.* St. Paul, MN: Borealis, 2004.

Tibbets, Alison Davis. *Henry Clay: From "War Hawk" to the "Great Compromiser."* (Historical American Biographies). Berkeley Heights, NJ: Enslow, 2003.

Internet

A map showing free states and slave states—http://www.rosecity.net/civilwar/capesites/warmap.html.

This Dred Scott time line shows the rise and fall of the Missouri Compromise—http://library.wustl.edu/vlib/dredscott/chronology.html.

Answers.com explains the Missouri Compromise, with links to the Fifth Amendment and *Dred Scott*—http://www.answers.com/topic/missouri-compromise-of-1820.

A detailed discussion of the *Dred Scott* case and its implications from the Freeman Institute—http://www.freemaninstitute.com/scott.htm.

PBS considers the Compromise of 1850 and the Fugitive Slave Act—http://www.pbs.org/wgbh/aia/part4/4p2951.html.

The Library of Congress shows original documents from the Missouri Compromise debate—http://www.loc.gov/rr/program/bib/ourdocs/Missouri.html.

History and time line of Liberia and the American Colonization Society from the Library of Congress—http://memory.loc.gov/ammem/gmdhtml/libhtml/liberia.html.

For the Teacher

The National Endowment for the Humanities has lesson plans for the Missouri Compromise in *The House Dividing: The Growing Crisis of Sectionalism in Antebellum America*—http://edsitement.neh.gov/view_lesson_plan.asp?id=658.

Find a Compromise

Have you ever had a conflict with your brother, sister, or classmate? You want your way, your sibling wants his or hers, and neither of you will give in. You need to learn the art of compromise! Next time a conflict arises, try to find a solution by which everyone gets some of what they want and yet everyone gives up a little to make the other person happy. PBS has some ideas for you—http://pbskids.org/itsmylife/family/vacations/article6.html.

Oklahoma Land Rush (1889)

On April 22, 1889, people who gathered on the Arkansas and Texas borders of Oklahoma could seek a parcel of unclaimed land and file for ownership with the federal government. Most of these people were from Kansas and Missouri, but people from all over the country were part of the pack. Buglers were stationed at intervals around the perimeters of the region and they announced the opening of the new land at noon. People burst westward in droves on the Sante Fe Railroad, in covered wagons, and on horseback. They rode frantically racing to secure the best parcels of land before anyone else could. The weather was perfect, sunny and dry, for the frantic quest.—Kellie Sisson Snider, © 2002 http://sdsd.essortment.com/oklahomalandru_rccj.htm

Words to Know

Boomers · Land Rush
Buffalo Soldiers · Reservations
Covered Wagons · Sod House
Eighty-Niners · Sooners
Free Homes Bill/Act of 1900 (Public Law 105)
Homestead Act · Unassigned Lands

Related Jumpstarts

Atchison, Topeka, and Santa Fe Railroad · Becoming a State · Buffalo Soldiers
Go West, Young Man · Trail of Tears · Where Cities Bloom

You Are There

It is April 22, 1889, and your family is on the Arkansas border waiting for the buglers to blow their horns. When that happens, everyone will rush forward to claim free land in the Oklahoma Territory. Buffalo soldiers and other men are placed at intervals all around the state watching the borders to make sure everyone starts together. The Santa Fe Railroad has an enormous load of passengers. Many men are on horseback and some are leading oxen or riding in covered wagons. You are in a covered wagon with your mother and brothers. Your father is in the driver's seat. Four mules are tied to the wagon. The bugle sounds! You rush forward with all the others, shouting and laughing. No one rents in Oklahoma!

Topics to Consider

All-Black Towns in Oklahoma	Homestead Act of 1862
Boomers and Sooners	The Land Rush
Broken Promises: Indian Lands and the Government	Life in a Sod House
Buffalo Soldiers and the Land Rush	Oklahoma Territory
Harrison's Horse Race	Settling in Oklahoma

Books

Search Words: Homestead Act; Oklahoma—History; Oklahoma Land Rush

Hauswald, Carol. *Westward Movement: Expanding America's Boundaries 1800–1900.* Tucson, AZ: Zephyr, 1998.

Isaacs, Sally Senzel. *The Great Land Rush.* (American Adventure). Chicago: Heinemann, 2004.

Johnson, Hannibal B. *Acres of Aspiration: The All-Black Towns in Oklahoma.* Austin, TX: Eakins, 2002.

Landau, Elaine. *The Homestead Act.* (True Book). New York: Children's Press, 2006.

McCaughrean, Geraldine. *Stop the Train.* New York: HarperCollins, 2003. (fiction)

Internet

The Oklahoma Land Rush is easy to understand—http://sdsd.essortment.com/oklahomalandru_rccj.htm.

Oklahoma Land Run has facts and statistics—http://www.sandplum.com/guthrie/landrun.htm.

Harrison's Horse Race and other info about Edmond—http://www.edmondhistory.org/exhi_harr.html.

Oklahoma Land Openings contains links to essays about the 1889–1907 land rush and those of the future. It is worth spending time here—http://marti.rootsweb.com/land/oklands.html.

Encyclopedia of Oklahoma History and Culture Index has a listing of essays about Oklahoma. Be sure to look at *Settlement Patterns*—http://www.ok-history.mus.ok.us/enc/ENCINDEX2.htm.

Life in a Sod House and other essays about not only Oklahoma but several other territories and the Homestead Act—http://www.museumoftheamericanwest.org/explore/exhibits/sod/daily.html.

The National Park Service (NPS) has a copy of the Homestead Act and a map of the states—http://www.nps.gov/home/homestead_act.html.

For the Teacher

Although the pictures are from the Nebraska, the museum has many worthwhile activities for your class on the Homestead Act—http://www.museumoftheamericanwest.org/explore/exhibits/sod/activities.html.

Rushing for Land

⅄ Learn a little Lakota Indian language—http://www.native-languages.org/dakota.htm.

⅄ Bunco history—get a bunco game together. Bunco was played in Oklahoma in the 1890s—http://www.worldbunco.com/history.html.

⅄ Research your own state. How and when did people locate there? Write about a significant event that happened during the early days of statehood—or when it was a territory.

Oldest Person in Town

The great secret that all old people share is that you really haven't changed in 70 or 80 years. Your body changes, but you don't change at all.—Doris Lessing, O Magazine, October 2003

Words to Know

Active   Lifestyle
Aged   Retirement
Elderly   Transcribe
Experiences   Volunteerism

Related Jumpstarts

Business of Doing Good

Lives and Times of My Grandparents

You Are There

In the picture above you see Professor Ed Peniche. Professor Peniche fought at the Battle of the Bulge in 1945. (See Ed Peniche, *World War II Journal*, http://kclibrary.nhmccd.edu/peniche.html.) He is a trained linguist in English, Spanish, Portuguese, French, and Vietnamese. Following a long career in the service (he fought in World War II, Korea, and Vietnam) he taught college. Retiring at the age of 75, he has continued to speak to college and high school students all over the world about the importance of education. At 83, Ed is still a dynamo. In 2005 the energetic Dr. Peniche went to Longchamps, Belgium, for the commemoration of the sixtieth anniversary of Battle of the Bulge. Then he left Longchamps to speak to friends at a reception in Holland. During the past 10 years, he has been asked to speak in Washington, D.C., and many other places, and has won awards from agencies worldwide. Both Ed's parents lived long and happy lives. For your report, find someone who remains an active part of the community. These oldsters have wonderful stories to tell. Tape your interview and then transcribe it.

Topics to Consider

Interview an elderly member of your community. Find someone who is at least 80 years old. Ask how he or she feels about being elderly. What is the best thing about being old? The worst? Try to get a good quote from the person about "aging." What is he or she doing today to remain strong and to keep active? How does he or she feel about some of the changes in the world since he or she was young? Does the person use technology? This can be a very good report. Many elderly feel like Doris Lessing in the quote we have at the top of this jumpstart: "Your body changes but you don't." Ask your interviewee if he or she feels that way.

Books

Search Words: Elderly; Interview; Interview Tips; Oral History

Brady, John. *The Craft of Interviewing.* New York: Vintage, 1977.

Brown, Cynthia Stokes. *Like It Was: A Complete Guide to Writing Oral History.* New York: Teachers & Writers, 1988.

Keats, Daphne M. *Interviewing: A Practical Guide for Students and Professionals.* Sydney: University of New South Wales Press, 2000.

LoVerde, Mary. *Touching Tomorrow: How to Interview Your Loved Ones to Capture a Lifetime of Memories on Video or Audio.* New York: Fireside, 2000.

Mabery, D. L. *Tell Me About Yourself: How to Interview Anyone from Your Friends to Famous People.* Minneapolis, MN: Lerner, 1985.

Mullen, Patricia B. *Listening to Old Voices: Folklore, Life Stories, and the Elderly.* Urbana: University of Illinois Press, 1991.

Internet

Interview questions for you—http://www.members.tripod.com/the_english_dept/projects/files/interviewplan.html.

History Matters—Oral History on tape and lots of good information about how to go about interviewing and collecting data—http://www.historymatters.gmu.edu/mse/oral/question1.html.

Hometown Heroes has examples of write-ups about people who are heroes. Good examples to read before you begin—http://www.weta.org/community/hometownheroes/heroes.php.

Oral history in your community. Hints for the interviewer and good explanations of the value and methods you can use—http://muextension.missouri.edu/explore/aging/gg0008.htm.

Fifty questions for family history interviews by kids. Select from this list for a good interview with the elderly person you choose—http://genealogy.about.com/cs/oralhistory/a/interview.htm.

Conducting oral history interviews—http://www.nebraskastudies.org/1100/1100_1002.html.

For the Teacher

The Learning Page from Library of Congress has good examples and lesson plans using oral history—http://memory.loc.gov/learn/lessons/oralhist/ohhome.html. Use the strategies to have students evaluate the histories they get from this project.

Who Will You Be When You Are Old?

Conduct an interview with your future, elderly self. Take time to reflect on what your life may be like. Include the questions found at http://sfhelp.org/01/future_self.htm.

Peer Pressure

Read, every day, something no one else is reading. Think, every day, something no one else is thinking. Do, every day, something no one else would be silly enough to do. It is bad for the mind to continually be part of unanimity.—Christopher Morley, http://www.quotegarden.com/conformity.html

Words to Know

Cliques
Conformity
Fads
Honor System

Nonconformist
Self-Confidence
Unanimity

Related Jumpstarts

Business of Doing Good

Fighting Prejudice

Flower Children

I Want That! Needs vs. Wants

Marketing to Kids

You Are There

You know the feeling. There is a big test in math, and you really haven't figured out how to do the problems. Sure, you should have studied more, but it's too late now. The test is in 10 minutes. As you try to cram during lunch, one of the cool kids, Cory, comes up to you. "Don't worry about the test," he whispers. "John borrowed a copy last night. Here are the answers." You look up at him in disbelief. "But . . . that's cheating!" "Don't worry about it," he assures you. "Everybody's doing it." "What if we get caught?" You worry. "No sweat," Cory says. "The teacher can't flunk us all." You look at the paper. All it gives are the answers. A, C, D, A, B. "Are you sure these are right? Who figured them out?" "The copy John borrowed had the answer key. What's wrong, are you chicken?" A little while later, you stare at the math test in front of you. As you start to work the first problem, Cory's words invade your thoughts. "What's wrong, are you chicken?" You start to write. A, C, D, A, B . . . .

Topics to Consider

Alcohol and Teens	Peer Relationships
Developing the Right Friends	Resisting Pressure
Developing Self-Esteem	Standing up for What's Right
Forming Cliques at School: The Good	Virtues of Being Different
and the Bad and the Ugly	What Is Peer Pressure?
Keeping up with the Joneses	

From *99 Jumpstarts for Kids' Social Studies Reports: Research Help for Grades 3–8* by Peggy J. Whitley and Susan Williams Goodwin. Westport, CT: Libraries Unlimited. Copyright © 2007.

Books

Search Words: Cliques (Sociology); Fads; Friendship in Adolescence; Peer Pressure

InVision Communications. *Peer Pressure* (videorecording). (Schlessinger Teen Health). Bala Cynwyd, PA: Schlessinger Video Productions, 1994.

Koubek, Christine Wickert. *Friends, Cliques and Peer Pressure: Be True to Yourself.* (Teen Issues). Berkeley Heights, NJ: Enslow, 2002.

Simmons, Rachel. *Odd Girl Speaks Out: A Girl Writes about Bullies, Cliques, Popularity and Jealousy.* Orlando, FL: Harcourt, 2004.

Slavens, Elaine. *Peer Pressure: How to Deal with It Without Losing Your Cool.* (Deal with It). Toronto: J. Lorimer, 2004.

Spangenburg, Ray, and Kit Moser. *Teen Fads: Fun, Foolish or Fatal?* (Teen Issues). Berkeley Heights, NJ: Enslow, 2003.

Internet

Kids Health discusses peer pressure—http://kidshealth.org/kid/feeling/friend/peer_pressure.html.

Peer Pressure . . . the Good and the Bad from ThinkQuest—http://library.thinkquest.org/3354/Resource_Center/Virtual_Library/Peer_Pressure/peer.htm.

The Cool Spot, from the Department of Health and Human Services helps you learn to resist peer pressure—http://www.thecoolspot.gov/pressures.asp.

Experiments that show the power of peer pressure, from I Am Next—http://www.iamnext.com/living/image.html.

Focus Adolescent Services discusses peer influence and peer relationships—http://www.focusas.com/PeerInfluence.html.

The National Institute on Drug Abuse presents a scholarly paper on peer relationships and substance abuse—http://www.nida.nih.gov/NIDA_notes/NNVol18N2/Relationships.html.

For the Teacher

Peer Pressure from the British Broadcasting Company (BBC) has experiments that illustrate this concept—http://news.bbc.co.uk/cbbcnews/hi/teachers/pshe_11_14/subject_areas/peer_pressure/newsid_2960000/2960308.stm.

A Taste of History

See if you can start a new trend yourself. Choose something new—wearing red shoes or a certain kind of bracelet, for example. Make it yourself or go to the store and look around for something different. When anyone asks you about it, say, "This is the latest thing. All the cool kids are wearing them." If you let one or two of your friends in on the secret, they can start wearing the same thing. All the other kids will believe that it is really becoming the in thing to do.

70

Pilgrim Harvest (1621)

Our corn did prove well, and God be praised, we had a good increase of Indian corn, and our barley indifferent good, but our peas not worth the gathering, for we feared they were too late sown. They came up very well, and blossomed, but the sun parched them in the blossom. Our harvest being gotten in, our governor sent four men on fowling, that so we might after a special manner rejoice together after we had gathered the fruit of our labors. They four in one day killed as much fowl as, with a little help beside, served the company almost a week. At which time, amongst other recreations, we exercised our arms, many of the Indians coming amongst us, and among the rest their greatest king Massasoit, with some ninety men, whom for three days we entertained and feasted, and they went out and killed five deer, which they brought to the plantation and bestowed on our governor, and upon the captain and others.—Edward Winslow, letter, December 12, 1621

Words to Know

Colonists	Ojibwa
Fowl	Pilgrims
Harvest	Plymouth Rock
Maize	Squanto
Massosoit	Thanksgiving
Myles Standish	Wampanoag
Myth	

Related Jumpstarts

13 Colonies	Abigail Adams	Aboard the *Mayflower*
Benjamin Franklin, Statesman	Boston Tea Party	Coming to America
Writing the Constitution		

You Are There

It is the fall of 1621, and 90 Wampanoag Indians and 52 English colonists are gathering for a three-day harvest feast. You are one of the Indians. The English arrived on your shores a year ago and, with the help of Squanto and other members of your tribe, have finally learned to hunt and to gather berries, and to grow corn, cranberries, and squash. The menu will include deer, fowl, likely turkey, and bass, cod, lobsters, and mussels. But the menu hardly matters. The colonists are celebrating the very fact that they are learning the skills of survival in a new land, and that they have survived thus far.

Topics to Consider

Corn as Part of America's History	Squanto and the Pilgrims
The First Thanksgiving	The Story of the Pilgrims
First Thanksgiving Table Feast	Surviving the First Winter in the New Land
Life with the Pilgrims	Symbols of Thanksgiving
Ojibwa Indians, Fathers of Corn	Thanksgiving: Becoming a Holiday
Plymouth Rock	The Wampanoag Indians

Books

Search Words: Pilgrims; Squanto; Thanksgiving; Wampanoag

Barth, Edna. *Turkeys, Pilgrims, and Indian Corn: The Story of the Thanksgiving Symbols.* New York: Clarion, 2000.

Bial, Raymond. *The Wampanoag.* (Lifeways). New York: Benchmark, 2004.

Bulla, Clyde Robert. *Squanto: Friend of the Pilgrims.* (Scholastic Biography). New York: Scholastic, 1954.

Curtin, Kathleen, Sandra L. Oliver, and the Plimoth Plantation. *Giving Thanks: Thanksgiving Recipes and History from Pilgrims to Pumpkin Pie.* New York: Clarkson Potter, 2005.

DeRubertis, Barbara. *Thanksgiving Day: Let's Meet the Wampanoag and the Pilgrims.* New York: Kane, 1992.

Hunter, Sally M. *Four Seasons of Corn: A Winnebago Tradition.* Minneapolis, MN: Lerner, 1997.

Peters, Russell. *Clambake—A Wampanoag Tradition.* (We Are Still Here). Minneapolis, MN: Lerner, 1992.

Internet

Diplomacy in New England: The First Thanksgiving—http://www.nmai.si.edu/education/files/harvest.pdf.

Daily Life in 1621—http://teacher.scholastic.com/thanksgiving/plimoth/daily.htm.

Pilgrim Hall Museum has good basic information—http://www.pilgrimhall.org/museum. htm. Includes the story of Plymouth Rock and other interesting information about the Pilgrims.

The First Thanksgiving by the *Christian Science Monitor* has good information with statistics, the menu, and participant accounts—http://www.csmonitor.com/2002/1127/p13s02-lign.html.

The Pilgrim's First Thanksgiving—http://www.defenselink.mil/news/Nov1999/n11221999_9911221.html.

Father of Corn, Ojibwah—the story of the *Legend of Indian Corn*—http://www.indians. org/welker/fathcorn.htm and http://www.rivernen.ca/legend_4.htm.

Life as a Plimoth Pilgrim contains transcripts describing life in 1621 New England from various people of different ages—http://teacher.scholastic.com/thanksgiving/plimoth/pilgrims.htm.

The First Thanksgiving at one of our favorite sites—http://people.howstuffworks.com/thanksgiving2.htm.

History of Thanksgiving, video, audio interviews, background information, and more at this excellent site by the History Channel—http://www.historychannel.com/thanksgiving/.

For the Teacher

Choose from several plans—*Colonial Times*—http://www.theteacherscorner. net/thematicunits/colonial.htm.

Preparing for Thanksgiving

This year ask your family if you can help plan a real traditional Thanksgiving meal. Do your homework before creating the menu and doing the preparation. Share the real Thanksgiving story with family—http://members.aol.com/calebj/thanksgiving.html.

71

Place Names

I was asking for something specific and perfect for my city,
Whereupon, lo! Up sprang the aboriginal name!
Now I see what there is in a name, a word, liquid, sane, unruly, musical, self-sufficient;
I see that the word of my city is that word up there,
Because I see that word nested in nests of water-bays, superb, with tall and wonderful spires . . . .

—Walt Whitman, "Mannahatta"

Words to Know

Gazetteer   Locality
Flora and Fauna   Nomenclature
Geographic Board   Toponymy
Legacy

Related Jumpstarts

Atchison, Topeka, and Santa Fe Railroad
Go West, Young Man
History of Main Street
Mighty Mississippi
Route 66
Where Cities Bloom

You Are There

You've been working on the railroad as it slowly builds a path across America. The company needs places to restock food and fuel, so every seven to ten miles they establish a train station and a town. And, of course, every town needs a name. This time, you get to choose the name. What should it be? You consider the options. Elk are all over the place. It might be a good idea to call it Elk River. It's very descriptive. Then again, you come from a nice town in Massachusetts named Salem. Maybe you ought to name your town Salem. That would remind you of home. Of course, this new town out in the prairie is nothing like your forested waterfront town, but the name might give you comfort. Even better, maybe you should name the town for your girlfriend, Adelaide, who's waiting for you back in Salem (you hope). With a town named for her, she might even come visit you! Not many people have the privilege of naming a town. It will be your legacy; you want to be sure to do it right.

Topics to Consider

Changing Place Names	Place Names That Honor People or Events
Changing the Name of the Airport	Truth or Consequences, N.Mex., Cut 'n Shoot,
How Towns Get Their Names	Tex., and Other Interesting Places
My Town: Humble, Texas	Use a Gazetteer (You Find out What That Is) to
Names for Old Area Families	Write a Poem or Story about Places
Naming New Streets and Roads	

Books

Search Words: Names, Geographical; United States Gazetteer

Jouris, David. *All Over the Map: An Extraordinary Atlas of the United States Featuring Towns That Actually Exist.* Berkeley, CA: Ten Speed Press, 1994.

Nelson, Derek. *Off the Map: The Curious Histories of Place Names.* New York: Kodansha, 1997.

Nestor, Sandy. *Indian Placenames in America.* Jefferson, NC: McFarland, 2003.

Stewart, George R. *American Place-names: A Concise and Selective Dictionary for the Continental United States of America.* New York: Oxford University Press, 1985.

Internet

H. L. Mencken discusses the eight categories of American geographical names—http://www.bartleby.com/185/50.html.

Locations for American place names. See if there's more than one of any given name!—http://www.placenames.com/.

Arizona State University links to many sites for place names—http://www.asu.edu/lib/hayden/govdocs/maps/geogname.htm#usstates.

The U.S. Board on Geographical Names is the official source for place names—http://geonames.usgs.gov/bgn.html.

The Handbook of Texas gives the origin of place names in Texas. You may find something similar for your state—http://www.tsha.utexas.edu/.

The impact of railroads on towns and American society, from Rutgers University—http://www.let.rug.nl/usa/E/ironhorse/ironhorse16.htm.

For the Teacher

National Geographic offers resources for teachers, including *Geo-Spy*, a fast moving place name game—http://www.nationalgeographic.com/education/. Or see the divsersity of U.S. place names—http://www.teachervision.fen.com/activity/maps/4981.html.

A Taste of History

Find a natural feature that isn't named. Develop a name for it, or use the local unofficial name. Propose the name to the U.S. Board on Geographical Names—http://geonames.usgs.gov/bgn.html. Who knows? You just might make it official! For fun, notice the names of the streets in your neighborhood. How did they get their names? Find out!

72

Political Cartoons

We seldom do cartoons about public officials that say: "Congratulations on keeping your hands out of the public till," or "It was awfully nice of you to tell the truth yesterday." Public officials are supposed to keep their hands out of the till and to tell the truth. With only one shot a day, cartoons are generally drawn about officials we feel are not serving the public interest. And we usually support the "good guys" by directing our efforts at their opponents.
—Herb Block, 1977, http://www.loc.gov/rr/print/swann/herblock/cartoon.html

Words to Know

Caricature	Picture Is Worth a Thousand Words
Bias	Propaganda
Herblock	Proponent
Irony	Public Opinion
Media	Satire
Opponent	Subtlety

Related Jumpstarts

Donkeys and Elephants
First Amendment
Right to Vote
Telling America's Story with Photographs
Who Runs Our Town?
Women Get the Vote

You Are There

You've just moved to America. You don't speak English very well, but you understand what is going on around you. You watch as politicians create empires for themselves, giving jobs to their friends instead of those who are qualified. You see things you consider ridiculous, like food being thrown away while nearby people are hungry. You hear people arguing heatedly about issues that don't really matter. You want to say something about it, but you feel that no one would pay attention to someone like you. You aren't very good at putting your ideas into words, at least not into English words. How can you express yourself? You've heard that a picture is worth a thousand words, so you try it. Now people understand, even agree with you, no matter what language they speak!

Topics to Consider

Choose 3 Recent Cartoons in Your Newspaper and Report on the Creator, the Meaning, and the Story Behind the Cartoon	Thomas Nast
	Using Irony in Cartoons
	Using Satire in Cartoons
Oil Shortage, or Other Economic Issue	Voting for Blacks or Women
Origins of Political Cartoons	What Is Propaganda?
Pick an Issue and Explore It through Cartoons: Any Presidential Campaign or Any War	Who Is Herb Block? (Herblock)

Books

Search Words: Caricatures and Cartoons; Cartooning; Political Satire

Hess, Stephen, and Milton Kaplan. *The Ungentlemanly Art: A History of American Political Cartoons*. New York: Macmillan, 1975.

Paine, Albert Bigelow. *Thomas Nast, His Period and His Pictures*. New York: Macmillan, 1904; reprint Princeton, NJ: Pyne, 1974.

Pflueger, Lynda. *Thomas Nast, Political Cartoonist*. (Historical American Biographies). Berkeley Heights, NJ: Enslow, 2000.

Weiss, Harvey. *Cartoons and Cartooning*. Boston: Houghton Mifflin, 1990.

Internet

Political cartoons from Graphic Witness and *Grolier Encyclopedia*—http://www.graphicwitness.org/group/cartoon.html.

The U. S. Senate discusses Nast's political cartoons—http://www.senate.gov/artandhistory/art/exhibit/nast_cartoons.htm.

Uniting Mugawumps and the Masses: Dan Backer of the University of Virginia discusses the history of cartoons and political culture in the Gilded Age—http://xroads.virginia.edu/~MA96/PUCK/intro.html.

The Library of Congress links to many sites about political cartoons—http://memory.loc.gov/learn/community/cc_pcartoon.php.

Current political cartoons by Daryl Cagle—http://cagle.msnbc.com/politicalcartoons/.

Dr. Seuss Went to War—http://orpheus.ucsd.edu/speccoll/dspolitic/.

Herblock's Cartoons, Political Cartoons from the Crash to the Millennium—http://www.loc.gov/rr/print/swann/herblock/.

For the Teacher

The American Memories site of the Library of Congress offers activities and teaching ideas about political cartoons—http://memory.loc.gov/learn/features/political_cartoon/index.html . Also, the *Teaching with Documents* lesson plans include a worksheet on political cartoons—http://www.archives.gov/education/lessons/.

A Taste of History

Create a political cartoon of your own. First, you'll have to think of an issue that you care about. It can be a local issue, right in your own school, or a state or national issue. Read about it and identify some irony. As you plan out your picture, you may find some help—http://kids-learn.org/cartoons/forstudents.htm.

Poverty in America

I used to think I was poor. Then they told me I wasn't poor, I was needy. Then they told me it was self-defeating to think of myself as needy, I was deprived. Then they told me deprived was a bad image, I was underprivileged. Then they told me underprivileged was overused, I was disadvantaged. I still don't have a dime. But I sure have a great vocabulary.—Jules Feiffer, http://www.memorablequotations.com/feiffer.htm

Words to Know

Colonial

Destitute

Food Stamps

Ghetto

Homeless

Income

Indigence

Needy

Penniless

Penury

Poorhouse

Save the Children

Sweatshops

Underprivileged

Unemployment

Welfare

Related Jumpstarts

American Sweatshops

Business of Doing Good

Fighting Prejudice

I Want That! Needs vs. Wants

Social Security

You Are There

Imagine living without toys. You can't afford them. You've never had new clothes. Yours are hand-me-downs from your brother or sister. If you're lucky, they sort of fit. Sometimes they're even hand-me-downs from your mother. Your mom shops at Goodwill or the Salvation Army. And while other kids may cheer for snow days and look forward to weekends, you think of them as the hungry days. At school, you get breakfast and lunch! Over 12 million children in the United States live in poverty. These children have to do without many of the things that everyone wants. Sometimes you feel sorry for yourself. It can seem as if you are the only one who has to go without things. Like the other day when it got so cold, and you had to go to school wearing only a sweater because your brother needed your jacket.

Topics to Consider

Child Labor	Poor Houses
Education and Income	Poverty in America
Food Stamps	School Lunch Program
Government Aid	Ways to End Poverty
Local Food Pantry	Welfare
Minimum Wage	What Is Poverty?

Books

Search Words: Children's Rights; Food Relief; Homelessness; Poor; Poverty

Doak, Melissa. *Homeless in America: How Could It Happen Here?* (Information Plus Reference). Detroit: Gale, 2006.

Griffin, Geoff, ed. *How Can the Poor Be Helped?* (At Issue: Social Issues). San Diego: Greenhaven, 2006.

Harrison, Jean. *Home.* (Children's Rights). North Mankato, MN: Smart Apple, 2005.

Iceland, John. *Poverty in America: A Handbook.* Berkeley: University of California Press, 2003.

Mason, Paul. *Poverty.* (Planet under Pressure). Chicago: Heinemann, 2006.

Stearman, Kaye. *Why Do People Live on the Streets?* (Exploring Tough Issues). Austin, TX: Raintree-Steck Vaughn, 2001.

Internet

Ohio State University has statistics on child poverty in America—http://ohioline.osu.edu/hyg-fact/5000/5704.html.

America's Children: Key National Indicators of Well-Being 2005 has statistics on poverty among children—http://www.childstats.gov/americaschildren/index.asp.

Facts about Poverty from the Office for Social Justice—http://www.osjspm.org/101_poverty.htm.

Learn about the National School Lunch Program from the U.S. Department of Agriculture—http://www.fns.usda.gov/cnd/Lunch/default.htm.

What happens to homeless children? From the National Resource & Training Center on Homelessness and Mental Illness—http://www.nrchmi.samhsa.gov/facts/facts_question_5.asp.

Learn what it was like to live through the Irish potato famine through this interactive game—http://www.irishpotatofamine.org/.

The Forgotten Americans, a PBS special on the "colonias." Find out how they developed and what problems they face—http://www.pbs.org/klru/forgottenamericans/.

For the Teacher

The National Center for Children in Poverty has resources for educators to promote school success and emotional well-being. Also includes State Economic Security profiles—http://www.nccp.org/.

Do Something!

When you read about children living in poverty, it makes you want to help! Read about what other kids are doing, then make plans. You can organize a fund drive in your classroom or neighborhood. For more information—http://www.savethechildren.org/involved/donations/moneybox.asp.

The President Has Been Shot!

Crook, do you know I believe there are men who want to take my life? And I have no doubt they will do it. . . . I know no one could do it and escape alive. But if it is to be done, it is impossible to prevent it.—Abraham Lincoln, April 14, 1865 (the day he was shot), according to policeman William Henry Crook

Words to Know

Abraham Lincoln
Assassination
Bay of Pigs
Cold War
Conspiracy
Jack Ruby

James Garfield
Lee Harvey Oswald
U.S.S.R. (Soviet Union)
Warren Commission
William McKinley

Related Jumpstarts

Cold War

Election of Abraham Lincoln

Lives and Times of My Grandparents

Man on the Moon

Rough Riders

You Are There

You are sitting in your classroom trying to concentrate on your assignment when the public announcement system comes on. It's a strange time for announcements, and you are only half listening until you hear the principal say, "The president has been shot." No! You can't believe it. President Kennedy is too popular, too good a president. Why would someone shoot him? It must be a mistake. But as you listen to the news reports that evening and all the next day, you find out it is for real. You watch during the days that follow as the whole country mourns its lost president.

Topics to Consider

Assassination of Martin Luther King Jr.	Presidents Who Were Assassinated:
Attempted Assassination of Ronald Reagan	John Kennedy
Chain of Command for Presidents	Abraham Lincoln
Conspiracy Theories	James Garfield
Jack Ruby	William McKinley
John Wilkes Booth	Secret Service
Lee Harvey Oswald	

From *99 Jumpstarts for Kids' Social Studies Reports: Research Help for Grades 3–8* by Peggy J. Whitley and Susan Williams Goodwin. Westport, CT: Libraries Unlimited. Copyright © 2007.

Books

Search Words: Assassination and Kennedy, Lincoln, McKinley, or Garfield

Anderson, Catherine Corley. *John F. Kennedy.* (Presidential Leaders). Minneapolis, MN: Lerner, 2004.

Kingsbury, Robert. *The Assassination of James A. Garfield.* (Library of Political Assassinations). New York: Rosen, 2002.

Marinelli, Deborah A. *The Assassination of Abraham Lincoln.*(Library of Political Assassinations). New York: Rosen, 2002.

Rivera, Shiela. *The Assassination of John F. Kennedy.* (American Moments). Edna, MN: Abdo & Daughters, 2004.

Spencer, Lauren. *The Assassination of John F. Kennedy.* (Library of Political Assassinations). New York: Rosen, 2002.

Wilson, Antoine. *The Assassination of William McKinley.*(Library of Political Assassinations). New York: Rosen, 2002.

Internet

The National Archives houses all the documents and evidence from Kennedy's assassination. You can see many of them online—http://www.archives.gov/research/jfk/.

The John F. Kennedy Presidential Library and Museum has photographs, audio speeches, biographical information, and historic events—http://www.jfklibrary.org/.

PBS has newspaper articles and transcripts of news shows from the days following the assassination of Kennedy. Feel like you were there!—http://www.pbs.org/newshour/bb/white_house/kennedy/.

The White House biography of Kennedy—http://www.whitehouse.gov/history/presidents/jk35.html.

Listen to John F. Kennedy's speeches through the History Channel! Choose "Speeches and Video," then search for John Kennedy—http://www.historychannel.com/.

Abraham Lincoln research site—http://members.aol.com/RVSNorton/Lincoln.html.

For the Teacher

The John F. Kennedy Presidential Library and Museum has a variety of resources for teachers at all grade levels, including chronologies, online exhibits, professional development, and an essay contest for students—http://www.jfklibrary.org/Education+and+Public+Programs/For+Teachers/Teaching+Resources.htm.

Protect the President

Make a plan to protect the president from assassins or others who might want to harm him. To get more details on a Secret Service agents' duties, check out the page for kids—http://www.secretservice.gov/kids_faq.shtml.

Prohibition and Gangsters (1920)

In an abandoned warehouse late at night
in the shipping yards
The gangsters keep a watchful eye for
the man in blue
As a loaded semi pulls up to an empty dock
The rear door opens to reveal the demon alcohol
CHORUS:
Restriction drinking's against the law
Prohibition the demon alcohol

A heavy profit's to be turned on this mountain dew
But if you're caught you might get killed or
thrown in jail
But what's the fuss it's soon to be legal anyway
So you may as well go with the flow of
things to come.
—Zoetrope, "Prohibition," *Life of Crime*
(Combat Records, 1987),
http://lyrics.rare-lyrics.com/Z/Zoetrope/
Prohibition.html

Words to Know

Al Capone	Organized Crime
Anti-Saloon League	Prohibition
Bootleggers	Roaring Twenties
Flappers	Saloons
Gangsters	Speakeasies
Moonshine	Still

Related Jumpstarts

American Sweatshops	Great Depression	Poverty in America
Supply and Demand	Taxes	Women Get the Vote

You Are There

You are 12 years old in 1918. Your family has moved to 7200 South Prairie Avenue in Cicero, Illinois, a Chicago suburb. Right down the street is a family of seven boys. What joy! Matthew Capone is your playmate. He has several older brothers, including Al. Sometimes the whole family goes into the street and plays ball. Al has a nasty scar on his face from a fight with Frank Gallucio. He dropped out of school after a fight with his teacher. And his brothers get into trouble, too. Your mom doesn't want you to play with the older boys. "Beware of the Capone boys," she says.

Topics to Consider

Al Capone	Jazz Age
Bootleggers and Speakeasies	The 1920s in America
Carrie Nation, Saloon Smasher	Prohibition and Crime
Chicago and Organized Crime	Temperance Movement in 1920
The Eighteenth Amendment	Volstead Act
Gangsters of the 1920s	What Is Prohibition?
Harlem in the 1920s	Why Prohibition Spawned Crime

 From *99 Jumpstarts for Kids' Social Studies Reports: Research Help for Grades 3–8* by Peggy J. Whitley and Susan Williams Goodwin. Westport, CT: Libraries Unlimited. Copyright © 2007.

Books

Search Words: Capone, Al; Eighteenth Amendment; Gangsters; Prohibition; Roaring Twenties

Harvey, Bonnie. *Carry A. Nation: Saloon Smasher and Prohibitionist.* (Historical American Biographies). New York: Enslow, 2002.

King, David C. *Al Capone and the Roaring Twenties.* (Notorious Americans and Their Times). Woodbridge, CT: Blackbirch, 1999.

Lieurance, Suzanne. *Prohibition Era in American History.* (In American History). Berkeley Heights, NJ: Enslow, 2003.

Lucas, Eileen. *The Eighteenth and Twenty-first Amendments: Alcohol, Prohibition, and Repeal.* (Constitution). Springfield, NJ: Enslow, 1998.

Orr, Tamra B. *Prohibition.* (People at the Center Of). San Diego: Blackbirch, 2004.

Internet

Prohibition and Gangsters—get started with the background information on this page. Look at *Jazz Age,* too—http://www.historylearningsite.co.uk/prohibition_and_the_gangsters.htm.

Prohibition is a background article about the Eighteenth Amendment and much more. Follow "Next" to other 1920s info—http://www.digitalhistory.uh.edu/database/article_display.cfm?HHID=441.

Prohibition tells what, where, why, how, and when—http://library.thinkquest.org/28892/index.shtm.

The Lawless Decade is both fun and informational. Follow through the years of the 1920s and select the topics that interest you most—http://www.paulsann.org/thelawlessdecade/index.html.

Al Capone's History File—http://www.chicagohs.org/history/capone.html.

University of Pennsylvania has many links about the jazz age and the gangster period of the 1920s—http://faculty.pittstate.edu/~knichols/jazzage.html.

Between the Wars has links to all you may need and much more. Bookmark it. It is easy to lose your way—http://www.chenowith.k12.or.us/tech/subject/social/depression.html.

American Cultural History: The Twenties—http://kclibrary.nhmccd.edu/decade20.html.

Bootleggers and Speakeasies—http://bootlegger1920.tripod.com/.

For the Teacher

The classroom activities at the Anti Saloon League site should be fun for your class. Editorial cartoons are discussed and recommended—prohibition.osu.edu/ASL/.

Mug Shots

Have fun with your digital camera creating a mug shot gallery of your friends and family. Put your shots in a notebook with "just the facts."

Religions of the World

Eye cannot see him, nor words reveal him;
by the senses, austerity, or works he is not known.
When the mind is cleansed by the grace of wisdom,

he is seen by contemplation —the One
without parts.
—Hinduism, Mundaka Upanishad 3.1.8,
http://www.unification. net/ws/theme001.htm

Words to Know

Agnostic	Muslim
Atheist	Mythology
Buddhism	Polytheism
Christianity	Ramadan
Eid-al-Fitr	Reincarnation
Hinduism	Scripture
Iftar	Secular
Islam	Sikhism
Judaism	Suhoor
Monotheism	Taoism

Related Jumpstarts

Ancient Greece	Cultures and Cuisines	Fighting Prejudice
I Am the Pharaoh	Pilgrim Harvest	Salem Witch Trials

You Are There

It is the ninth lunar month, the month of Ramadan. As a Muslim, you and every-one else who is 12 or older are fasting. You awaken early, before the sun rises, to have suhoor, or breakfast, because once the sun is up, you will not eat or drink anything until the sun sets again. That really means anything; you can't even have a drink of water. All day while you are thirsty and your stomach is rumbling, you think about how fortunate you are. If you were very poor, you would have to be hungry like this all the time. At night, you will have iftar and you can eat and drink your fill. Most of all, you look forward to Eid-al-Fitr, the Breaking of the Fast, when you celebrate with special foods and gifts.

Topics to Consider

Atheism	Mohammed
Christmas	Prayer in School
Easter	Protestant Religions
Hannukkah	Religions in the United States
Hinduism—What Is It?	Religions of the World
Islam—What Is It?	Religious Holidays
Judaism—What Is It?	Weddings in Different Religions

Books

Search Words: Country Name and Social Life and Customs; Cults; Mythology; Names of Specific Religions; Religion

> Barnes, Trevor. *Hinduism and Other Eastern Religions: Worship, Festivals and Ceremonies from Around the World.* (World Faiths). Boston: Kingfisher, 2005.
>
> Barnes, Trevor. *Islam: Worship, Festivals and Ceremonies from Around the World.* (World Faiths). Boston: Kingfisher, 2005.
>
> Barnes, Trevor. *Judaism: Worship, Festivals and Ceremonies from Around the World.* (World Faiths). Boston: Kingfisher, 2005.
>
> Melton, J. Gordon. *Encyclopedia of American Religions.* Wilmington, NC: McGrath, 1978– .

Internet

> Mr. Dowling tells kids about the three major Western religions, Christianity, Judaism, and Islam—http://www.mrdowling.com/605westr.html.
>
> The University of Wyoming has facts and lifestyles for the five major religions of the world, including Buddhism and Hinduism—http://uwacadweb.uwyo.edu/religionet/ER/.
>
> Compare the writings of sacred texts from different religions at this Unitarian Church Web site—http://www.unification.net/ws/.
>
> Older students who want to delve more deeply into religions can find a thorough list of Web sites in the *Virtual Religion Index*—http://virtualreligion.net/vri/.
>
> *The Book of Days* tells about holidays of the world and the background behind them. This includes secular as well as religious holidays—http://www.shagtown.com/days/.
>
> Odyssee takes you on an interactive journey through Africa, ancient America, and the Mediterranean. You can read about mythology, rituals, and burial rites—http://carlos.emory.edu/ODYSSEY/.

For the Teacher

> *A Teacher's Guide to Religion in the Public Schools* discusses the First Amendment and methods to appropriately introduce the study of comparative religion in the classroom—http://www.phschool.com/professional_development/teaching_tools/social_studies/guide_to_religion.html.

Check It Out

Go to a religious ceremony with a friend from another religion, and invite that friend to visit yours. It would be especially helpful if you attend a religious education class. Ask the instructor for more information about rituals that are different than yours. If you go only to a ceremony and don't have a teacher to talk with, ask your friend's parents for the background.

77

Reshaping the Land

I've got a mule, her name is Sal,
Fifteen years on the Erie Canal.
She's a good ol' worker and a good ol' pal,
Fifteen years on the Erie Canal.

We've hauled some barges in our day,
Filled with lumber, coal, and hay,
And we know ev'ry inch of the way,
From Albany to Buffalo.
—"The Erie Canal," folksong

Words to Know

Canals   Levees
Dikes   Lightning Rods
Dousing   Locks
Habitat   William Seward
Hydroelectric Dams Windcatchers
Irrigation

Related Jumpstarts

Atchison, Topeka, and Santa Fe Railroad

Brooklyn Bridge

Mighty Mississippi

Where Cities Bloom

You Are There

You have been growing your crops—potatoes, corn and squash—for years. Every year the crop gets bigger. You have way more food than you need. You hear that in the city there is not nearly enough food. You hitch up your mule to a cart and bring the produce to the city to sell. Unfortunately, it takes a week to get there by road, and too many of the vegetables spoil. The government just finished building a canal, a straight, shallow river, all the way from Lake Erie to the Hudson River. You would think the water would all run downhill and spill out into the Hudson, but those engineers figured out how to make locks. Can you imagine locking in water? Amazing! And now you can get your crops to the city in a day, fresh and ready to cook!

Topics to Consider

Adapting Land for Farming	Hoover Dam
Building the Erie Canal	Making Tunnels
Crossing Great Rivers	New Orleans Landfills
Down at the Levee	Planning for New Roads
From Farm to Subdivision	Roads, from Footpath to Pavement
Getting Water to the Desert	What Do Windmills do?

From *99 Jumpstarts for Kids' Social Studies Reports: Research Help for Grades 3–8* by Peggy J. Whitley and Susan Williams Goodwin. Westport, CT: Libraries Unlimited. Copyright © 2007.

Books

Search Words: Canals; Dams; Floods; Nature, Effect of Human Beings on

Allaby, Michael. *Floods*. (Facts on File Science Library). New York: Facts on File, 2003.

Barter, James. *The Colorado*. (Rivers of the World). San Diego: Lucent, 2003.

Brimner, Larry Dane. *Subway: The Story of Tunnels, Tubes and Tracks*. Honesdale, PA: Boyd's Mills, 2004.

DuTemple, Lesley A. *The Hoover Dam*. (Great Building Feats). Minneapolis, MN: Lerner, 2003.

Landau, Elaine. *Canals*. (True Book). New York: Children's Press, 2001.

Leslie, Jacques. *Deep Water: The Epic Struggle Over Dams, Displaced People and the Environment*. New York: Farrar, Straus & Giroux, 2005.

Macaulay, David. *Building Big*. Boston: Houghton Mifflin, 2000.

Internet

Adapting to Climate Extremes discusses the ways a body, animal or human, adapts to the environment—http://anthro.palomar.edu/adapt/adapt_2.htm.

The Kids Site of Canadian Trains talks about building railway tunnels, with pictures—http://www.collectionscanada.ca/trains/kids/h32-2130-e.html.

The Circle of Ancient Iranian Studies explains windcatchers, an ancient means of air conditioning—http://www.cais-soas.com/CAIS/Architecture/wind.htm.

The history and use of tunnels is described at the PBS site *Building Big: Tunnels*. You can also link to information on dams, bridges, and domes—http://www.pbs.org/wgbh/buildingbig/tunnel/.

Building of the Erie Canal—http://www.canals.org/erie.htm.

History Central offers William Seward's account of the building of the Erie Canal—http://www.historycentral.com/documents/EirieCanal.html.

For the Teacher

Dams, their benefits, and their environmental problems are covered in this lesson about the Three Gorges dam—http://school.discovery.com/lessonplans/programs/threegorges/.

A Taste of History

You can take a ride down the Erie Canal! While it is no longer a major trade route, the Erie Canal is still working, with 34 locks and a rise of 169 feet from sea level. Marvel at what untrained engineers were able to accomplish almost 200 years ago!—http://www.canals.state.ny.us/exvac/landwater/lwerie.html.

78

Riding in the Back of the Bus (1960)

Back in Montgomery during my growing up there, it was completely legally enforced racial segregation, and of course, I struggled against it for a long time. I felt that it was not right to be deprived of freedom when we were living in the Home of the Brave and Land of the Free. Of course, when I refused to stand up, on the orders of the bus driver, for a white passenger to take the seat, and I was not sitting in the front of the bus, as many people have said, and neither was my feet hurting, as many people have said. But I made up my mind that I would not give in any longer to legally-imposed racial segregation and of course my arrest brought about the protests for more than a year.—Rosa Parks, interview, June 2, 1995, Williamsburg, Virginia

Words to Know

Activism
Boycott
Civil Rights Movement
Freedom Rides
Jim Crow Laws
Ku Klux Klan

NAACP
Passive Resistance
Prejudice
Racism
Segregation
Supreme Court

Related Jumpstarts

Buffalo Soldiers
Fighting Prejudice
Jackie Robinson Breaks Baseball's Color Barrier

You Are There

You are 12 years old in 1955. You live in Montgomery, Alabama, and you are African American. You have grown up knowing that the Jim Crow laws demand segregation of whites and colored people in places such a,s restaurants, theaters, hotels, cinemas, and public baths. Trains and buses also segregate races. You drink from water fountains marked "Colored." Now, you hear from your parents that a lady in your neighborhood, Rosa Parks, has been arrested for refusing to give her seat to a white man on the bus. Everyone is talking about it and about a young man named Martin Luther King. What will happen next?

Topics to Consider

Awards and Honors for Rosa Parks	Marching for Freedom
Boycotting the Montgomery Buses	Martin Luther King Becomes an Activist
Fighting for Civil Rights	The Mother of the Civil Rights Movement
Integrating the Public Schools	NAACP History
Jim Crow Laws	Rosa Parks as a Young Girl
Life of an African American in the Fifties	Rosa Rides on the Bus

From *99 Jumpstarts for Kids' Social Studies Reports: Research Help for Grades 3–8* by Peggy J. Whitley and Susan Williams Goodwin. Westport, CT: Libraries Unlimited. Copyright © 2007.

Books

Search Words: Boycotts; Civil Rights Movement; Jim Crow; Parks, Rosa; Segregation

Dubowski, Cathy East. *Rosa Parks: Don't Give In!* (Defining Moments). New York: Bearport, 2006.

Hull, Mary. *Rosa Parks: Civil Rights Leader.* (Black Americans of Achievement). Philadelphia: Chelsea, 2005.

Parks, Rosa, with Gregory J. Reed. *Quiet Strength: The Faith, the Hope, and the Heart of a Woman Who Changed a Nation: Reflections by Rosa Parks.* Grand Rapids, MI: Zondervan, 1994.

Parks, Rosa, with Jim Haskins. *Rosa Parks: My Story.* New York: Scholastic, 1992.

Walsh, Frank. *The Montgomery Bus Boycott.* (Landmark Events in American History). Milwaukee, WI: World Almanac, 2003.

Williams, Donnie. *The Thunder of Angels: The Montgomery Bus Boycott and the People Who Broke the Back of Jim Crow.* Chicago: Lawrence Hill, 2006.

Internet

Academy of Achievement salutes Rosa Parks—http://www.achievement.org/autodoc/page/par0pro-1.

Rosa Parks Portal is a collection of Internet links, by main headings—http://www.e-portals.org/Parks/.

Remembering Rosa Parks—transcript, audio and video of Parks on the bus. Be sure to read the transcript about Parks—http://www.pbs.org/newshour/bb/race_relations/july-dec05/parks_10-25.html.

AfricanAmericans.com page for Rosa Parks. This is a wonderful site for more information about African Americans—http://www.africanamericans.com/RosaParks.htm.

Back to the Back of the Bus, essays before and since Rosa's ride on the bus. Excellent information—http://www.thenation.com/doc/20001225/wypijewski.

The Rosa Parks Story includes a time line of Parks and a time line of the civil rights movement. Supreme Court case ending bus segregation—http://www.kidsnet.org/cbs/rosaparks/timeline/frame.html.

For the Teacher

Scholastic Teacher's Plans for Rosa has excellent information, links, and background. It covers from 1955 until her death in 2005—http://teacher.scholastic.com/rosa/index.htm.

Riding the Bus

Talk to your grandparents and other people who were alive in the 1950s and 1960s. Ask them what they remember about segregation. What was it like? Create a chart and list methods people used to change the law. Name people and organizations who helped. Research using the Internet and books.

The Right to Vote

The right of citizens of the United States to vote shall not be denied or abridged by the United States or by any State on account of race, color, or previous condition of servitude.
—United States Constitution, Amendment XV, February 3, 1870

The right of citizens of the United States to vote shall not be denied or abridged by the United States or by any State on account of sex.—United States Constitution, Amendment XIX, August 18, 1920

Words to Know

Absentee Ballots
Candidate
Constitutional Amendments
Democrats
Electoral College
Governor
Independents
Media Bias

Political Parties
Politicians
Polling Place
Precinct
Representative
Republicans
Senator
Suffrage

Related Jumpstarts

Becoming a Citizen
Who Runs Our Town?

Coming to America
Women Get the Vote

Donkeys and Elephants
Writing the Constitution

You Are There

As you walk into the voting booth, you enter your code into a computer and up pops a screen with the first candidates. You look at the list and wonder. Are you really qualified to choose the leaders of your city, your state, and your country? You have done your homework. You listened to candidates debating, you read about them in the newspapers, and you have discussed them with your friends. You probably know as much about them as anyone. Later that evening, after all the polling places have closed, you listen to the results. As more precincts report in, your candidate pulls ahead. Yeah! It looks like you've chosen a winner!

Topics to Consider

Absentee Ballots	Learning about the Candidates
Constitutional Amendments about Voting	Presidential Debates
Electoral College	Voting Machines
Exit Polls	Voting Rights Act of 1965
Felons and the Right to Vote	Voting Rights for Kids
League of Women Voters	Women's Suffrage

Books

Search Words: Election Monitoring; Elections: Voting; Political Corruption; Suffrage

> Frost-Knappman, Elizabeth, and Kathryn Cullen-Dupont. *Women's Suffrage in America.* (Eyewitness History). New York: Facts on File, 2005.
>
> Horn, Geoffrey M. *Political Parties, Interest Groups, and the Media.* (World Almanac Library of American Government). Milwaukee, WI: World Almanac, 2004.
>
> LeVert, Suzanne. *Electoral College.* (Watts Library). New York: Franklin Watts, 2004.
>
> Ring, Susan. *Election Connection: Official Nick Guide to Electing the President.* San Francisco, Chronicle, 2004.
>
> Thurber, James, and Candice Nelson. *Campaigns and Elections American Style.* (Transforming American Politics). Boulder, CO: Westview, 2004.

Internet

> PBS takes you *Inside the Voting Booth* to look at controversial elections—http://pbskids.org/democracy/vote/.
>
> Ben Franklin and the Government Printing Office explain the election process for students—http://bensguide.gpo.gov/9-12/election/.
>
> Political parties, elections, and candidates are discussed in this multimedia site by the Library of Congress—http://learning.loc.gov/learn/features/election/home.html.
>
> The American Museum of the Moving Image shows television campaign advertisements from 1952 until now—http://livingroomcandidate.movingimage.us/index.php.
>
> Improve your election vocabulary at Comic Strip University!—http://www.vocabulary.com/election12cs.html.
>
> The Constitutional Rights foundation lays out the groundwork for equal voting rights—http://www.crfc.org/equal.html.
>
> Full text of the constitution—http://www.usconstitution.net/.

For the Teacher

Kids Voting USA has civics lessons and classroom activities to make learning about politics and voting relevant to students—http://www.kidsvotingusa.org/.

An Election to Remember

Run for office! If it's time for student council elections, nominate yourself or a friend for a candidate. Make campaign posters, give a speech, and encourage everyone to vote. Most important, after the election is over, whether you win or lose, be a good sport! Find campaign ideas—http://www.kidzworld.com/site/p4878.htm.

Rosie the Riveter (1940–1945)

These fantastic women filled the gap when the men were needed on the front lines. Yet the need for war production only increased, and the women of this nation met that need. They were uniformly called "Rosie the Riveter" meaning production workers.
—DC3 Aviation Museum, http://www.centercomp.com/cgi-bin/dc3/memorial?14515

Words to Know

American Icon	Rationing
Contributions	Recycling
Factory	Riveter
Homefront	Symbol
Production Workers	Victory Bonds
Propaganda	Victory Garden

Related Jumpstarts

Changing Family

Child Labor

Life and Times of My Grandparents

Women Get the Vote

Women on the Home Front

You Are There

It is 1945. You are 12 years old and your father is away fighting for his country. Your mother, who has always stayed home taking care of your sister and you, is now working in the local airplane plant. She is helping other women make parts for the planes that will be shipped to the army. It is a little hard for you and your sister, now that your mother works long hours. You have added chores. You set the table, get dinner started, and help around the house. Your mother enjoys her work at the plant. She believes she is contributing to the war effort. But what will happen when your dad comes home from the war? Will your mom lose her job? Will this be hard for her? After five years of working, will she want to continue? Will she be satisfied returning home to care for you and your sister and the home? This is a topic of conversation you hear often among your mother and her friends. Also, you have grown independent during this time. How will your mom's return to being a housewife affect you?

Topics to Consider

From Rosie to Lucy: Women after the War	War Journals by Women at Home
The Home Front During WWII	What Did You Do in the War,
Oveta Culp Hobby, Commander of the	Grandma?
Women's Army Corps	What Kids Did for the War Effort
Rosie and Women's Rights	Women During WWII
Rosie the Riveter, American Icon	

Books

Search Words: Home Front; Rosie the Riveter; Women in World War II

Colman, Penny. *Rosie the Riveter: Women Working on the Home Front During World War II*. New York: Crown, 1995.

Petersen, Christine. *Rosie the Riveter*. (Cornerstones of Freedom). New York: Children's Press, 2005.

Sinnott, Susan. *Doing Our Part: American Women on the Home Front During World War II*. (First Book). New York: Franklin Watts, 1995.

Thomas, Mary Martha. *Riveting and Rationing in Dixie: Alabama Women and the Second World War* (e-book). Tuscaloosa: University of Alabama Press, 1987. Available at http://www.questia.com/PM.qst?a=o&d=54415892.

Yellin, Emily. *Our Mother's War: American Women at Home and at the Front During World War II*. New York: Free Press, 2004.

Internet

Kingwood College Library's *American Cultural History*—http://kclibrary.nhmccd.edu/decade40.html.

Rosie the Riveter, a Web site for women of World War II—http://www.rosietheriveter.org/.

WWII Women—links to many excellent sites—http://www.teacheroz.com/WWIIHomefront.htm.

Library of Congress's Rosie site, links and Webcast—http://www.loc.gov/rr/program/journey/rosie.html.

BBC's *Women in World War I*—http://www.bbc.co.uk/history/war/wwone/women_employment_01.shtml.

Women from 1900 to 1945; choose WWI and WWII to find the information you need for your report—http://www.historylearningsite.co.uk/women%201900_1945.htm.

The American Family in World War II (link to Rosie, too)—http://www.u-s-history.com/pages/h1692.html.

Children Aid the War—http://www.foxvalleyhistory.org/wwII/resources/Children-Aid-the-War-Effort.pdf.

For the Teacher

Rosie the Riveter Web site has a wonderful collection of information for the classroom—http://www.rosietheriveter.org/index.htm.

Selling Rosie

Norman Rockwell painted the"Rosie" cover for the *Saturday Evening Post* issue of May 29, 1943 (http://www.curtispublishing.com/News/May%2029.htm). It represents Rosie as the working woman on the home front during the war. The original painting sold at auction for almost $5 million. Have a little fun. Use the Internet to discover the marketing power of Rosie the Riveter. What items can you find for sale with Rosie's picture on them today? A mug? A shirt? Make a list!

Rough Riders (1898)

It is now known that 251 men and 2 officers of the United States battleship Maine *lost their lives in consequence of the explosion, burning and sinking of that vessel in this harbor last night . . . the night was intensely dark, the clouds hanging low with the heavy rain that began to fall soon after the catastrophe occurred.—*"Not a Sound of Warning," New York Times, *February 17, 1898, p. 1*

Words to Know

Battleship *Maine*
Buffalo Soldiers
Cavalry
Imperialism
Medal of Honor
Puerto Rico

Regiment
Spanish–American War
Teddy Bear
Treaty of Paris
Yellow Fever
Yellow Journalism

Related Jumpstarts

Battle of New Orleans
Boston Tea Party
Buffalo Soldiers
Custer's Last Stand
Women at War
Yellow Fever Attacks Philadelphia

You Are There

When you read the newspaper article about the battleship *Maine,* you were so angry that you wanted to strike out at someone! How dare the Spanish sink one of our ships in the middle of the night with all men on board? You decided then and there to enlist in the army so you could get back at the Spanish. But it wasn't that easy. Many other men felt the same way, and the regiments were full. Then you heard about Teddy Roosevelt, who was gathering a regiment of Harvard students, and you wrote to him. You were one of the lucky ones, you thought. Until today. You are looking up at San Juan Hill, where the Spanish soldiers are firing down at anyone who moves. But when Teddy rides out from the trees and leads the charge, you follow.

Topics to Consider

Buffalo Soldiers in the Spanish–American War	Riding with Teddy Roosevelt
Cavalry	Sinking of the Battleship *Maine*
Cuba	Spanish American War
Discuss the Countries That the U.S. Won as a Result of the War	The Story of the Teddy Bear
	Treaty of Paris
Journalism and the War	Weapons of the War
Medal of Honor	Yellow Fever: Causes, Symptoms, and Treatment

Books

Search Words: Spanish–American War, 1898; Theodore Roosevelt

Brannen, Daniel E., Julie Carnegie, and Allison McNeill, eds. *Spanish-American War.* Detroit: UXL, 2003.

Chant, Christopher. *The Military History of the United States.* Vol. 7. New York: Marshall Cavendish, 1992.

Golay, Michael. *The Spanish American War.* (America at War). New York: Facts on File, 2003.

Kupferberg, Audrey E. *The Spanish American War.* (People at the Center). San Diego: Blackbirch, 2005.

Santella, Andrew. *Roosevelt's Rough Riders.* (We the People). Minneapolis, MN: Compass Point, 2006.

Internet

Teddy Roosevelt's memoirs, *Rough Riders,* full text—http://www.bartleby.com/51/.

The Theodore Roosevelt Association summarizes the events surrounding the Spanish–American War—http://www.theodoreroosevelt.org/life/Rough_Riders.htm.

Read an eyewitness account of the battle of San Juan Hill—http://www.eyewitnesstohistory.com/roughriders.htm.

See a biography of President Roosevelt from the White House—http://www.whitehouse.gov/history/presidents/tr26.html.

The Spanish–American War, courtesy of the Library of Congress, has information on Cuba, Guam, the Philippines and Puerto Rico—http://www.loc.gov/rr/hispanic/1898/intro.html.

The Spanish–American War Web site gives background details on medicine, music, weapons, African Americans, and much more—http://www.spanamwar.com/.

The Crucible of Empire is a PBS Web site that explores the Spanish–American War—http://www.pbs.org/crucible/.

For the Teacher

This five-day project from Historical Thinking Matters aims at helping students develop critical thinking skills—http://historicalthinkingmatters.org/inquiry.php?moduleID=1&teacher=1.

It's As If You Were There

The Spanish–American War marked a change in the way the public learned about war. The motion picture industry was just beginning, and cameramen filmed the wreckage of the battleship *Maine* and showed the human side of the war. Journalists weren't able to film the war itself, so they filmed reenactments. If you have a video camera, try being a journalist yourself. Get some friends to stage a mock battle and film it to show to your class. Be sure to plan the battle so no one really gets hurt! Some other ideas are provided by CNN—http://cgi.turnerlearning.com/cnnstudentnewsjc/manual/across.html.

Route 66 (1926–1985)

If you ever plan to motor west
Travel my way, take the highway that's the best
Get your kicks on Route 66.
It winds from Chicago to L.A.
More than 2,000 miles all the way
Get your kicks on Route 66.
You go through St. Louie, Joplin, Missouri
And Oklahoma City looks mighty pretty.

You'll see Amarillo, Gallup, New Mexico
Flagstaff, Arizona, don't forget Winona
Kingman, Barstow, San Bernadino.
Won't you get hip to this timely tip
When you make that California trip
Get your kicks on Route 66.
— Bobby Troop, "Get Your Kicks on
    Route 66"

Words to Know

Burma Shave Signs
Cyrus Stevens Avery
Dixie Highway
Interstate Highway System

Landmarks
Main Street of America
The Mother Road
Roadside Architecture

Related Jumpstarts

Atchison, Topeka, and Santa Fe Railroad
Brooklyn Bridge
Dust Bowl
Place Names
Reshaping the Land
Where Cities Bloom

You Are There

It is 1958 and you are 11 years old. Disneyland has opened in California with 18 attractions, including the Jungle Cruise, Tomorrowland, Autopia, Mr. Toad's Wild Ride, and the Mark Twain. You have waited all year and now you, your brothers, and your sisters are on the way to the greatest attraction in America. You will drive from Chicago along Route 66. There are many things to see along the way. You may get to stay in a teepee in Wigwam Village. Your mom promises that in Texas you will see 10 Cadillacs planted nose down. You will be on the road for three whole weeks. What a time you will have along the way!

Topics to Consider

Burma Shave Signs	Mother Road Race
Compare the Dixie Highway with Route 66	One of the States along the Route
Events on Route 66 Today	Paving the Way—Blazing the Trail Racing on Route 66
Landmarks of Route 66	
The Marketing Campaign for Route 66	Traveling Route 66 Today
Migrants Travel Route 66 (See Dust Bowl)	Why Route 66 Is Disappearing

From *99 Jumpstarts for Kids' Social Studies Reports: Research Help for Grades 3–8* by Peggy J. Whitley and Susan Williams Goodwin. Westport, CT: Libraries Unlimited. Copyright © 2007.

Books

Search Words: Burma Shave; Roadside Architecture; Route 66 (as a keyword)

Benson, Sara. *Lonely Planet Road Trip: Route 66*. Oakland, CA: Lonely Planet, 2003.

Freeth, Nick, and Paul Taylor. *Traveling Route 66: 2,250 Miles of Motoring History from Chicago to L.A.* Norman: University of Oklahoma Press, 2001.

Kaszynski, William. *Route 66: Images of America's Main street.* Jefferson, NC: McFarland, 2003.

Olsen, Russell A. *Route 66, Lost and Found: Ruins and Relics Revisited.* Stillwater, MN: Voyageur, 2006.

Rowsome, Frank. *Verse by the Side of the Road: The Story of the Burma Shave Signs and Jingles.* New York: Stephen Greene Publishing, 1990.

Internet

National Geographic essay—http://news.nationalgeographic.com/news/2002/01/0102_020104wir66.html.

Why is Route 66 so important?—http://www.national66.org/66hstry.html.

Route 66 includes paving it, driving it, mapping it, and getting your kicks on it—http://xroads.virginia.edu/~UG02/carney/route66home.html.

National 66 Organization has background information, why it was built, how it is different from past highways, its demise, and highway architecture—http://www.national66.org/66hstry.html.

Facts about Route 66. Good site for landmarks—http://www.legendsofamerica.com/66-Facts.html.

Route 66 Clicks claims to be the largest Route 66 site on the Web. It has an enormous number of links by subject. Find your topic here—http://www.route66clicks.com/8states.html.

National Park Service *Corridor Preservation Program for Rte 66*—http://www.cr.nps.gov/rt66/index.htm.

For the Teacher

Cline Library in Flagstaff, Arizona, has an enormous collection of resources and links—http://jan.ucc.nau.edu/~rse/route66.htm.

Help Save a Bridge on Old 66

Join preservationists in their effort to save another Route 66 landmark bridge in Edwardsville, Illinois. IDOT (Illinois Department of Transportation) plans to demolish this historic landmark as part of a highway relocation plan. The bridge is part of Schoolhouse Trail. Read about it and e-mail or call the names listed—http://www.historic66.com and http://www.goedwardsville.com. Become part of this important effort. Learn early that your vote and efforts count.

Salem Witch Trials (1692)

The same method of trying them, which was by the evidence of the afflicted persons who when they were brought into the Court as soon as the suspected witches looked upon them instantly fell to the ground in strange agonies and grevious torments.—William Phips, Governor of Massachusetts, February 1693

Words to Know

Capital Punishment   Goody or Goodwife
Carib Indian   Mass Hysteria
Cotton   Mather Testimony
Fortune Telling   Voodoo
Gallows   Witchcraft

Related Jumpstarts

13 Original Colonies
Aboard the *Mayflower*
Fighting Prejudice
Jury System
Peer Pressure
Pilgrim Harvest
Religions of the World

You Are There

You live in Salem, Massachusetts, in 1620. Whenever the witch trials are happening, you go to watch them. They're fascinating, and you can't keep yourself away. You really can't believe this is happening. At first you wondered: Can it be true? Can Tituba really be a witch? And you convinced yourself that she could, because she looked so strange (she was a Carib Indian). She had a strange accent, and she spoke of voodoo and fortune telling. But Nurse Rebecca? You've known her all your life, and you never knew a person more unlikely to be a witch. Even the jury agreed. At first they said she was not guilty. But when the judge sent them back to reconsider, they realized that they'd better say she was guilty. You wish you could stand up and shout out, "No! Not Goody Nurse! She can't be a witch!" You wish you could, but you won't. You know that if you defend her, you will be accused of witchcraft, too.

Topics to Consider

Capital Punishment	The Salem Witch Trials
Cotton Mather	Separation of Church and State
The Crucible, by Arthur Miller	Theories about the Reasons for the Hysteria
Mass Hysteria: What Is It?	Voodoo
Religion in Nineteenth-Century New England	Witchcraft in the Nineteenth Century

From *99 Jumpstarts for Kids' Social Studies Reports: Research Help for Grades 3–8* by Peggy J. Whitley and Susan Williams Goodwin. Westport, CT: Libraries Unlimited. Copyright © 2007.

Books

Search Words: History; Salem, Mass.; Trials (Witchcraft)

Burgan, Michael. *The Salem Witch Trials.* (We the People). Minneapolis, MN: Compass, 2005.

Jackson, Shirley. *The Witchcraft of Salem Village.* New York: Random House, 1956.

Kallen, Stuart A. *Figures of the Salem Witch Trials.* (History Makers). Detroit: Lucent, 2005.

Martin, Michael. *The Salem Witch Trials.* (Graphic History). Mankato, MN: Capstone, 2005.

Miller, Arthur. *The Crucible: A Play in Four Acts.* New York: Penguin, 2003 (and other editions).

Yolen, Jane, and Heidi Elisabet Yolen Stemple. *The Salem Witch Trials: An Unsolved Mystery from History.* New York: Simon & Schuster, 2004.

Internet

An account of the witchcraft hysteria, with a list of the accused and the testimony in their trials, from the University of Missouri Kansas City School of Law—http://www.law.umkc.edu/faculty/projects/ftrials/salem/SALEM.HTM.

Court records and biographies of important persons in the Salem witch trials—http://etext.virginia.edu/salem/witchcraft/home.html.

National Geographic lets you experience the trials—http://www.nationalgeographic.com/features/97/salem/.

The Salem Witch Museum has FAQs and gives you an idea of the geography—http://www.salemwitchmuseum.com/.

Watch a Flash movie about the trials—http://school.discovery.com/schooladventures/salemwitchtrials/story/.

PBS examines the hysteria of the Salem witch trials in *Secrets of the Dead.* Choose the "Witches Curse"—http://www.pbs.org/wnet/secrets/.

For the Teacher

Discovery School has a project and lesson plans for using the Salem witch trials for grades 5–8—http://school.discovery.com/schooladventures/salemwitchtrials/tips.html.

Act It Out

You wouldn't want to go back in history and be a participant in the Salem witch trials, but you can get a taste of what it was like. Older students can read the play, *The Crucible*, by Arthur Miller. Get some friends, or better yet, your class, and discuss the play after doing some research on the topic.

Seward's Folly (1866–1885)

Sing of gold, gold, gold, Sing of lumpy chunky gold;
We are hustlin', we are prying, we are achin', we are dying, To get in and send aflyin',
The gravel from the gold, from the lumpy, clunky, very chunky gold.

Sing of feet, feet, feet, Sing of frigid, arctic feet;
We are goin' up a-diggin', With allot of Klondike riggin', an' most like we'll come back jiggin' on
our feet, feet, feet,
On our very frigid, very arctic feet.
—Roger S. Phelps, "Klondike Gold," 1898, http://library. state.ak.us/goldrush/

Words to Know

Aleut	Gold Rush
Arctic Circle	Iceberg
Aurora Borealis	Inuit
Boom Towns	Klondike
Eskimo	Pipeline
Exxon Valdez	Treaty
Ghost Towns	William Seward
Glacier	Yukon

Related Jumpstarts

Becoming a State

Go West, Young Man

Gold Rush

Indian Tribes in Your State

John Muir

The President Has Been Shot!

Where Cities Bloom

You Are There

It doesn't take much to be special in an Alaskan boom town. There aren't many children, so just being a child can do it. You walk down the street with your father, and people reach out to touch you. You shake a miner's hand, and he gives you a gold nugget. When a woman saw you, she started crying. Anywhere else, you will see lots of children, but here in Alaska where there are so few, adults get excited when they see you. As a matter of fact, you would be excited to see another child, too. You have heard that a school will be built soon for the 10 children here. You can't wait! It will be so nice to have other children to play with.

Topics to Consider

Alaska Pipeline	Drilling for Oil in Alaska
Alaska's Native Americans	Manifest Destiny
Alaska's Natural Resources	Mining
Alaska's Path to Statehood	Panning for Gold
Call of the Wild or Another	The Pursuit of Gold
Jack London Story	Russians in Alaska
Children in Alaska	William Seward, Secretary of State

Books

Search Words: Alaska, History; Russians—Alaska History; Seward, William Henry

Doherty, Craig A., and Katherine M. Doherty. *The Trans-Alaska Pipeline.* (Building America). Woodbridge, CT: Blackbirch Press, 1998.

Freemon, David K. *The Alaska Purchase in American History.* (In American History). Springfield, NJ: Enslow, 1999.

Kent, Zachary. *William Seward: The Mastermind of the Alaska Purchase.* (Historical American Biographies). Berkeley Heights, NJ: Enslow, 2001.

London, Jack. *Call of the Wild.* 1903. Various print editions or online—http://www.online-literature.com/london/callwild/.

Murphy, Claire Rudolf, and Jane G. Haigh. *Children of the Gold Rush.* Boulder, CO: Roberts Reinhart, 2001.

Whitcraft, Melissa. *Seward's Folly.* (Cornerstones of Freedom). New York: Children's Press, 2002.

Internet

The Library of Congress *American Memories* explains the background and significance of Seward's purchase of Alaska—http://memory.loc.gov/ammem/today/mar30.html.

The history of Alaska, from the city of Fairbanks, gives details on Seward's Folly—http://fairbanks-alaska.com/alaska-history.htm.

Full text of the treaty between Russia and the United States, *The Alaska Purchase Treaty of 1867*—http://www.historicaldocuments.com/AlaskaPurchaseTreaty.htm.

Where to Find Gold in Alaska charts gold production in Alaska—http://www.akmining.com/mine/akgold.htm.

The discovery of gold, and the life of a miner, from the Alaska State Library—http://library.state.ak.us/goldrush/.

The Alaska Department of the Interior explores oil, including oil platforms, crude oil, and oil spills—http://www.mms.gov/alaska/kids/shorts/shorts.htm.

For the Teacher

The *Teachers' Guide* at the Alaska State Library Web site on the gold rush explains learning with primary source materials—http://library.state.ak.us/goldrush/. See also *Teaching with Documents* from the National Archives—http://www.archives.gov/education/lessons/alaska/index.html.

Pan for Gold

You can still pan for gold in Alaska! Go to http://www.alaska.com/activities/goldpan/story/4652577p-4608744c.html to learn where you can pan for gold without being shot! If Alaska is too far to go, you can also find places to pan for gold throughout the country, from North Carolina to California.

Social Security (1936)

An act to provide for the general welfare by establishing a system of Federal old-age benefits, and by enabling the several States to make more adequate provision for aged persons, blind persons, dependent and crippled children, maternal and child welfare, public health, and the administration of their unemployment compensation laws; to establish a Social Security Board; to raise revenue; and for other purposes.
—Preamble to the Social Security Act of 1935

Words to Know

Dependant	Retirement
Disability	Revenue
Great Depression	SSN (Social Security Number)
New Deal	Unemployment Insurance
Pension	Welfare
Poorhouse	Widows and Orphans

Related Jumpstarts

Banking
Great Depression
Poverty in America
Stocks and Bonds
Taxes

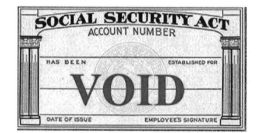

You Are There

Times are hard. Your father owns the gas station in town. Farmers come to the gas station to fuel their tractors, but they don't have any money to pay for the gas. One farmer gave your father a horse to pay what he owed. You didn't mind that; you got the horse! Others pay him in vegetables. But your father still has to pay the Standard Oil Company for the gas. You have to move into the basement of your uncle's house to save money. You know you're luckier than many of your friends. Their fathers don't have a job at all. But yesterday, President Roosevelt signed the Social Security Act. It gives unemployment insurance to the people who lost their jobs. Everyone who works will register and get a Social Security number. They'll pay a special tax. Money from the tax will help the unemployed and people like your grandparents, who are retired, to survive.

Topics to Consider

Changing the Retirement Age	Should the United States Have a National Identification Card?
Disability and Social Security	
Getting Your Social Security Card	Social Security Benefits for Children
History of the Social Security Program	Social Security Reform
Identity Theft	Taxes and the Social Security Number
The New Deal	Timeline of Social Security
	What Is Social Security? Will I Get It?

Books

Search Words: Pension Plans; Social Security, United States

Beland, Daniel. *Social Security: History and Politics from the New Deal to the Privatization Debate.* (Studies in Government and Public Policy). Lawrence: University of Kansas Press, 2005.

Benavie, Arthur. *Social Security under the Gun: What Every Informed Citizen Needs to Know about Pension Reform.* New York: Palgrave Macmillan, 2006.

Bonello, Frank J. *Taking Sides: Clashing View on Economic Issues.* 12th ed. Blacklick, OH: Dushkin, 2005.

Gedney, Mona K. *The Story of the Great Depression.* (Monumental Milestones). Hockessin, DE: Mitchell Lane, 2005.

Hanes, Sharon M., and Richard C. Hanes. *Great Depression and the New Deal: Almanac.* (UXL Great Depression and New Deal Reference Library). Detroit: UXL, 2003.

Internet

Social Security Online Kids page tells you in brief what Social Security is all about—http://www.ssa.gov/kids/kids.htm.

A Social Security primer from About.com tells you about retirement and disability benefits and how to file for them—http://usgovinfo.about.com/blssaprimer.htm.

An introduction to Social Security from the Economic Policy Institute discusses the purposes of Social Security—http://www.epinet.org/content.cfm/issueguide_socialsecurity.

History and development of Social Security from the Social Security Administration, including video and audio clips—http://www.ssa.gov/history/history.html.

Interesting stories about Social Security numbers—http://www.ssa.gov/history/ssn/ssncards.html.

How Stuff Works explains how the Social Security number works—http://people.howstuffworks.com/social-security-number.htm.

An article in *The Nation* shows you what people in the 1930s thought about Social Security, both as unemployment insurance and old age pensions—http://newdeal.feri.org/nation/na35261.htm.

For the Teacher

The IRS (Internal Revenue Service) offers a comprehensive lesson plan on Social Security that includes calculating taxes, understanding the Social Security Act of 1935, and the history. Other tax-related lesson plans are also at this site—http://www.irs.gov/app/understandingTaxes/jsp/whys/lp/IWT2L4lp.jsp.

What's in a Name?

The Social Security Administration theoretically has everyone over the age of five in the United States registered. That means it has the names of almost everyone in America. Check to see the most popular names for everyone born in the same year as you were . . . or your parents . . . or even check for twin names or popular names by state—http://www.ssa.gov/OACT/babynames/.

Stocks and Bonds

After your research, you're convinced it's a solid company that . . . offers both stocks and bonds. With the bonds, the company agrees to pay you back your initial investment in ten years, plus pay you interest twice a year at the rate of 8% a year. If you buy the stock, you take on the risk of potentially losing a portion or all of your initial investment if the company does poorly or the stock market drops in value. But you also may see the stock increase in value beyond what you could earn from the bonds. If you buy the stock, you become an "owner" of the company.—U.S. Security and Exchanges Commission, http://www.sec.gov/investor/pubs/roadmap/choice.htm

Words to Know

American Stock Exchange (AMEX)
Bear Market
Bull Market
Dividends
Gambling
Initial Public Offering (IPO)
Investing

Mutual Funds
New York Stock Exchange (NYSE)
P/E Ratio
Portfolio
Savings Bonds
Shares
Stock Market

Related Jumpstarts

Banking
Great Depression
I Want That! Needs vs. Wants
Making Money
Marketing to Kids
Supply and Demand

You Are There

Woo-hoo! You've just won the lottery! You are now officially a multimillionaire. Now what do you do with the money? Spending it sounds like a great idea! But then, if you spend it, you won't have it anymore! You could put it in the bank. How boring. You'd rather have some fun with it. Well, then, how about investing it. Investing? What does that mean? In a way, it means that you let other people use your money and they pay you for the privilege. With the right investments, you can have your money and spend it too! You'd better be careful, though. If you invest your money with the wrong company, you may not get it back. It's time to do your homework and learn what investing is all about.

Topics to Consider

Bull Market and Bear Market	History of the Stock Market
Compare New York, London, and Tokyo Stock Markets	Initial Public Offerings (IPOs)
Compare Stocks and Bonds	Interest Rates
Compare Two Stocks for a Month	Mutual Funds
Day Trading	New York Stock Exchange
Gambling vs. Investing	Savings Bonds
	Technology Bonds

Books

Search Words: Stock Exchanges; Stock Market; Stocks

Blumenthal, Karen. *Six Days in October: The Stock Market Crash of 1929.* (Wall Street Journal Book). New York: Atheneum, 2002.

Fuller, Donna Jo. *The Stock Market.* (How Economics Works). Minneapolis, MN: Lerner, 2006.

Harman, Hollis Page. *Money Sense for Kids.* 2d ed. Hauppauge, NY: Barrons, 2004.

Loewen, Nancy. *Ups and Downs: A Book about the Stock Market.* (Money Matters). Minneapolis, MN: Picture Window, 2005.

McGowen, Eileen Nixon, and Nancy Lagow Dumas. *Stock Market Smart.* Brookfield, CT: Millbrook, 2002.

Internet

Thinkquest has all sorts of information about understanding and investing in stocks and bonds—http://library.thinkquest.org/3298/.

Kiplinger answers questions kids ask about the stock market—http://www.kiplinger.com/personalfinance/basics/managing/kids/faqs/kfaq_stocks.htm.

Check NASDAQ to see how an individual stock is doing—http:/www.nasdaq.com/.

The official Web site of the New York Stock Exchange has a glossary and symbol lookup—http://www.nyse.com/.

Investing 101 from PBS tells about stock exchanges and how to get started investing—http://www.pbs.org/newshour/on2/money/stocks.html.

What is an IPO (Initial Public Offering), and how does it work? From How Stuff Works—http://money.howstuffworks.com/ipo.htm.

Savings bonds for kids. Details are at the U.S. Treasury Web site—http://www.publicdebt.treas.gov/sav/savkids.htm.

The SEC (Securities Exchange Commission) explains the difference between stocks and bonds—http://www.sec.gov/investor/pubs/roadmap/choice.htm.

For the Teacher

A global stock market game, sponsored by the University of Georgia, designed to help teach students about the stock market. Teachers can create a customized stock game for the class—http://investsmart.coe.uga.edu/C001759/help.htm.

Follow the Stock Market

Choose two or three stocks that interest you, such as Hershey (HSY), Kellogg (K), or Toys R Us (TOY). "Buy" 100 shares of each. Record how much the shares cost you. Check the newspaper every week to track your stock. Make a chart. Get friends to "buy" shares of their own favorites and compare your fortunes at the end of the semester. Stock symbols can be found through http://biz.yahoo.com/i/.

Supply and Demand

[A] period of freezing weather killed a large number of orange trees in Florida. The sharp decline in the supply of oranges caused a large increase in orange juice prices, which encouraged people to drink other beverages, thus allocating the smaller supply of oranges. The higher price of orange juice also attracted Brazilian producers to the U.S. market, providing a large increase in the supply of frozen juice concentrate available to U.S. consumers. The higher prices also encouraged U.S. farmers to replant farther south in Florida, and after a few years U.S. production recovered. The combination of the short-term Brazilian and long-term U.S. response to the supply shortage brought prices back down—Robert M. Dunn Jr., USINFO, http://usinfo.state.gov/products/pubs/market/mktsb6.htm

Words to Know

Allocation   Price Controls
Black Market   Price Fixing
Competition   Rarity
Glut   Short- and Long-term Solutions
Overproduction   Subsidies
Shortages

Related Jumpstarts

Dust Bowl

Gold Rush

I Want That! Needs vs. Wants

Marketing to Kids

Prohibition and Gangsters

Stocks and Bonds

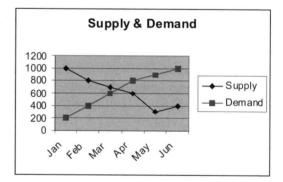

You Are There

Pretend that Wacky Boppers are the latest fad, and they come in five colors: red, yellow, blue, green, and gold. Only one in a hundred Wacky Boppers is gold, though. Everyone seems to want the gold Wacky Bopper. You go to the toy store just as a new batch of Boppers is being unloaded. You dig through the pile, rejecting red ones and green ones and blue ones. There's a gold Wally Bopper! Really! It really is a gold one! When you show it off to your friends, they're envious. "I'll give you ten dollars for it." "I'll trade you three reds, a yellow and a green." But you hold on to the gold one. A month later, you realize that you don't even like gold. You would much rather own a red one. But when you try to trade, no one wants it any more. "No, thanks. I've got two gold boppers now. But I'll sell you the red one for $10.00."

Topics to Consider

Cable Television	Supply and Demand
Farm Subsidies	Weather and Prices
Oil Prices	Why Are All the Stores Out of the Most
Price Controls	Popular New Games?
Price Fixing	Why Is Gold Valuable?
Price of Diamonds	

Books

Search Words: Business; Economics: Finance, Personal; Supply and Demand

Adil, Janeer. *Supply and Demand.* (First Facts). Mankato, MN: Capstone, 2006.

Fodor, R. V. *Nickels, Dimes, and Dollars: How Currency Works.* New York: Morrow, 1980.

Gunderson, Cory Gideon. *The Need for Oil.* (World in Conflict: Middle East). Edina, MN: Abdo, 2003.

Loewen, Nancy. *Lemons and Lemonade: A Book about Supply and Demand.* (Money Matters). Minneapolis, MN: Picture Window, 2005.

Seidman, David. *Young Zillionaire's Guide to Supply and Demand.* (Be a Zillionaire). New York: Rosen, 2000 (and other books in this series).

Internet

Social Studies for Kids explains the basic facts of supply and demand—http://www.socialstudiesforkids.com/articles/economics/supplyanddemand1.htm.

Economics: I'll Buy That!—http://www.uen.org/utahlink/tours/tourFames.cgi?tour_id=14721.

St. Joseph's College explains supply and demand for older students—http://ingrimayne.saintjoe.edu/econ/DemandSupply/OverviewSD.html.

Learn about the law of supply and demand using a tree farm as an example—http://www.realtrees4kids.org/ninetwelve/supply.htm.

Econopolis, a ThinkQuest site, has games to teach you about supply and demand while you have fun—http://library.thinkquest.org/3901/.

The *Energy Kids Page* from the Department of Energy has a time line of oil exploration that illustrates supply and demand and the effect on prices—http://www.eia.doe.gov/kids/history/timelines/petroleum.html.

Real Trees 4 Kids, Supply & Demand—http://www.realtrees4kids.org/ninetwelve/supply.htm.

The World Gold Council discusses the value of gold as an investment—http://www.gold.org/value/invest/whybuy/index.html.

For the Teacher

The National Council on Economic Education (NCEE) has 470 economics lesson plans and new ways to teach economics for grades K–12—http://www.ncee.net/.

Spot the Trends

See if you can spot economic trends in historic places! This example uses the Gold Rush. Work through it, or read it and try to find another example of your own—http://www.econedlink.org/lessons/index.cfm?lesson=EM328.

Taxes

No government can exist without taxation. This money must necessarily be levied on the people; and the grand art consists of levying so as not to oppress.—Frederick the Great, eighteenth-century Prussian king

If you make any money, the government shoves you in the creek once a year with it in your pockets, and all that don't get wet you can keep.—Will Rogers

Words to Know

THE HOME OF THE AMERICAN CITIZEN AFTER THE TAX BILL HAS PASSED.

Excise Tax
Expenses
Income Tax
Internal Revenue
Levy

Percentage
Reallocation
Sales Tax
Service Tax Reform
Treasury

Related Jumpstarts

Becoming a Citizen
Boston Tea Party
Business of Doing Good
I Want That! Needs vs. Wants
Making Money
Right to Vote
Social Security
Who Runs Our Town?
Writing the Constitution

You Are There

You worked hard all day, helping to clean up the kitchen. You had to take everything out of the cupboards, clean it, sort it by size and use, and stack it all up again. It's not your favorite way to spend your Saturday, but your Mom promised you that if you did all that work, she'd pay you five dollars. Five dollars! You know just what you will do with that money. At the end of the day, you hold out your hand for the money. She counts out "One, two, three, four, five," then takes back the last dollar. "You only get four dollars," she says. "The other dollar is for taxes. "But that's not fair," you shout. "I earned that money. It's mine. Why should I have to pay taxes?" Why indeed? What does tax money pay for? And if there were no taxes, how would those things get done?

Topics to Consider

Back-to-School Tax Free Weekend	Income Tax Reform
Compare Different Tax Proposals	Local Taxes
Compare Taxes in Different States	Progressive Tax
Excise, Luxury, or Cigarette Taxes	Should Necessities Be Taxed?
Funding Schools	Taxes in Different Countries
History of Taxation	Why Are Taxes Important?
How We Pay Taxes	

Books

Search Words: Income Tax; Internal Revenue Service; Taxation

De Capua, Sarah. *Paying Taxes.* (True Book). New York: Children's Press, 2002.

Giesecke, Ernestine. *Your Money at Work: Taxes.* (Heinemann Know-it: Everyday Economics). Chicago: Heinemann, 2003.

Grote, JoAnne A. *The Internal Revenue Service.* (Your Government: How It Works). Philadelphia: Chelsea House, 2001.

Hamilton, John. *Funding the Nation.* (Government in Action). Edina, MN: ABDO, 2005.

Internet

How Stuff Works explains how income taxes work and gives the history of taxes in America—http://people.howstuffworks.com/income-tax.htm.

History for Kids briefly tells the history of taxes—http://www.historyforkids.org/learn/economy/taxes.htm.

Understanding Taxes for Students, by the Internal Revenue Service—http://www.irs.gov/app/understandingTaxes/jsp/s_student_home.jsp.

Social Security Kids Stuff uses fables and games to explain Social Security tax for younger students—http://www.ssa.gov/kids/kids.htm.

The United States Department of the Treasury answers questions about the history of taxes and how they work, for older students—http://www.treas.gov/education/faq/taxes/.

Tax rates around the world in brief, for older students—http://www.worldwide-tax.com/.

The Tax History Museum has information, cartoons, and presidential tax returns, by tax analysts. For older students—http://www.taxhistory.org/.

For the Teacher

The Internal Revenue Service offers 36 tax lessons for students—http://www.irs.gov/app/understandingTaxes/jsp/s_student_lessons.jsp.

Collecting Taxes

Play SimCity™. At the end of each year, you have to determine the taxes for the coming year. The higher the taxes, the less people like you, but you have more money! This article discusses the SimCity™ model, if you really want to analyze why you are playing it—http://www.firstmonday.org/issues/issue4_4/friedman/index.html.

Telling America's Story with Photographs (1839–Present)

From the first, I regarded myself as under obligation to my country to preserve the faces of its historic men and mothers.—Mathew Brady, 1891

Words to Know

Daguerre
Daguerreotype
Documentary
Farm
Landscape
Life Magazine
Look Magazine

Photography
Photojournalism
Photography Portrait
Security Administration Tenement
Time Magazine
U.S. National Child Labor

Related Jumpstarts

Any jumpstart after 1840 would be useful as a topic for your photo history.

You Are There

We owe the term "photography" to Sir John Herschel, who first used it in 1839, the year the photographic process became public. You were 10 years old when this came about. In 1860, when you were 30, you joined the Confederates, leaving your wife and three small children at home while you went off to fight for the South. In 1865 you were with General Robert E. Lee when he surrendered to Ulysses S. Grant. A few days later, the famous Civil War photographer Mathew Brady took photographs of General Lee. Lee wore the same uniform he had worn to surrender and, with the encouragement of his wife, allowed Mr. Brady to take his picture. General Lee made history—and you were a part of it all. Maybe the photograph Mr. Brady took will tell your grandchildren and great grandchildren a story.

Topics to Consider

Tell a story using photographs of an event or time period. The photographs you select to tell your story are extremely important. Your captions are crucial. They move the story along. Stick to 10 pictures if you can. Good examples for topics are the pictures taken by the photographers listed below.

1860 Mathew Brady and the Civil War
1870 William Jackson and Tim O'Sullivan Photograph the Old West
1890 Jacob Riis Photographs Tenement Life in New York City
1900 Alfred Stieglitz Photographs New York at the Turn of the Century
1909 Lewis Hine Photographs Children mill workers
1930 American Landscapes by Ansel Adams, Edward Weston, Imogen Cunningham (Biography)
1935 Walker Evans, Dorothea Lange, Arthur Rothstein
1940 World War II Photographers: Paul Strand, Margaret Bourke-White, or Robert Capa

Books

Search Words: Documentary Photography; Name of Photographer; Photographers; Photojournalism

Don't forget to use magazines for this project: *Time, Life, National Geographic,* and others.

Armstrong, Jennifer. *Photo by Brady: A Picture of the Civil War.* New York: Atheneum, 2006.

Light, Ken. *Witness in Our Time: Working Lives of Documentary Photographers.* Washington, DC: Smithsonian, 2000.

Venezia, Mike. *Dorothea Lange.* New York: Children's Press, 2000.

Webb, Alex. *Crossings: Photographs from the U.S.–Mexico Border.* New York: Monacelli, 2003.

Internet

Every Picture Tells a Story helps you understand the importance of selecting the right photo. Try the activities and learn from photographers of the past—http://chnm.gmu.edu/fsa/.

The History of Photography has good information about photography and is a great place to find short biographies of photographers, like Brady—http://www.rleggat.com/photohistory/index.html.

Time Magazine or *Life Magazine* archives will be one of your best resources. Use search terms, like Vietnam or John F. Kennedy—http://www.time.com/time/archive/ or http://www.life.com/Life.

War time photography—information and links. There is lots more information here, so be sure to use the index—http://photography.about.com/library/weekly/aa110899a.htm.

Mathew Brady: Civil War Newspapers—http://memory.loc.gov/learn/lessons/98/brady/home.html.

National Geographic knows as much about telling a story with pictures as anyone else. Select "History" and learn—http://www.nationalgeographic.com/?fs=www9.nationalgeographic.com.

Walker Evans and Documentary Photography—http://xroads.virginia.edu/~UG97/fsa/welcome.html.

The Daguerreotype Society, information and examples—http://www.daguerre.org/gallindex.php.

For the Teacher

American Memory has lesson plans for using photography to tell a story. These lessons have something for every age and subject, using a wonderful Library of Congress photograph collection—http://memory.loc.gov/learn/lessons/index.htm.

Tell a Story in Five Frames

Create your own story with five photographs and post it online—http://www.flickr.com/groups/visualstory/. You must follow the Flickr rules. First photo: establish characters and location. Second photo: create a situation with possibilities of what might happen. Third photo: involve the characters in the situation. Fourth photo: build to probable outcomes. Fifth photo: have a logical, but surprising, end. This is fun.

Trail of Tears (1838–1839)

No better symbol exists of the pain and suffering of the "Trail Where They Cried" than the Cherokee Rose. The mothers of the Cherokee grieved so much that the chiefs prayed for a sign to lift the mother's spirits and give them strength to care for their children. From that day forward, a beautiful new flower, a rose, grew wherever a mother's tear fell to the ground. The rose is white, for the mother's tears. It has a gold center, for the gold taken from the Cherokee lands, and seven leaves on each stem that represent the seven Cherokee clans that made the journey. To this day, the Cherokee Rose prospers along the route of the "Trail of Tears." The Cherokee Rose is now the official flower of the State of Georgia.—The Legend of the Cherokee Rose, Cherokee-pride.com

Words to Know

Aniyunwiya	The Removal Act
Cherokee Nation	Sequoyah
Displacement	Syllabary
Keetoowah	Treaty
Principal Chief	Treaty of New Echola

Related Jumpstarts

Becoming a State
Go West, Young Man
Indian Tribes in Your State
Lewis & Clark Expedition
Mesa Verde Cliff Dwellings
Oklahoma Land Rush
Place Names

You Are There

The year is 1838. You, your parents, your grandparents, and all your friends and kin are being forced out of Georgia and removed to a land far away. This is the saddest of times. Your family has lived in Georgia since many generations before the white man arrived. Yet the president has signed a treaty that forces you to go west of the Mississippi River. Along with 15,000 other Cherokee Indians, you and your family head west. Along the way, you meet hardship after hardship. Faced with hunger, disease, drought, freezing weather, and exhaustion, more than 4,000 of your friends and kin die along the way. What must it have been like? We can hardly imagine. Find out.

Topics to Consider

The Cherokee Language	Indian Removal
Cherokee Rose	Life on the Trail
Cherokees Today	The Removal Act—What Was It?
Chief John Ross, Principal Chief of the Oklahoma Cherokee Nation	Sequoyah (aka George Gist)
	U.S. Government Treaties with American Indians
General Winfield Scott and the Trail of Tears	Why Were the Cherokee Indians Forced Out
History of the Cherokee Indians	of Georgia?

From *99 Jumpstarts for Kids' Social Studies Reports: Research Help for Grades 3–8* by Peggy J. Whitley and Susan Williams Goodwin. Westport, CT: Libraries Unlimited. Copyright © 2007.

Books

Search Words: Cherokee Indians, History; Ross, John; Sequoyah; Trail of Tears

Birchfield, D. L. *The Trail of Tears.* (Landmark Events in American History). Milwaukee, WI: World Almanac Library, 2004.

Byars, Ann. *The Trail of Tears: A Primary Source History of the Forced Relocation of the Cherokee Nation.* (Primary Sources in American History). New York: Rosen, 2004.

Kent, Deborah. *The Trail of Tears.* (Cornerstones of Freedom). New York: Children's, 2005.

Rozema, Vicki. *Voices from the Trail of Tears.* (Real Voices, Real History). Winston-Salem, NC: J.F. Blair, 2003.

Rumford, James. *Sequoyah: The Cherokee Man Who Gave His People Writing.* Boston: Houghton Mifflin, 2004.

Internet

History of the Cherokee is an excellent page of links to history, genealogy, newspapers, and books—http://www.cherokeehistory.com/ and http://www.rosecity.net/tears/.

Pitter's Cherokee Indians—Pitter Seabaugh is editor of the *Cherokee Trails Newsletter.* Articles on this Web site are reprinted here from the newsletter—http://www.rosecity.net/cherokee/.

The Trail of Tears is from the North Georgia Web site. An excellent starting place to learn the short history of the Cherokee removal—http://ngeorgia.com/history/nghisttt.html.

The University of Georgia page for the Trail of Tears. Links. Includes the address to the Cherokee Indians by General Winfield Scott—http://www.cviog.uga.edu/Projects/gainfo/trailtea.htm.

Sequoyah and the Syllabary—background on Sequoyah and his invention of the written Cherokee alphabet—http://college.hmco.com/history/readerscomp/naind/html/na_035400_sequoyah.htm.

Indian Removal is the topic of this PBS Web site and includes earlier removals plus the Trail of Tears—http://www.pbs.org/wgbh/aia/part4/4p2959.html.

For the Teacher

Trail of Tears for grades 5–8. This excellent lesson plan includes information, links, plans, topics for discussion, and several ideas for student exploration—http://www.42explore2.com/trailoftears.htm.

On the Trail

Create a Trail of Tears travel journal. Try some research on the actual trail. Think about the outside forces that would affect your journey, like weather, lack of food, and water. Make your own journal—as though you are on the trail with the other Cherokees families and friends in 1838–1839—http://www.rosecity.net/tears/trail/map.html.

Underground Railroad (1830–1865)

I looked at my hands, to see if I was de same person now I was free. Dere was such a glory ober eberything, de sun came like gold trou de trees, and ober de fields, and I felt like I was in heaven.—Harriet Tubman

Words to Know

Abolitionists
Conductors
The Drinking Gourd
Frederick Douglass
Freedom Train

Harriet Tubman
Quilt Code
Sojourner Truth
Stations
Underground Railroad

Related Jumpstarts

Buffalo Soldiers

Cultures and Cuisines

King Cotton

Missouri Compromise

Riding in the Back of the Bus

Right to Vote

You Are There

You are born a slave in South Carolina in 1843. Now you are 15 years old. Your father was sold to another plantation. Your brothers were sold in Georgia. Your mother is a house slave. She lives with you and others in the slave quarters in Charleston. Your mother always says, "Child, if you have a chance to run away—do it. Never miss an opportunity to run to freedom." You have learned the quilt code used by other slaves from Georgia and Charleston. You know to follow the drinking gourd. Then, one day you have a chance to run with two friends. The conductor leads you along the Appalachian Mountains into Ohio. The path is scary and hard. You travel at night. You hide in homes and fields. But at last you are free. You are in Canada, where you will start a new life.

Topics to Consider

Biographies of Several Conductors	Signs and Signals for Slaves
Following the Drinking Gourd	A Specific Route on the Trail
Harriet Tubman (or Another Conductor)	The Underground Railroad in Your State
Henry Box Brown, Runaway Slave	The Underground Railroad Quilt Code
Personal Accounts by Other Runaway Slaves	Unusual Hiding Places on the Under-
Preservation of the Underground Railroad	ground Railroad
(What Is Being Done Today)	

Books

Search Words: Abolitionists; Fugitive Slaves; Slavery—Documents; Tubman, Harriet (or Any of the Other Abolitionists); Underground Railroad and Quilts

Ford, Carin. *Slavery and the Underground Railroad: Bound for Freedom.* (Civil War Library). Berkeley Heights, NJ: Enslow, 2004.

Hudson, Wade. *The Underground Railroad.* (Cornerstones of Freedom). New York: Children's Press, 2005.

Landau, Elaine. *Abolitionists Movement.* (Cornerstones of Freedom). New York: Children's Press, 2004.

Landau, Elaine. *Flying to Freedom on the Underground Railroad: The Courageous Slaves, Agents and Conductors.* (People's History). Minneapolis, MN: Twenty-first Century, 2006.

McKissack, Pat. *Days of Jubilee: The End of Slavery in the United States.* New York: Scholastic, 2003.

Tobin, Jacqueline, and Raymond G. Dobard. *Hidden in Plain View: The Secret Story of Quilts and the Underground Railroad.* New York: Anchor, 2000.

Internet

The Underground Railroad from National Geographic has something for everyone. Follow the links at http://www.nationalgeographic.com/features/99/railroad/j1.html.

Maryland and Kentucky Underground Railroad information—http://pathways.thinkport.org/about/ and http://www.ket.org/underground/. Take time at these excellent sites.

Time line of the Underground Railroad—http://www.nps.gov/boaf/urrchronology.htm.

The National Park System has an excellent site—http://209.10.16.21/TEMPLATE/FrontEnd/index.cfm#.

Harriet Tubman and the Underground Railroad by a second grade class at Pocantico Hills School in Sleepy Hollow, New York—http://www2.lhric.org/pocantico/tubman/tubman.html.

The Lee Coffin House is an Underground Railroad site—http://www.waynet.org/nonprofit/coffin.htm.

Underground Quilt Code has plenty of information—http://www.ugrrquilt.hartcottagequilts.com/.

For the Teacher

⌐ This lesson plan for grades 4–6 contains activities, tests, and lyrics—http://www.lessonplanspage.com/SSLAMusicCivilWarUnitB-UndergroundRailroad46.htm.

⌐ Share *Jacob Lawrence: The Frederick Douglass and Harriet Tubman Series of 1938–1940* (Hampton, VA: Hampton University Museum, 1991) or the Jacob Lawrence books, *Harriet Tubman and the Promised Land* (New York: Simon & Schuster, 1993) and *The Great Migration, an American Story* (New York: HarperCollins, 1993).

Quilting a Secret Message

Make your own secret message quilt for Slaves who are trying to escape. Use the Underground quilt code. What message will you send?—http://pathways.thinkport.org/secrets/secret_quilt.cfm and http://www.ugrrquilt.hartcottgequilts.com/.

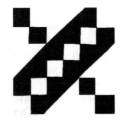

Wal-Mart Comes to Our Town

For a hundred years Bath, Maine, had done just fine, thank you. Downtown-business owners worked hard, sometimes flourished, and always sustained a small but vital economic community that was the lifeblood of the town. Then Wal-Mart arrived.—Edward Welles, *Inc. Magazine*, July 2003

Words to Know

Competition
Discount
Mega-Stores
Mom and Pop Stores
Retailer

Sourcing or Outsourcing Importing Goods
Stores Sprawl Busters
Superstores
Supply and Demand
Zoning

Related Jumpstarts

American Sweatshops
Going to Market: From Seed to Sale
History of Main Street
Supply and Demand

You Are There

Imagine this: You live in a small town in east Texas. Your family has lived there for three generations and your dad owns the only hardware store in town; the one that his grandfather opened 50 years ago. Everyone visits his store, and he knows everyone in town. You have a happy life in your small town. But along comes Wal-Mart. They build a superstore right on the highway about three miles from downtown. The prices are cheaper, there is more variety, and the one-stop shopping makes it easier for families. Not only that, but restaurants and other retail stores have moved to the Wal-Mart area. Over a short period, everything changes. Small shops around your dad's hardware store begin to close. Downtown is changed forever. Your dad fears that he will have to close his store.

Topics to Consider

Are Superstores a National Trend?	Sprawl-Busters: Who Are They?
Can the Mom and Pop Stores Survive?	Superstores (Barnes & Noble and Others)
Five Reasons People Hate Wal-Mart	The Story of What Happened When
Five Reasons People Love Wal-Mart	Wal-Mart Came to Our Town
How Can Downtown Be Saved?	The Wal-Mart Story—Sam Walton
Should Wal-Mart Outsource Products?	Why Is Wal-Mart So Successful?

Books

Search Words: Discount Houses; Wal-Mart—History; Walton, Sam

Dicker, John. *The United States of Wal-Mart.* New York: Penguin, 2005.

Greenberg, Keith Elliot. *Sam Walton.* (Made in America). Vero Beach: Rourke, 1993.

Quinn, Bill. *How Wal-Mart Is Destroying America and What You Can Do About It.* Berkeley, CA: Ten Speed Press, 1998.

Save Our Land, Save Our Towns (videorecording). Reading, PA: Bullfrog Films, 2000.

Store Wars: When Wal-Mart Comes to Town (videorecording). Produced by Teddy Bear Films. Oley, PA: Bullfrog Films, 2001.

Internet

Information about Wal-Mart, including statistics and history—http://www.explainplease.com/wal-mart.htm.

Wal-Mart Comes to Town from PBS covers several of the issues—good site—http://www.pbs.org/itvs/storewars/.

An *Inc. Magazine* article, "When Wal-Mart Comes to Town: How One Small Town Reacted to Wal-Mart's Opening Three Stores"—http://www.inc.com/magazine/19930701/3644.html.

Sprawl-Busters.com fights for the American hometown—http://www.sprawl-busters.com/.

Milford Residents Battle Wal-Mart—http://www.wcpo.com/news/2004/local/04/06/Wal-Mart.html. Be sure to watch the video, which describes how both residents and this mega-company operate.

Statistics and other information from Wal-Mart—http://www.walmartfacts.com/.

Why Do Mom and Pop Stores Hate Wal-Mart?—http://answers.google.com/answers/threadview?id=481435.

For the Teacher

Teachable Moment has an excellent lesson plan—http://www.teachablemoment.org/high/walmart.html.

Shopping Wal-Mart

Make a list of 15 products that you and your family use regularly. Go to your local Wal-Mart and two other stores. Check the prices on these products at every store. Then create a comparison chart of prices at Wal-Mart and the other stores in your area. Is Wal-Mart the best buy? Is one-stop shopping important? Draw conclusions about your findings.

Where Cities Bloom

The distribution and density of Earth's population reflect the planet's topography, soils, vegetation, and climate types (ecosystems); available resources; and level of economic development.—National Geographic Xpeditions, 2001, http://www.nationalgeographic.com/xpeditions/standards/09/

Words to Know

Agglomeration
Census
Climate
Demographics
Employment
Environment
Immigration

Migration
Mobility
Population Density
Settlement Patterns
Sustainability
Urbanization
Utopia

Related Jumpstarts

Atchison, Topeka, and Santa Fe Railroad
Coming to America
Go West, Young Man
Indians Tribes in Your State
Mighty Mississippi
Place Names
Reshaping the Land

You Are There

You have just arrived in America. America, the Land of Opportunity! You have always heard about it and dreamed about just what you would do when you arrived. But until you got here, you didn't realize just how big the country was. The first thing you are going to have to decide is where you want to go. Would you like to move to the Great Plains, where most of the people are farmers? If you raise cattle or sheep or grow crops, you will never go hungry. You also think about moving to a city. In a city, there are plenty of jobs. You could sell things in a store or work in a factory. You wouldn't have to worry about the hard work people do on a farm. When your job is done, you can go home and relax. Whichever lifestyle you choose, you also have to worry about how you will get there. You can go by boat, by train, or by car. That means that your destination will probably be near a river, railroad tracks, or a highway.

Topics to Consider

Compare Indian Settlements to Current Day	Overpopulation
Compare Rural to Urban Economies	Reasons for Settlement in Your Area
Differences Between Population Distribution Today and Long Ago	Rivers and Their Effect on Population
	Settlement Patterns for a Certain Nationality
Occupations	Sustainability
	Transportation and Towns

Books

Search Words: Frontier and Pioneer Life—U.S.; Human Geography; Land Settlement Patterns; Population, Environmental Aspects

Ciovacco, Justine, Kathleen A. Feeley, and Kristen Behrens. *State-by-State Atlas*. New York: DK Publishing, 2003.

Davenport, John. *Louisiana Territory*. (Arbitrary Borders). Philadelphia: Chelsea House, 2005.

Gale Encyclopedia of Multicultural America: Primary Documents. 2d ed. (2 vols.). Detroit: Gale, 2000.

Harrison, Paul, and Fred Pearce. *AAAS Atlas of Population and Environment*. Berkeley: University of California Press, 2000.

Savageau, David, and Ralph D'Agostino. *Places Rated Almanac*. Indianapolis, IN: Macmillan, 1981– .

Internet

Germans, Czechs, Finns, Luxembourgers, Portuguese, and Slovaks in America, from the Library of Congress Reading Room—http://www.loc.gov/rr/european/specproj.html.

NASA satellites track the growth of cities through night photography—http://www.nasa.gov/vision/earth/everydaylife/Growing_Cities_AGU.html.

Where do immigrants come from? Current statistics are available in the *World Almanac for Kids*—http://www.worldalmanacforkids.com/explore/population5.html.

Internet Geography explains population density—http://www.geography.learnontheinternet.co.uk/topics/popn1.html#density.

Settlement patterns in the United States, by the *Encyclopedia Britannica*—http://www.britannica.com/eb/article-77981.

Foundations of Human Activity, by the U.S. Department of State—http://usinfo.state.gov/products/pubs/geography/geog03.htm.

The Geography of U.S. Diversity from the 2000 census shows where people of different racial origins currently live in the United States—http://www.census.gov/population/www/cen2000/atlas.html.

For the Teacher

Making Sense of Census, put out by the U.S. Census Bureau, has kits for teachers to use in the classroom. More information—http://www.census.gov/dmd/www/teachers.html.

A Place of Your Own

If you were coming to America today, where would you choose to live? Maybe you don't want to start with a real place, but one in your imagination. What would your ideal place be like? Would it have beaches to play on or mountains for skiing? Would it be full of people or would you like to be alone? Design your ideal place, your utopia. Then see if you can find a place that comes close. Or try drawing it with this tool from the NIEHS (National Institute of Environmental Health Sciences) *Kids' Page*—http://www.niehs.nih.gov/kids/draweasy/home.htm.

Who Runs Our Town?

I know my town and I love my town
And I want to help it be
As great a town to everyone
As it seems to be to me.
I praise my town and cheer my town
And I try to spread its fame
And I know what a splendid thing 'twould be
If all would do the same.
—J. P. Dunn, "My Town,"
http://skyways.lib.ks.us/poetry/dunn/mytown.html

Words to Know

City Council   Politics
City Manager   Public Works
Mayor   Sanitation Department
Municipal   School Board

Related Jumpstarts

History of Main Street
Place Names
Right to Vote
Taxes
Where Cities Bloom
Women Get the Vote

You Are There

Every day when you ride your bike home from school, you run into that same pothole. Every day, you tell yourself that you are going to do something about it, but you forget. Today, when you run into the pothole, your bike topples over and you crash and scrape up your elbow and your chin. That's just too much! Today, when you get home, you remember. But what are you going to do? You're ready to call the mayor. Will it do any good? Will the mayor listen to a kid? You call, and the person who answers the phone doesn't treat you like a kid. She very politely tells you to call Public Works. That's the department that takes care of potholes. Maybe you should learn more about who runs your town.

Topics to Consider

How Your City Government Works	Taxes for Schools
How Your Town Got Its Name	Transportation in Our Town
Law Enforcement	Underneath the City—What Goes On?
Local Parks	What Does the Mayor Do?
Origin of Your Town	What Happens to the Garbage?
Running Local Elections	What Is Your Town Famous For?
School Principal	Where Do the Roads Go?

Books

Search Words: Cities and Towns; United States Politics and Government

America's Top-rated Cities: A Statistical Handbook. 12th ed. (4 vols.). Millerton, NY: Grey House, 2005.

Bowden, Rob. *Cities.* (Sustainable World). San Diego: Kidhaven Press, 2004.

Comparative Guide to American Suburbs. Milpatas, CA: Towcan Valley, 1997.

Friedman, Mark. *How Local, State and Federal Government Works.* (Our Government and Citizenship). Chanhassen, MN: Child's World, 2005.

Silate, Jennifer. *Mayor: Local Government in Action.* (Primary Source Library of American Citizenship). New York: Rosen, 2004.

Internet

Student Voices helps you find your elected officials and learn more about your community by zip code—http://student-voices.org/.

What does the mayor do? It varies with the town or city. Here's what the mayor of Philadelphia does—http://student-voices.org/philadelphia/mayor/.

Find a connection to your local government's Web site—http://www.statelocalgov.net/local.cfm.

The U. S. Conference of Mayors provides an idea what mayors all over the country are doing. Includes video clips, best practices, and new laws—http://www.usmayors.org/uscm/home.asp.

Housing and Urban Development tells about people who help in your town, including you—http://www.hud.gov/kids/.

Great Government for Kids helps you learn how local government works by going on a city council scavenger hunt—http://www.cccoe.net/govern/.

For the Teacher

The Democracy Project by PBS provides activities to help students learn more about government at work. This site is designed for students in grades 3–6—http://pbskids.org/democracy/educators/index.html.

If I Ran the Town

"Things sure would be different if I were the mayor." Would they? What would you do differently if you were the mayor? Identify a problem in your town and come up with a solution that really could work. Describe it well enough that other people can understand what you're talking about. Then write a letter to the mayor asking him or her to consider your idea. Or, start small. Identify a problem in your school—something you need or want. Find a solution and write the principal. Run a campaign.

Women at War

History raves about the heroics of men in war . . .
but few instances are mentioned in which
female courage was displayed.
Yet during every conflict, and the peaceful years between, they too were there.

—Captain Barbara A. Wilson,
http://userpages.aug. com/captbarb/femvets.html

Words to Know

Armed Forces	Marksman
Clara Barton	Patriotism
Courage	WACS
Espionage	WASP
Jennie Hodges	WAVE

Related Jumpstarts

Abigail Adams
Civil War Spies
Women Get the Vote
Women on the Home Front

MADAM VELASQUES IN FEMALE ATTIRE.

You Are There

It is 1864. You watch as your 15-year-old brother, dressed in his new uniform, marches off to fight for the country, for truth and freedom. You are proud of him, but you're also a little envious. You're just as much of a patriot as he is. You believe in your country and you believe that this war is necessary. You are an expert marksman, while your brother misses the target half the time. Why, you even beat him in arm wrestling! You brood over this for weeks. Finally, one day you decide to prove yourself. If the army won't take women, you will pretend you are a boy. You cut your hair short, dress in your brother's clothes, and run off to join the army. (The photograph above shows a woman who did this.) They don't notice that you don't have a beard. Maybe you're too young to grow one. There are no physical tests, not in the 1800s. If you're willing to fight, you can join. You don't know what is going to happen when you get to the battle front, but you do know one thing. If your brother can do it, so can you.

Topics to Consider

Female Soldiers vs. Male Soldiers	WAVES (Women Accepted for Volunteer
Jessica Lynch, Soldier	Emergency Service)
Molly Pitcher, Soldier	Women in Today's Military
My Mom Is a soldier	Women Soldiers of the Civil War
Nurses at War	Women Soldiers of the Revolution
WACS (Women's Army Corps)	Women Spies
WASP (Women's Air Service)	

Books

Search Words: United States History—Civil War—Women; Women Soldiers, United States; World War 1939–1945—Female; World War 1939–1945—Women

> Ford, Carin T. *Daring Women of the Civil War.* (Civil War Library). Berkeley Heights, NJ: Enslow, 2004.
>
> Hasan, Heather. *American Women of the Gulf War.* (American Women at War). New York: Rosen, 2004.
>
> Nathan, Amy. *Count on Us: American Women in the Military.* Washington, DC: National Geographic, 2004.
>
> Payment, Simone. *American Women Spies of World War II.* (American Women at War). New York: Rosen, 2004.

Internet

> *American Women in Uniform,* by Captain Barbara Wilson, USAF Retired, shows women who fought in wars throughout American history—http://userpages.aug.com/captbarb/femvets.html.
>
> The British Broadcasting Company discusses *Women at War,* including the reasons women were excluded from soldiering before the twentieth century—http://www.bbc.co.uk/history/lj/warslj/women_01.shtml.
>
> *Women of the U.S. Marine Corps* home page—http://www.womenmarines.org/history.php.
>
> *Women of the U.S. Navy,* with pictures and biographies of women WAVES of World War II—http://www.history.navy.mil/ac/women/women1.html.
>
> *Women of the U.S. Air Force* includes an informative Flash video—http://www.waspwwii.org/news/movie.htm.
>
> The U.S. Army Women's Museum has history and lots of photos of women in uniform —http://www.awm.lee.army.mil/.
>
> *Women Spies for the Confederacy*—http://home.att.net/~smerela/belleboyd.html.
>
> The U.S. Army has a war game available for free download. See what war is like . . . virtually —http://www.americasarmy.com/.

For the Teacher

The *American Memories* site of the Library of Congress offers teaching ideas about the home front during World Wars I and II—http://memory.loc.gov/learn/features/homefront/index.html.

A Good Soldier

Many of the skills that both men and women need to be good soldiers can be learned in Girl Scouts or Boy Scouts. Yes, both of these organizations are still segregated. But if you join a troop, you will learn about taking care of yourself outdoors, practice marksmanship, and progress in rank, much like the military. For more information—http://www.scouting.org/ or http://www.girlscouts.org/.

Women Get the Vote (1840–1920)

Different groups at different times have turned to founding documents of the United States to meet their needs and to declare their entitlement to the promises of the Revolution of 1776. At Seneca Falls, New York in the summer of 1848, a group of American men and women met to discuss the legal limitations imposed on women during this period. Their consciousness of those limitations had been raised by their participation in the anti-slavery movement; eventually they used the language and structure of the Declaration of Independence to stake their claim to the rights they felt women were entitled to as American citizens.—ERIC Digest, http://www.ericdigests.org/2002-1/women.html

Words to Know

Amelia Bloomer
Carrie Catt
Declaration of Sentiments
Elizabeth Cady Stanton
Susan B. Anthony

Equal Rights Amendment
Nineteenth Amendment
Seneca Falls
Women's Suffrage

Related Jumpstarts

Abigail Adams
Right to Vote
Women at War
Women on the Home Front
Writing the Constitution

You Are There

It is 1848 and you live in Seneca Falls, New York. You are acquainted with Mrs. Stanton, Miss Anthony, and Mrs. Mott. They believe that the U.S. Constitution gave women the same rights as men. For the past several years, these ladies and others have planned a women's rights conference. Your mother is attending and has promised you can go as well. After all, you are 12 years old and quickly moving from childhood. July 19 finally arrives; 240 people attend, including 40 men. The participants issue the Declaration of Sentiments, listing ways in which women have been oppressed. You are surprised that women can't attend college or have a profession. When you grow up, you will help change these unfair laws. What an opportunity for you to work alongside the women who will help make voting and inclusion in professional life a reality for women!

Topics to Consider

Anti-suffragettes	League of Women Voters
Biography of a Suffragette	The Men Who Helped Women Vote
Declaration of Sentiment	Parading for the Vote
History of Voting for Women	Women of Seneca Falls
Going Hungry for the Vote	Nineteenth Amendment

Books

Search Words: Seneca Falls, Suffragists—Biography; Suffragettes; Women's Rights

Adams, Colleen. *Women's Suffrage: A Primary Source History of the Women's Rights Movement in America.* (Primary Sources in American History). New York: Rosen, 2003.

Crewe, Sabrina, and Dale Anderson. *Seneca Falls Women's Rights Convention.* (Events That Shaped America). Milwaukee: G. Stevens, 2005.

Kops, Deborah. *Women's Suffrage.* (People at the Center Of). San Diego: Blackbirch, 2005.

Landau, Elaine. *Women's Right to Vote.* (Cornerstones of Freedom). New York: Children's Press, 2005.

Rossi, Ann. *Created Equal: Women Campaign for the Right to Vote, 1840–1920.* (Crossroads America). Washington, DC: National Geographic, 2005.

Somervill, Barbara A. *Votes for Women: The Story of Carrie Chapman Catt.* Greensboro, NC: Morgan Reynolds, 2003.

Internet

Wikipedia's *History of Women Suffrage in the United States* has good info and links—http://en.wikipedia.org/wiki/History_of_women%27s_suffrage_in_the_United_States.

League of Women Voters has information about its history and issues today—http://www.lwv.org/.

Suffragettes and Women's Right to Vote has one of the best collections of links to these topics, from the movement to antisuffragettes—http://www.betterworldlinks.org/book41zh.htm.

The National Archives (search "Women's Rights") has primary documents—http://www.archives.gov/.

Women's Rights Convention, 1848, Seneca Falls report—http://www.luminet.net/~tgort/convent.htm.

National Women's Hall of Fame has biographies of women who made a difference, including Susan B. Anthony, Elizabeth Cady Stanton, and Carrie Chapman Catt—http://www.greatwomen.org/women.php.

For the Teacher

The National Archives offers lesson resources, including a reading (by multiple students) of the *Failure is Impossible* script—http://www.archives.gov/education/lessons/woman-suffrage/script-intro.htm.

Sufferin' Suffrage

Songs of the nineteenth century—Learn and teach them to your friends—http://www.geocities.com/Athens/Academy/7316/Suff.html or http://memory.loc.gov/ammem/smhtml/audiodir.html#7601869.

Women on the Home Front

If all the women in the factories stopped work for twenty minutes, the Allies would lose the war.—French Field Marshal Joffre, World War I, http://www.greatwar.nl/frames/default-quotes.html

Words to Know

Air Raid Drills
"Any Soldier"
Censor
Rationing
Rosie the Riveter
Rolling Bandages

Scrap Drive
Tin
Victory Gardens
War Bonds
War Relief

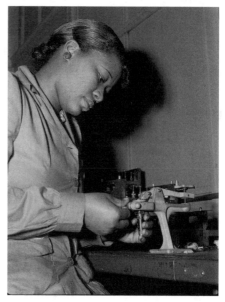

Related Jumpstarts

Abigail Adams

Civil War Spies

Rosie the Riveter

Women at War

Women Get the Vote

You Are There

You miss the men in your life: your father, your brother, and your uncle. They are all gone off to fight in the war. You worry about them and wish you could do something to help. When your neighbor asks you to join the Women's War Relief, you're excited. It's good to be able to do something. At the meetings, you talk about the news from the front. When someone receives a letter from a soldier, she tells everyone else about it. Meanwhile, you knit socks and fold bandages and think about how the men in the field will appreciate receiving them. How the socks will keep them warm. How your bandages may save lives. Now you have a letter from your brother to share. It doesn't say a whole lot. Many of the words have been cut out by the censors. Your brother must have said something that the censors thought would help the enemy if the letter were intercepted. Still, it's good to hear from him. At least you know he's still doing okay.

Topics to Consider

Air Raids	Women's Rights
Betsy Ross	Women's War Relief
Changing Roles of Women	Working Women of World War II
Civil War	World War I
Rosie the Riveter	World War II
Revolutionary War	World War II in Great Britain
Victory Gardens	

Books

Search Words: Revolution 1775–1783—Women; United States History, Civil War—Women; War Work; Women at War

Burgan, Michael. *Great Women of the American Revolution.* (We the People). Minneapolis, MN: Compass Point, 2005.

Colman, Penny. *Rosie the Riveter: Women Working on the Home Front in World War II.* New York: Crown, 1995.

Raatma, Lucia. *Great Women of the Civil War.* (We the People). Minneapolis, MN: Compass Point, 2005.

Redmond, Shirley Raye. *Patriots in Petticoats: Heroines of the American Revolution.* New York: Random House, 2004.

Sinnott, Susan. *Doing Our Part:; American Women on the Home Front During World War II.* (First Book). New York: Franklin Watts, 1995.

Internet

What Did You Do During the War, Grandma? Women during World War II, interviewed by high school students—http://www.stg.brown.edu/projects/WWII_Women/tocCS.html.

Civil War Women—Diaries of women written during the Civil War, from Duke University—http://scriptorium.lib.duke.edu/women/cwdocs.html.

The Civil War Home Front from the National Park Service talks about the lives of women who stayed behind during the war—http://www.cr.nps.gov/history/online_books/rthg/chap6.htm.

The Learning Curve presents *The Home Front 1939–1945* in Great Britain—http://www.learningcurve.gov.uk/homefront/default.htm.

World War II: The Home Front, by History on the Net, includes evacuation, rationing, and Home Guard in Britain—http://www.historyonthenet.com/WW2/home_front.htm.

The National Archives has pictures, radio clips, and records on rationing, women's war work, and other home front details—http://www.archives.gov/northeast/boston/exhibits/homefront/#women.

Betsy Ross home page—http://www.ushistory.org/betsy/index.html.

For the Teacher

The American Memories site of the Library of Congress offers teaching ideas about the home front during World Wars I and II—http://memory.loc.gov/learn/features/homefront/index.html.

A Taste of History

You can be a part of war relief even now. Write letters and collect treats to send in packages to American soldiers serving in foreign lands. If you know someone serving in the Armed Forces, write to him or her. If not, send your letters and packages to "Any Soldier" overseas today. For more information, see http://www.anysoldier.com/index.cfm.

98

Writing the Constitution

[The Constitution of the United States] was not, like the fable Goddess of Wisdom, the offspring of a single brain. It ought to be regarded as the work of many heads and many hands.—James Madison, March 10, 1834

Words to Know

Amendment
Bill of Rights
Checks and Balances
Compromise
Continental Congress

Equal Rights
Magna Carta
Ratify
Rebellion
Taxation

Related Jumpstarts

Abigail Adams
Becoming a State
Declaration of Independence
Donkeys and Elephants
The First Amendment
Jury System
Making Money
Right to Vote
Taxes

You Are There

You represent your state at the Constitutional Convention in Philadelphia. You're a long way from your home and family, and you're tired of sitting in that hot room everyday listening to people argue about rights. Should the constitution protect the rights of the states to do what they believe right? Or should the federal government be more powerful and make laws that affect everyone in every state? You agree with both points of view. After all, what do the people in Georgia know about how things work in Rhode Island? How does a state that's mostly urban understand a state that's mostly agricultural? But if the federal government doesn't have any power, how will it raise an army? And if every state makes its own money, will a dollar from New York be good in Maryland? You are proud that you are part of the group that will help to form this new country, and you want to make sure that the constitution will be good for a long time . . . at least 200 years.

Topics to Consider

Alexander Hamilton	Federalists and Anti-Federalists
Amendments to the Constitution	James Madison
Articles of Confederation	Magna Carta
Bill of Rights	Ratifying the Constitution
Checks and Balances	Three Branches of Government

 From *99 Jumpstarts for Kids' Social Studies Reports: Research Help for Grades 3–8* by Peggy J. Whitley and Susan Williams Goodwin. Westport, CT: Libraries Unlimited. Copyright © 2007.

Books

Search Words: Constitutional History—United States; United States Constitution, Signers

Fradin, Dennis B. *The Founders: The 39 Stories Behind the U. S. Constitution.* New York: Walker, 2005.

Patrick, John J. *The Bill of Rights: A History in Documents.* (Pages from History). New York: Oxford, 2003.

Payan, Gregory. *The Federalists and Anti-federalists: How and Why Political Parties Were Formed in Young America.* (Life in the New American Nation). New York: Rosen, 2004.

Price Hossell, Karen. *The United States Constitution.* (Heinemann Know It. Historical Documents). Chicago: Heinemann, 2004.

Sherman, Josepha. *The Constitution.* (Primary Source Library of American Citizenship). New York: Rosen, 2004.

Internet

Ben's Guide to the Government discusses writing the constitution—http://bensguide. gpo.gov/3-5/documents/constitution/about.html.

James Madison writes about the Constitutional Convention of 1787 and the Bill of Rights—http://rs6.loc.gov/ammem/collections/madison_papers/mjmconst.html.

The Constitution for Kids explains the constitution in simple terms—http://www. usconstitution.net/constkids4.html.

Congress for Kids takes you to the Constitutional Convention—http://www. congressforkids.net/Constitution_delegates.htm.

The National Archives invites you to meet the Founding Fathers and to learn about changes to the constitution—http://www.archives.gov/national-archives-experience/ charters/constitution.html.

For the Teacher

The National Archives resources for educators has lesson plans and online resources for teaching with documents—http://www.archives.gov/education/index. html.

A Taste of History

Join a club or group. If you can't find one that suits your interests, form a club of your own. Most schools encourage you to do just that! Whatever your passion might be, baseball or collecting or making something, you can form a club for it. And of course, when you have an organization, you will need a constitution. For help in writing your constitution, check http://wiki.ehow.com/Write-a-Constitution.

99

Yellow Fever Attacks Philadelphia (1793)

On August 17, 1793, Philadelphia's renowned Dr. Benjamin Rush conferred with two other local doctors about a disease that he had observed over the last two weeks. Symptoms included fever, nausea, skin eruptions, black vomit, incontinence, jaundice-and finally death. In the early weeks of the epidemic, the disease centered on the waterfront district. Rush and his fellow physicians diagnosed the disease as yellow fever and suspected the cause to be putrefied air-miasma-from a spoiled cargo of Santo Domingo coffee that had been dumped on the docks. Rush believed that the seriousness of the outbreak called for drastic purging and bleeding-removing as much as four-fifth of an infected person's blood.—Atwater Kent Museum of Philadelphia

Words to Know

Black Death
Bleeding
Dr. Benjamin Rush
Dr. Jean Deveze
Epidemic
Plague

Public Health
Richard Allen and Absalom Jones
Water Works
Yellow Fever
Yellow Jack

Related Jumpstarts

Abigail Adams
Declaration of Independence
Great Chicago Fire
Reshaping the Land

You Are There

In 1793, you are 10 years old. You and your family, including your grandparents, live in Philadelphia, the country's largest city and the capital. Dr. Benjamin Rush, a signer of the Declaration of Independence, is your family doctor. He has told your dad that during the past two weeks many people in Philadelphia have died of yellow fever. Your family has a dilemma. Do you stay in the city or flee as President and Mrs. Washington and many others have done?

Topics to Consider

Account of any U.S. Epidemic	Fleeing the City in During the Epidemic
African Americans Come to the Aid	Flying the Yellow Jack
Book Report—Fever 1793 by L. Anderson	History of Yellow Fever in the United States
Causes and Treatments of the Yellow Fever Epidemic of 1793	Keeping Records of the Philadelphia Yellow Fever in 1793
Children During the Epidemic	Living in Colonial America
Dr. Benjamin Rush	Philadelphia in the 1790s
Dr. Jean Deveze	Philadelphia's Water Works

Books

Search Words: Epidemics; Philadelphia; Rush, Benjamin; Yellow Fever

Anderson, Laurie Halse. *Fever 1793*. New York: Simon & Schuster, 2000. (fiction)

Arnebeck, Bob. *Benjamin Rush, Yellow Fever and the Birth of Modern Medicine* (e-book). Available at http://www.geocities.com/bobarnebeck/fever1793.html.

Defrey, Holly. *Yellow Fever*. (Epidemics). New York: Rosen, 2002.

Krebs, Laurie. *A Day in the Life of a Colonial Doctor*. (Library of Living and Working in Colonial Times). New York: PowerKids, 2004.

Murphy, Jim. *An American Plague: The True and Terrifying Story of the Yellow Fever Epidemic of 1793*. Philadelphia: Clarion, 2003.

Powell, J. H. *Bring Out Your Dead: The Great Plague of Yellow Fever in Philadelphia in 1793*. (Studies in Health, Illness and Caregiving). Philadelphia: University of Pennsylvania Press, 1993.

Internet

City History contains background info—http://www.philadelphiahistory.org/akm/lessons/yellowFever/.

Eyewitness account of Dr. Benjamin Rush—http://www.eyewitnesstohistory.com/yellowfever.htm.

Philadelphia's Water Works includes the essays *The Diseased City* and *Writing the Fever* (writings about the fever by journalists)—http://xroads.virginia.edu/~MA96/forrest/WW/fever.html and http://xroads.virginia.edu/~MA96/forrest/WW/home.html.

Benjamin Rush and the Epidemic, an e-book for browsing. Find Dr. Deveze here, too—http://www.geocities.com/bobarnebeck/fever1793.html.

The History of Philadelphia—http://www.ushistory.org/philadelphia/index.html.

Support links for *Fever 1793* by Laurie Anderson—http://www.arches.uga.edu/~rutndot/Fever1793.htm.

U.S. Army doctors discovered the cause of yellow fever in 1900. Details from America's Library—http://www.americaslibrary.gov/cgi-bin/page.cgi/jb/progress/yellow_1.

For the Teacher

Fever 1793: Discussion Guides, Activities and Links for teachers of grades 5–8. Help across the curriculum—http://www.writerlady.com/fever1793_teachers.html.

Fact Sheet: Yellow Fever Today

Write a fact sheet about yellow fever in the world today. Where is it in the world? What are the symptoms and treatments? What precautions should travelers take? Sample fact sheets—http://www.kidsplanet.org/factsheets/map.html. See also http://www2.ncid.cdc.gov/travel/yb/utils/ybGet.asp?section=dis&obj=yellowfever.htm.

Bibliography

12 Angry Men (videorecording). Santa Monica, CA: MGM, 2001.

Aaseng, Nathan. *The Space Race.* (World History Series). San Diego: Lucent, 2001.

Abrams, Floyd. *Speaking Freely: Trials of the First Amendment.* New York: Viking, 2005.

Ackroyd, Peter. *Ancient Greece.* (Voyages Through Time). New York: DK Publishing, 2005.

———. *Cities of Blood* (Voyages Through Time). London: DK Publishing, 2005.

Adams, Colleen. *Women's Suffrage : A Primary Source History of the Women's Rights Movement in America.* (Primary Sources in American History). New York: Rosen, 2003.

Adil, Janeer. *Supply and Demand.* (First Facts). Mankato, MN: Capstone, 2006.

Allaby, Michael. *Floods.* (Facts on File Science Library). New York: Facts on File, 2003.

Alter, Judy. *Exploring and Mapping the American West.* (Cornerstones of Freedom). New York: Children's Press, 2001.

———. *Williamsburg.* (We the People). Minneapolis, MN: Compass Point, 2003.

American Citizenship (videorecording). (American Government for Children). Wynnewood, PA: Schlessinger Media, 2005.

American Doughboys: Heroes of World War I (videorecording). Los Angeles: OnDeck, 2004.

American Immigrant Cultures: Builders of Nations. 2 vols. Edited by David Levinson and Melvin Ember. New York: Macmillan Reference, 1997.

America's Top-Rated Cities: A Statistical HandBook. 12th ed. 4 vols. Millerton, NY: Grey House, 2005.

Ancona, George. *Mi Comida = My Foods.* New York: Children's Press, 2005.

Anderson, Catherine Corley. *John F. Kennedy.* (Presidential Leaders). Minneapolis: Lerner, 2004.

Anderson, Dale. *The Anasazi Culture at Mesa Verde.* (Landmark Events in American History). Milwaukee, WI: World Almanac, 2003.

Anderson, Laurie Halse. *Fever 1793.* New York: Simon & Schuster, 2000. (fiction)

Armstrong, John H. *Railroad: What It Is, What It Does.* 4th ed. New York: Simmons-Boardman, 1998.

Arnebeck, Bob. *Benjamin Rush, Yellow Fever and the Birth of Modern Medicine* (e-book). Available at http://www.geocities.com/bobarnebeck/fever1793.html.

Arnold, James R., and Roberta Weiner. *The Industrial Revolution.* Danbury, CT: Grolier, 2005.

Banquieri, Eduardo. *Secrets of the Earth.* (Our Planet). Philadelphia: Chelsea House, 2006.

Baquedano, Elizabeth. *Aztec, Inca and Maya.* (DK Eyewitness). New York: DK Publishing, 2005.

Barnes, Trevor. *Hinduism and Other Eastern Religions: Worship, Festivals and Ceremonies from Around the World.* (World Faiths). Boston: Kingfisher, 2005.

———. *Islam: Worship, Festivals and Ceremonies from Around the World.* (World Faiths). Boston: Kingfisher, 2005.

———. *Judaism: Worship, Festivals and Ceremonies from Around the World.* (World Faiths). Boston: Kingfisher, 2005.

Barter, James. *The Colorado.* (Rivers of the World). San Diego: Lucent, 2003.

———. *Life in a Medieval Village.* (Way People Live). San Diego: Lucent, 2003.

Barth, Edna. *Turkeys, Pilgrims, and Indian Corn: The Story of the Thanksgiving Symbols.* New York: Clarion, 2000.

Bartoletti, Susan Campbell. *Kids on Strike!* Boston: Houghton Mifflin, 2003.

Bates, Richard F., and Thomas Schwartz. *The Great Chicago Fire and the Myth of Mrs. O'Leary's Cow.* Jefferson, NC: McFarland, 2005.

Beal, Eileen. *Ritalin: Its Use and Abuse.* (Drug Abuse Prevention Library). New York: Rosen, 2003.

Beland, Daniel. *Social Security: History and Politics from the New Deal to the Privatization Debate.* (Studies in Government and Public Policy). Lawrence: University of Kansas Press, 2005.

Benavie, Arthur. *Social Security under the Gun: What Every Informed Citizen Needs to Know About Pension Reform.* New York: Palgrave Macmillan, 2006.

Benson, Sara. *Lonely Planet Road Trip: Route 66.* Oakland, CA: Lonely Planet, 2003.

Berger, Leslie. *The Grand Jury.* (Crime, Justice and Punishment). Philadelphia: Chelsea House, 2000.

Bernstein, Daryl. *Better Than a Lemonade Stand: Small Business Ideas for Kids.* Hillsboro, OR: Beyond Words, 1992.

Bial, Raymond. *Cow Towns.* (American Community). New York: Children's Press, 2004.

———. *The Wampanoag.* (Lifeways). New York: Benchmark, 2004.

Bingham, Jane. *Why Do Families Break Up?* (Exploring Tough Issues). Chicago: Raintree, 2004.

Birchfield, D. L. *The Trail of Tears.* (Landmark Events in American History). Milwaukee, WI: World Almanac Library, 2004.

Bloom, Barbara Lee. *The Mexican Americans.* (Immigrants in America). San Diego: Lucent, 2004.

Blumenthal, Karen. *Six Days in October: The Stock Market Crash of 1929.* (Wall Street Journal Book). New York: Atheneum, 2002.

Bombeck, Erma. *Family: The Ties That Bind—and Gag.* New York: McGraw-Hill, 1987.

Bonello, Frank J. *Taking Sides: Clashing Views on Economic Issues.* 12th ed. Blacklick, OH: Dushkin, 2005.

Bosco, Peter. *World War I.* (America at War). New York: Facts on File, 2003.

Boskey, Madeline. *Natural Disasters: A Chapter Book.* (True Tales). New York: Children's Press, 2003.

Bowden, Rob. *Cities.* (Sustainable World). San Diego: Kidhaven Press, 2004.

———. *Settlements of the Mississippi River.* (Rivers Through Time). Chicago: Heinemann, 2004.

Boy Scouts of America. *Citizenship in the Community.* (Merit Badge). Irving, TX: Boy Scouts of America, 2005.

———. *Citizenship in the Nation.* (Merit Badge). Irving, TX: Boy Scouts of America, 2005.

Brady, John. *The Craft of Interviewing.* New York: Vintage, 1977.

Bramwell, Martyn. *How Maps Are Made.* (Maps and Mapmaking). Minneapolis, MN: Lerner, 1998.

Brannen, Daniel E., Julie Carnegie, and Allison McNeill, eds. *Spanish-American War.* Detroit: UXL, 2003.

Brenner, Barbara. *If You Were There in 1776.* (If You Were There). New York: Simon & Schuster, 1994.

Brimner, Larry Dane. *Subway: The Story of Tunnels, Tubes and Tracks.* Honesdale, PA: Boyd's Mills, 2004.

Brooks, Phillip. *The McCarthy Hearings.* (20th Century Perspectives). Chicago: Heinemann, 2005.

Brown, Cynthia Stokes. *Like It Was: A Complete Guide to Writing Oral History.* New York: Teachers & Writers, 1988.

Bryant, Keith. *History of the Atchison, Topeka and Santa Fe Railway.* (Railroads of America). New York: Macmillan, 1974.

Bulla, Clyde Robert. *Squanto: Friend of the Pilgrims.* (Scholastic Biography). New York: Scholastic, 1954.

Burchard, Brendan. *The Student Leadership Guide.* 2d ed. Missoula: University of Montana Press, 2003.

Burgan, Michael. *Empire of Ancient Rome.* (Great Empires of the Past). New York: Facts on File, 2005.

———. *Great Women of the American Revolution.* (We the People). Minneapolis, MN: Compass Point, 2005.

———. *The Missouri Compromise.* (We the People). Minneapolis: Compass Point, 2006.

———. *The Salem Witch Trials.* (We the People). Minneapolis, MN: Compass, 2005.

———. *Samuel Adams: Patriot and Statesman.* (Signature Lives). Minneapolis, MN: Compass Point, 2005.

———. *The Stamp Act of 1765.* (We the People). Minneapolis, MN: Compass Point, 2005.

Byars, Ann. *The Trail of Tears: A Primary Source History of the Forced Relocation of the Cherokee Nation.* (Primary Sources in American History). New York: Rosen, 2004.

Carlson, Laurie. *Classical Kids: An Activity Guide to Ancient Greece and Rome.* Chicago: Chicago Review, 1998.

Carter, E. J. *The Mayflower Compact.* (Heinemann Know It). Chicago: Heinemann, 2004.

Ceban, Bonnie J. *Tornadoes: Disaster & Survival.* (Deadly Disasters). Berkeley Heights, NJ: Enslow, 2005.

Cernan, Eugene, and Don Davis. *The Last Man on the Moon: Astronaut Eugene Cernan and America's Race in Space.* New York: St. Martin's, 1999.

Chancellor, Deborah. *Maps and Mapping.* (Kingfisher Young Knowledge). New York: Kingfisher, 2004.

Chant, Christopher. *The Military History of the United States.* Vol. 7. New York: Marshall Cavendish, 1992.

Chasek, Ruth. *Essential Gardening for Teens.* (Outdoor Life). New York: Children's Press, 2000.

Ching, Jacqueline. *Abigail Adams: Revolutionary Woman.* (Library of American Lives and Times). New York: Power Books, 2002.

Ciovacco, Justine, Kathleen A. Feeley, and Kristen Behrens. *State-by-State Atlas.* New York: DK Publishing, 2003.

Coleman, Wim, and Pat Perrin. *Colonial Williamsburg.* (Virtual Field Trips). Berkeley Heights, NJ: Myreportlinks.com, 2005.

Collier, Chris, and James Lincoln Collier. *A Century of Immigration: 1820–1924.* (Drama of American History). New York: Marshall Cavendish, 2000.

Colman, Penny. *Rosie the Riveter: Women Working on the Home Front during World War II.* New York: Crown, 1995.

Comparative Guide to American Suburbs. Milpatas, CA: Towcan Valley, 1997.

Cooke, Jacob Ernest, and Milton M. Klein, eds. *North America in Colonial Times: An Encyclopedia for Students.* 4 vols. New York: Scribner's, 1998.

Cooper, Jason. *Around the World with Money.* (Money Power). Vero Beach, FL: Rourke, 2003.

———. *Money Through the Ages.* (Money Power). Vero Beach, FL: Rourke, 2003.

Cooper, Michael. *Dust to Eat: Drought and Depression in the 1930's.* New York: Clarion, 2004.

Corum, Vance, Marcie Rosenzweig, and Eric Gibson. *The New Farmer's Market: Farm-Fresh Ideas for Producers, Managers, and Communities.* Auburn, CA: New World, 2005

Cothran, Helen, ed. *National Security: Opposing Viewpoints.* San Diego: Greenhaven, 2005.

Cox, Clinton. *The Forgotten Heroes: The Story of the Buffalo Soldiers.* New York: Scholastic, 1993.

Cox, Kurt Hamilton. *Custer and His Commands: From West Point to Little Bighorn.* (GI Series). West Langhorn, PA: Chelsea House, 2001.

Crewe, Sabrina, and Dale Anderson. *Seneca Falls Women's Rights Convention.* (Events That Shaped America). Milwaukee, WI: G. Stevens, 2005.

Cribb, Joe. *Money.* (DK Eyewitness). New York: DK Publishing, 2005.

Curlee, Lynn. *The Brooklyn Bridge.* New York: Atheneum for Young Readers, 2001.

Curtin, Kathleen, Sandra L. Oliver, and the Plimoth Plantation. *Giving Thanks: Thanksgiving Recipes and History from Pilgrims to Pumpkin Pie.* New York: Clarkson Potter, 2005.

D'Aulaire, Ingri, and Edgar Parin D'Aulaire. *Benjamin Franklin.* New York: Doubleday, 1987.

Dave, Shilpa, Leilani Nishime, and Tasha Oren. *East Main Street: Asian American Popular Culture.* New York: New York University Press, 2005.

Davenport, John. *Louisiana Territory.* (Arbitrary Borders). Philadelphia: Chelsea House, 2005.

———. *Ponce de Leon and His Lands of Discovery.* (Explorers of New Lands). Philadelphia: Chelsea House, 2006.

Davidson, Tish. *Prejudice.* (Life Balance). New York: Franklin Watts, 2003.

Day, Nancy. *Advertising: Information or Manipulation?* (Issues in Focus). Springfield, NJ: Enslow, 1999.

Day, Nancy. *Censorship or Freedom of Expression?* Minneapolis, MN: Lerner, 2001.

De Capua, Sarah. *Becoming a Citizen.* (True Book: Civics). Children's Press, 2002.

———. *Paying Taxes.* (True Book). New York: Children's Press, 2002.

Defrey, Holly. *Yellow Fever.* (Epidemics). New York: Rosen, 2002.

DeKeyser, Stacy. *Sacagawea.* (Watts Library). New York: Franklin Watts, 2004.

DeRubertis, Barbara. *Thanksgiving Day: Let's Meet the Wampanoag and the Pilgrims.* New York: Kane, 1992.

Dicker, John. *The United States of Wal-Mart.* New York: Penguin, 2005.

Doak, Melissa. *Homeless in America: How Could It Happen Here?* (Information Plus Reference). Detroit: Gale, 2006.

Doak, Robin S. *Christopher Columbus: Explorer of the New World.* (Signature Lives). Minneapolis, MN: Compass Point, 2005.

Doeden, Matt. *John Sutter and the California Gold Rush.* (Graphic History). Mankato, MN: Graphic Library, 2005.

Doherty, Craig A., and Katherine M. Doherty. *The Trans-Alaska Pipeline.* (Building America). Woodbridge, CT: Blackbirch Press, 1998.

Dolan, Sean. *Juan Ponce De Leon.* (Hispanics of Achievement). Philadelphia: Chelsea House, 1995.

Drobot, Eve. *Money, Money, Money: Where It Comes from, How to Save It, Spend It and Make It.* Toronto: Maple Tree, 2004.

Dubowski, Cathy East. *Rosa Parks: Don't Give In!* (Defining Moments). New York: Bearport, 2006.

Ducker, James H. *Men of the Steel Rails: Workers on the Atchison, Topeka and Santa Fe Railroad, 1869–1900.* Lincoln: University of Nebraska Press, 1983.

DuTemple, Lesley A. *The Hoover Dam.* (Great Building Feats). Minneapolis, MN: Lerner, 2003.

Dyson, Marianne J. *Home on the Moon.* Washington, DC: National Geographic, 2003.

Eastwood, Kay. *Women and Girls in the Middle Ages.* (Medieval World). New York: Crabtree, 2003.

Egendorf, Laura K. *The Legal System: Opposing Viewpoints.* San Diego: Greenhaven Press 2003.

Eli Whitney (videorecording). (Inventors of the World). Wynnwood, PA: Schlessinger, 2001.

Emert, Phyllis Raybin. *All That Glitters: Men and Women of the Gold and Silver Rushes.* (Perspectives on History). Auburn, MA: History Compass, 1995.

Engstrand, Iris Wilson. *John Sutter: Sutter's Fort and the California Gold Rush.* (Library of American Lives and Times). New York: Rosen, 2004.

Epstein, Dwayne. *Lawmen of the Old West.* (History Makers). Detroit: Lucent, 2005.

Erickson, Paul. *Daily Life on a Southern Plantation, 1853.* New York: Lodestar, 1998.

Erlbach, Arlene. *The Kids' Business Book.* Minneapolis, MN: Lerner, 1998.

———. *The Kids' Volunteering Book.* Minneapolis, MN: Lerner, 1998.

Farish, Leah. *The First Amendment: Freedom of Speech, Religion, and the Press.* (Constitution). Springfield, NJ: Enslow, 1998.

Featherstone, Liza. *Students Against Sweatshops.* New York: Verso, 2002.

Feinstein, Stephen. *The 1930s From the Great Depression to the Wizard of Oz.* (Decades of the 20th Century). Berkeley Heights, NJ: Enslow, 2001.

———. *The 1960s from the Vietnam Era to Flower Power.* (Decades of the 20th Century). Berkeley Heights, NJ: Enslow, 2000.

———. *The Moon.* (Solar System). Berkeley Heights, NJ: MyReportLinks.com, 2005.

Ferris, Jeri. *Remember the Ladies: A Story About Abigail Adams.* (Creative Minds Biography). Minneapolis, MN: Carolrhoda, 2001.

Figley, Marty Rose. *Washington Is Burning.* (On My Own History). Minneapolis, MN: Millbrook Press, 2006.

Fischer, Laura. *Life in a Mississippi River Town.* (Picture the Past). Chicago: Heinemann, 2003.

Fish, Bruce, and Betty Durost Fish. *The History of the Democratic Party.* (Your Government: How It Works). Philadelphia: Chelsea, 2000.

Flanagan, Alice. *The Buffalo Soldiers.* (We the People). Minneapolis, MN: Compass Point, 2005.

Fodor, R. V. *Nickels, Dimes, and Dollars: How Currency Works.* New York: Morrow, 1980.

Folsom-Dickerson, W. E. S. *Cliff Dwellers.* San Antonio, TX: Naylor, 1968.

Ford, Carin T. *Daring Women of the Civil War.* (Civil War Library). Berkeley Heights, NJ: Enslow, 2004.

———. *Slavery and the Underground Railroad: Bound for Freedom.* (Civil War Library). Berkeley Heights, NJ: Enslow, 2004.

Foster Grandparent Program: Operations Handbook. Washington, DC: National Senior Service Corps, 2000.

Fox, Michael D., and Suzanne G. Fox. *Meriwether Lewis and William Clark: The Corps of Discovery and the Exploration of the American Frontier.* (Library of American Lives and Times). New York: Rosen, 2005.

Fradin, Dennis B. *The Founders: The 39 Stories Behind the U. S. Constitution.* New York: Walker, 2005.

———. *The Signers: The 56 Stories Behind the Declaration of Independence.* New York: Walker, 2002.

———. *The Thirteen Colonies.* Chicago: Children's Press, 2000.

Frank, Kim, and Susan J. Smith. *Getting a Grip on ADD: A Kids' Guide to Understanding and Coping with Attention Disorders.* Minneapolis, MN: Educational Media, 1994.

Franklin, Benjamin. *The Autobiography and Other Writings.* New York: Penguin, 2003. Also available as an e-book at http://www.earlyamerica.com/Lives/franklin/index.html.

Franklin, Paula. *Melting Pot or Not?: Debating Cultural Identity.* (Multicultural Issues). Springfield, NJ: Enslow, 1995.

Freedman, Russell. *Cowboys of the Wild West.* New York: Clarion, 1985.

———. *Kids at Work: Lewis Hine and His Campaign Against Child Labor.* New York: Clarion Books, 1998.

Freemon, David K. *The Alaska Purchase in American History.* (In American History). Springfield, NJ: Enslow, 1999.

Freeth, Nick, and Paul Taylor. *Traveling Route 66: 2,250 Miles of Motoring History from Chicago to L.A.* Norman: University of Oklahoma Press, 2001.

Friedman, Mark. *How Local, State and Federal Government Works.* (Our Government and Citizenship). Chanhassen, MN: Child's World, 2005.

Frisch, Carlienne. *Hearing the Pitch: Evaluating All Kinds of Advertising.* (Life Skills Library). New York: Rosen, 1994.

Fritz, Harry W. *The Lewis and Clark Expedition.* (Greenwood Guides to Historic Events). Westport, CT: Greenwood Press, 2004.

Fritz, Jean. *What's the Big Idea, Ben Franklin?* New York: Putnam, 1976.

———. *Will You Sign Here, John Hancock?* New York: Putnam, 1997. (reissue.)

Frommer, Harvey. *Rickey and Robinson: The Men Who Broke Baseball's Color Barrier.* New York: Macmillan, 1982.

Frost-Knappman, Elizabeth, and Kathryn Cullen-Dupont. *Women's Suffrage in America.* (Eyewitness History). New York: Facts on File, 2005.

Fuller, Donna Jo. *The Stock Market.* (How Economics Works). Minneapolis, MN: Lerner, 2006.

Furbee, Mary Rodd. *Outrageous Women of the American Frontier.* New York: J. Wiley, 2002.

Fuson, Robert Henderson. *Juan Ponce de Leon and the Spanish Discovery of Puerto Rico and Florida.* Blacksburg, VA: McDonald & Woodward, 2000.

Gale Encyclopedia of Multicultural America: Primary Documents. 2d ed. 2 vols. Detroit: Gale, 2000.

Gard, Carolyn. *The Attack on the Pentagon on September 11, 2001.* (Terrorist Attacks). New York: Rosen, 2003.

Gay, Kathlyn. *Cultural Diversity: Conflicts and Challenges: The Ultimate Teen Guide.* (It Happened to Me). Lanham, MD: Scarecrow Press, 2003.

Gedney, Mona K. *The Story of the Great Depression.* (Monumental Milestones). Hockessin, DE: Mitchell Lane, 2005.

Geisert, Bonnie, and Arthur Geisert. *Mountain Town.* (Small Town U.S.A.). Boston: Houghton Mifflin, 2000.

George, Charles, and Linda George. *The Maya.* (Life During the Great Civilizations). San Diego: Blackbirch, 2004.

Giblin, James Cross. *Secrets of the Sphinx.* New York: Scholastic Press, 2004.

Giesecke, Ernestine. *Everyday Banking: Consumer Banking.* (Everyday Economics). Chicago: Heinemann, 2003.

———. *Money Business: Banks and Banking.* (Everyday Economics). Chicago: Heinemann, 2003.

———. *Your Money at Work: Taxes.* (Heinemann Know-it: Everyday Economics). Chicago: Heinemann, 2003.

Glass, Maya. *Abigail Adams: Famous First Lady.* (Primary Sources of Famous People in American History). New York: Rosen, 2004.

Goist, Park Dixon. *From Main Street to State Street: Town, City, and Community in America.* Port Washington, NY: Kennikat Press, 1977.

Golay, Michael. *The Spanish American War.* (America at War). New York: Facts on File, 2003.

Gold, Susan Dudley. *Engel v. Vitale: Prayer in the Schools.* New York: Marshall Cavendish, 2006.

Gonzalez, Catherine Troxell. *Lafitte: The Terror of the Gulf.* Burnet, TX: Eakin, 1981.

Goodall, John. *The Story of a Main Street.* New York: Margaret K. McElderry, 1987.

Goodman, Susan. *Stones, Bones, and Petroglyphs: Digging into Southwest Archaeology.* New York: Atheneum Books for Young Readers, 1998.

Gow, Mary. *The Stock Market Crash of 1929: Dawn of the Depression.* (American Disasters). Berkeley Heights, NJ: Enslow, 2003.

Grant, R. G. *The Sixties.* (Look at Life In). Austin, TX: Raintree Steck, 2000.

Gratz, Roberta Brandes, and Norman Mintz. *Cities Back from the Edge: New Life for Downtown.* Hoboken, NJ: Wiley, 2000.

Graves, Kerry A. *Going to School During the Great Depression.* (Going to School in History). Mankata, MN: Blue Earth, 2002.

Graydon, Shari. *Made You Look: How Advertising Works and Why You Should Know.* New York: Annick, 2003.

Green, John, and William Kaufman. *Life in Ancient Rome.* New York: Dover, 1997.

Greenberg, Keith Elliot. *Sam Walton.* (Made in America). Vero Beach, FL: Rourke, 1993.

Greenwald, Maurine Weiner. *Women, War, and Work: The Impact of World War I on Women Workers in the United States.* Ithaca, NY: Cornell University Press, 1990.

Gresko, Jessica A. *The 1960's.* (American History by Decade). San Diego: Kidhaven Press, 2004.

Griffin, Geoff, ed. *How Can the Poor Be Helped?* (At Issue: Social Issues). San Diego: Greenhaven, 2006.

Grote, JoAnne A. *The Internal Revenue Service.* (Your Government: How It Works). Philadelphia: Chelsea House, 2001.

Gunderson, Cory Gideon. *The Need for Oil.* (World in Conflict: Middle East). Edina, MN: Abdo, 2003.

Gunderson, Mary. *Cowboy Cooking.* (Exploring History Through Simple Recipes). Mankato, MN: Blue Earth, 2000.

———. *Food Journal of Lewis and Clark: Recipes for an Expedition.* Yankdon, SD: History Cooks, 2003.

———. *Southern Plantation Cooking.* (Exploring History Through Simple Recipes). Mankato, MN: Blue Earth, 2000.

Haerens, Margaret, ed. *Immigration: Opposing Viewpoints.* San Diego: Greenhaven, 2006.

Halpern, Monica. *Railroad Fever: Building the Transcontinental Railroad 1830–1870.* (Crossroads America). Washington, DC: National Geographic, 2004.

Hamilton, John. *Funding the Nation.* (Government in Action). Edina, MN: ABDO, 2005.

Hanes, Sharon M. *Great Depression and the New Deal: Biographies.* (Great Depression and New Deal Reference Library). Detroit: UXL, 2003.

Hanes, Sharon M., and Richard C. Hanes. *Great Depression and the New Deal: Almanac.* (UXL Great Depression and New Deal Reference Library). Detroit: UXL, 2003.

Hansen, Ole Steen. *Amazing Flights: The Golden Age.* (Story of Flight). New York: Crabtree, 2003.

Harman, Hollis Page. *Money Sense for Kids.* 2d ed. Hauppage, NY: Barrons, 2004.

Harmon, Daniel E. *LaSalle and the Exploration of the Mississippi.* (Explorers of New Worlds). Philadelphia: Chelsea House, 2001.

Harness, Cheryl. *Abe Lincoln Goes to Washington 1837–1863.* Washington, DC: National Geographic, 2003.

———. *Young Abe Lincoln: The Frontier Days 1809–1837.* Washington, DC: National Geographic, 1996.

Harrison, Jean. *Home.* (Children's Rights). North Mankato, MN: Smart Apple, 2005.

Harrison, Paul, and Fred Pearce. *AAAS Atlas of Population and Environment.* Berkeley: University of California Press, 2000.

Harvey, Bonnie. *Carry A. Nation: Saloon Smasher and Prohibitionist.* (Historical American Biographies). New York: Enslow, 2002.

Hasan, Heather. *American Women of the Gulf War.* (American Women at War). New York: Rosen, 2004.

Hatt, Christine. *The End of the Cold War.* (Cold War). Milwaukee, WI: World Almanac, 2002.

Haulley, Fletcher. *The Department of Homeland Security.* (This Is Your Government). New York: Rosen, 2005.

Hauswald, Carol. *Westward Movement: Expanding America's Boundaries 1800–1900.* Tucson, AZ: Zephyr, 1998.

Herbert, Janis. *American Revolution for Kids: A History with 21 Activities.* Chicago: Chicago Review, 2002.

Hess, Stephen, and Milton Kaplan. *The Ungentlemanly Art: A History of American Political Cartoons.* New York: Macmillan, 1975.

Historical Times Encyclopedia of the Civil War. New York: Harper & Row, 1986.

Hixson, Walter L. *Charles A. Lindbergh, Lone Eagle.* (Library of American Biography). New York: Pearson Longman, 2007.

Honan, Linda. *Spend the Day in Ancient Egypt: Projects and Activities That Bring the Past to Life.* NY; John Wiley, 1999.

Hooker, Forrestine C. *Child of the Fighting Tenth: On the Frontier with the Buffalo Soldiers.* New York: Oxford University Press, 2003.

Horn, Geoffrey M. *The Bill of Rights and Other Amendments.* (Library of American Government). Milwaukee, WI: World Almanac, 2004.

———. *Political Parties, Interest Groups, and the Media.* (World Almanac Library of American Government). Milwaukee, WI: World Almanac, 2004.

Hudson, Wade. *The Underground Railroad.* (Cornerstones of Freedom). New York: Children's Press, 2005.

Hull, Mary. *The Boston Tea Party in American History.* (In American History). Springfield, NJ: Enslow, 1999.

———. *Rosa Parks: Civil Rights Leader.* (Black Americans of Achievement). Philadelphia: Chelsea, 2005.

Hunter, Dette. *38 Ways to Entertain Your Grandparents.* Toronto: Annick, 2002.

Hunter, Sally M. *Four Seasons of Corn: A Winnebago Tradition.* Minneapolis, MN: Lerner, 1997.

Hurd, Michael. *Grow Up, America.* Washington, DC: Living Resources, 2000.

Hurley, Jennifer A. *The 1960's.* (Opposing Viewpoints Digests). San Diego: Kidhaven Press, 2000.

Iannone, Catherine. *Sitting Bull: Lakota Leader.* (Book Report Biography). New York: Franklin Watts, 1998.

Iceland, John. *Poverty in America: A Handbook.* Berkeley: University of California Press, 2003.

Ichord, Loretta Frances. *Skillet Bread, Sourdough and Vinegar Pie: Cooking in Pioneer Days.* Brookfield, CT: Millbrook Press, 2003.

Ingram, W. Scott. *Japanese Immigrants.* (Immigration to the United States). New York: Facts on File, 2005

InVision Communications. *Peer Pressure* (videorecording). (Schlessinger Teen Health). Bala Cynwyd, PA: Schlessinger Video Productions, 1994.

Isaacs, Sally Senzel. *The Great Land Rush.* (American Adventure). Chicago: Heinemann, 2004.

Isserman, Maurice. *Across America: The Lewis and Clark Expedition.* (Discovery and Exploration). New York: Facts on File, 2005.

Jackson, Shirley. *The Witchcraft of Salem Village.* New York: Random House, 1956.

Janke, Katelan. *Survival in the Storm: The Dust Bowl Diary of Grace Edwards.* (Dear America). New York: Scholastic, 2002. (fiction)

January, Brendan. *The Dred Scott Decision.* (Cornerstones of Freedom). New York: Children's Press, 1998.

Jocoby, Tamar. *Reinventing the Melting Pot: The New Immigrants and What It Means to Be American.* New York: Basic, 2004.

Johnson, Hannibal B. *Acres of Aspiration: The All-Black Towns in Oklahoma.* Austin, TX: Eakins, 2002.

Jones, Charlotte Foltz. *Westward Ho!: Eleven Explorers of the West.* New York: Holiday House, 2005.

Jordan, Shirley. *Ancient Egypt: Moments in History.* (Cover to Cover). Logan, IA: Perfection Learning, 2000.

Jouris, David. *All Over the Map: An Extraordinary Atlas of the United States Featuring Towns That Actually Exist.* Berkeley, CA: Ten Speed Press, 1994.

Kallen, Stuart A. *Figures of the Salem Witch Trials.* (History Makers). Detroit: Lucent, 2005.

Kalman, Bobbie. *A Slave Family.* (Colonial People). New York: Crabtree, 2003.

Kasser, Tim. *The High Price of Materialism.* Cambridge, MA: MIT, 2002.

Kaszynski, William. *Route 66: Images of America's Main Street.* Jefferson, NC: McFarland, 2003.

Keats, Daphne M. *Interviewing: A Practical Guide for Students and Professionals.* Sydney: University of New South Wales Press, 2000.

Keeley, Jennifer. *Containing the Communists: America's Foreign Entanglements.* (American War Library. Cold War Series). San Diego: Lucent, 2003.

Kelley, Allison. *First to Arrive: Firefighters at Ground Zero.* (United We Stand). Philadelphia: Chelsea House, 2003.

Kent, Deborah. *The Trail of Tears.* (Cornerstones of Freedom). New York: Children's Press, 2005.

Kent, Susan. *Let's Talk About Living with a Grandparent.* (Let's Talk About). New York: PowerKids, 2000.

Kent, Zachary. *The Story of the Brooklyn Bridge.* (Cornerstones of Freedom). Chicago: Children's Press, 1988.

———. *William Seward: The Mastermind of the Alaska Purchase.* (Historical American Biographies). Berkeley Heights, NJ: Enslow, 2001.

———. *Williamsburg.* (Cornerstones of Freedom). Chicago: Children's Press, 1992.

Kerrod, Robin. *Dawn of the Space Age.* (History of Space Exploration). Milwaukee, WI: World Almanac, 2005.

———. *Space Shuttles.* (History of Space Exploration). Milwaukee, WI: World Almanac, 2005.

Kettman, Susan M. *The 12 Rules of Grandparenting: A New Look at Traditional Roles and How to Break Them.* New York: Facts on File, 2000.

Kielburger, Craig. *Free the Children! A Young Man's Personal Crusade.* New York: HarperCollins, 1998.

King, David C. *Al Capone and the Roaring Twenties.* (Notorious Americans and Their Times). Woodbridge, CT: Blackbirch, 1999.

Kingsbury, Robert. *The Assassination of James A. Garfield.* (Library of Political Assassinations). New York: Rosen, 2002.

Kirby, John T. *World Eras.* Vol. 6, *Classical Greek Civilization 800–323 B.C.E.* Detroit: Gale, 2001.

Kneib, Martha. *Christopher Columbus: Master Italian Navigator in the Court of Spain.* (Library of Explorers and Exploration). New York: Rosen, 2003.

Koenig, Viviane. *The Ancient Egyptians: Life in the Nile Valley.* (Peuples du Passé). Brookfield, CT: Millbrook, 1992.

Kopper, Philip. *The Smithsonian Book of North American Indians.* Washington, DC: Smithsonian, 1986.

Kops, Deborah. *Ancient Rome.* (Civilizations of the Ancient World). Berkeley Heights, NJ: MyReportLinks.com, 2005.

———. *Women's Suffrage.* (People at the Center Of). San Diego: Blackbirch, 2005.

Koubek, Christine Wickert. *Friends, Cliques and Peer Pressure: Be True to Yourself.* (Teen Issues). Berkeley Heights, NJ: Enslow, 2002.

Krebs, Laurie. *A Day in the Life of a Colonial Doctor.* (Library of Living and Working in Colonial Times). New York: PowerKids, 2004.

———. *A Day in the Life of a Colonial Indigo Planter.* New York: PowerKids, 2004.

Kuitenbrouwer, Peter. *7 Secrets of Highly Successful Kids.* (Millennium Generation). Toronto: Lobster, 2001.

Kuklin, Susan. *Families.* New York: Hyperion, 2006.

Kupferberg, Audrey E. *The Spanish American War.* (People at the Center). San Diego: Blackbirch, 2005.

Kyi, Tanya Lloyd. *Blue Jean Book: The Story Behind the Seams.* Toronto: Annick, 2005.

Lakin, Patricia. *Grandparents Around the World.* (We All Share). Farmington Hills, MI: Blackbirch, 1999.

Lamachia, John. *So What Is Tolerance Anyway?* (Students' Guide to American Civics.) New York: Rosen, 2002.

Landau, Elaine. *Abolitionist Movement.* (Cornerstones of Freedom). New York: Children's Press, 2004.

———. *Canals.* (True Book). New York: Children's Press, 2001.

———. *Exploring Ancient Egypt with Elaine Landau.* (Exploring Ancient Civilizations with Elaine Landau). Berkeley Heights, NJ: Enslow Elementary, 2005.

———. *Flying to Freedom on the Underground Railroad: The Courageous Slaves, Agents and Conductors.* (People's History). Minneapolis, MN: Twenty-first Century, 2006.

———. *Friendly Foes: A Look at Political Parties.* (How Government Works). Minneapolis, MN: Lerner, 2004.

———. *The Homestead Act.* (True Book). New York: Children's Press, 2006.

———. *Witness the Boston Tea Party with Elaine Landau.* (Explore Colonial America with Elaine Landau). Berkeley Heights, NJ: Enslow, 2006.

———. *Women's Right to Vote.* (Cornerstones of Freedom). New York: Children's Press, 2005.

Laney, Garrine P. *Statehood Process of the Fifty States.* Hauppage, NY: Nova Science, 2002.

Lassieur, Allison. *The Ancient Greeks.* (People of the Ancient World). New York: Franklin Watts, 2004.

Lee, Andrew W. *Backyard Market Gardening: The Entrepreneur's Guide to Selling What You Grow.* Burlington, VT: Good Earth, 1993.

Leslie, Jacques. *Deep Water: The Epic Struggle Over Dams, Displaced People and the Environment.* New York: Farrar, Straus & Giroux, 2005.

Lester, Julius. *Let's Talk About Race.* New York: HarperCollins, 2005.

LeVert, Suzanne. *Electoral College.* (Watts Library). New York: Franklin Watts, 2004.

Levey, Richard H. *Dust Bowl: The 1930's Black Blizzards.* (X-treme Disasters That Changed America). New York: Bearport, 2005.

Levy, Debbie. *Bigotry.* (Lucent Overview). San Diego: Lucent, 2002.

Lewis, Barbara A. *The Kid's Guide to Service Projects: Over 500 Service Ideas for Young People Who Want to Make a Difference.* Minneapolis, MN: Free Spirit, 1995.

Lewis, Cynthia Copeland. *Hello, Alexander Graham Bell Speaking: A Biography.* Minneapolis, MN: Dillon, 1999.

Lieurance, Suzanne. *Prohibition Era in American History.* (In American History). Berkeley Heights, NJ: Enslow, 2003.

———. *The Triangle Shirtwaist Fire and Sweatshop Reform in American History.* Berkeley Heights, NJ: Enslow, 2003.

Light, Ken. *Witness in Our Time: Working Lives of Documentary Photographers.* Washington, DC: Smithsonian, 2000.

Lincoln, Abraham. *Abraham Lincoln the Writer: A Treasury of His Greatest Speeches and Letters.* Edited by Harold Holzer. Honesdale, PA: Boyds Mills, 2000.

Lindbergh, Charles A. *The Spirit of St. Louis.* New York: Scribner's, 1953.

Link, Theodore. *Communism: A Primary Source Analysis.* (Primary Sources of Political Systems). New York: Rosen, 2005.

———. *George Armstrong Custer: General in the U.S. Cavalry.* (Primary Sources of Famous People in American History). New York: Rosen, 2004.

Linn, Susan E. *Consuming Kids: The Hostile Takeover of Childhood.* New York: New Press, 2004.

Loewen, Nancy. *Cash, Credit Cards or Checks: A Book About Payment Methods.* (Money Matters). Minneapolis, MN: Picture Window, 2005.

———. *Lemons and Lemonade: A Book About Supply and Demand.* (Money Matters). Minneapolis, MN: Picture Window, 2005.

———. *Ups and Downs: A Book About the Stock Market.* (Money Matters). Minneapolis, MN: Picture Window, 2005.

London, Jack. *Call of the Wild.* 1903. Various print editions or online at http://www.online -literature.com/london/callwild/.

LoVerde, Mary. *Touching Tomorrow: How to Interview Your Loved Ones to Capture a Lifetime of Memories on Video or Audio.* New York: Fireside, 2000.

Lowe, David. *The Great Chicago Fire: In Eyewitness Accounts and 70 Contemporary Photographs and Illustrations.* New York: Dover, 1979.

Lucas, Eileen. *The Eighteenth and Twenty-first Amendments: Alcohol, Prohibition, and Repeal.* (Constitution). Springfield, NJ: Enslow, 1998.

Lutz, Norma Jean. *The History of Third Parties.* (Your Government: How It Works). Philadelphia: Chelsea, 2000.

Mabery, D. L. *Tell Me About Yourself: How to Interview Anyone from Your Friends to Famous People.* Minneapolis, MN: Lerner, 1985.

Macaulay, David. *Building Big.* Boston: Houghton Mifflin, 2000.

———. *Pyramid.* Boston: Houghton Mifflin, 1975.

MacDonald, Fiona. *The Plague and Medicine in the Middle Ages.* (World Almanac Library of the Middle Ages). Cleveland, OH: World Almanac, 2005.

Madame Blueberry (videorecording). (VeggieTales Classics). Burbank, CA: Warner Home Video, 2003.

Manheimer, Ann. *Child Labor and Sweatshops.* (At Issue). Detroit: Greenhaven, 2006.

Mann, Elizabeth. *The Brooklyn Bridge: A Wonders of the World Book.* New York: Mikaya, 1996.

Map Skills for Children: Making and Reading Maps (videorecording). Wynnewood, PA: Schlessinger, 2004.

Marcovitz, Hal. *Benjamin Franklin: Scientist, Inventor, Printer and Statesman.* (Leaders of the American Revolution). West Langhorn, PA: Chelsea House, 2006.

Margulies, Philip. *Al Qaeda: Osama Bin Laden's Army of Terrorists.* (Inside the World's Most Infamous Terrorist Organizations). New York: Rosen, 2003.

Marinelli, Deborah A. *The Assassination of Abraham Lincoln.* (Library of Political Assassinations). New York: Rosen, 2002.

Marquette, Scott. *America Under Attack.* (America at War). Vero Beach, FL: Rourke, 2003.

Marrin, Albert. *Commander in Chief: Abraham Lincoln and the Civil War.* New York: Dutton, 2003.

Marsh, Carole. *The Here and Now Reproducible Book of the Day That Was Different: September 11, 2001: When Terrorists Attacked America.* [Here and Now]. Peachtree City, GA: Gallopade International, 2001.

Martin, Michael. *The Salem Witch Trials.* (Graphic History). Mankato, MN: Capstone, 2005.

Marx, Christy. *The Great Chicago Fire of 1871.* (Tragic Fires Throughout History). New York: Rosen Central, 2004.

Mason, Andres. *The Vietnam War: A Primary Source History.* (In Their Own Words). Milwaukee, WI: Gareth Stephens, 2006.

Mason, Paul. *Poverty.* (Planet Under Pressure). Chicago: Heinemann, 2006.

McArthur, Debra. *The Dust Bowl and the Depression in American History.* (In American History). Berkeley Heights, NJ: Enslow, 2002.

McBride, Bill. *Santa Fe Railroad: A History in Advertising 1937–1961* (CD-ROM). Hartford, CT: Archives of Advertising, n.d.

McCarthy, Pat. *Abigail Adams: First Lady and Patriot.* (Historical American Biographies). Berkeley Heights, NJ: Enslow, 2002.

———. *Henry Ford: Building Cars for Everyone.* (Historical American Biographies). Berkeley Heights, NJ: Enslow, 2002.

———. *The Thirteen Colonies from Founding to Revolution in American History.* (In American History). Berkeley Heights, NJ: Enslow, 2004.

McCaughrean, Geraldine. *Stop the Train.* New York: HarperCollins, 2003.

McGillian, Jamie Kyle. *The Kid's Money Book: Earning, Saving, Spending, Investing, Donating.* New York: Sterling, 2003.

McGlone, Catherine. New York Times v. Sullivan *and the Freedom of the Press Debate: Debating Supreme Court Decisions.* Berkeley Heights, NJ: Enslow, 2005.

McGowen, Eileen Nixon, and Nancy Lagow Dumas. *Stock Market Smart.* Brookfield, CT: Millbrook, 2002.

McGowen, Tom. *World War I.* (First Book). Danbury, CT: Franklin Watts, 1993.

McGregor, Cynthia. *Jigsaw Puzzle Family: The Stepkids' Guide to Fitting It Together.* (Rebuilding Books, for Divorce and Beyond). Atascadero, CA: Impact, 2005.

McKissack, Pat. *Days of Jubilee: The End of Slavery in the United States.* New York: Scholastic, 2003.

Meachum, Virginia. *Charles Lindbergh: American Hero of Flight.* (People to Know). Berkeley Heights, NJ: Enslow, 2002.

Mead, Gary. *Doughboys: America and the First World War.* Woodstock, NY: Overlook, 2000.

Melton, J. Gordon. *Encyclopedia of American Religions.* Wilmington, NC: McGrath, 1978-.

Meyer, Carolyn, and Charles Gallenkamp. *Mystery of the Ancient Maya.* New York: Atheneum, 1985.

Miller, Arthur. *The Crucible: A Play in Four Acts.* New York: Penguin, 2003 (and other editions).

Miller, Debra. *Hurricane Katrina : Devastation on the Gulf Coast.* (Lucent Overview). San Diego: Lucent, 2006.

Miller, Ron. *Earth and the Moon.* (Worlds Beyond). Brookfield, CT: 21st Century Books, 2003.

Monroe, Judy. *The Lindbergh Baby Kidnapping Trial: A Headline Court Case.* (Headline Court Cases). Berkeley Heights, NJ: Enslow, 2000.

Morley, Jacqueline, Mark Bergin, and John James. *An Egyptian Pyramid.* (Inside Story). New York: Peter Bedrick Books, 1991.

Morrison, Taylor. *Wildfire!* Boston: Houghton Mifflin, 2006.

Mullen, Patricia B. *Listening to Old Voices: Folklore, Life Stories, and the Elderly.* Urbana: University of Illinois Press, 1991.

Murdock, David Hamilton. *North American Indian.* (DK Eyewitness). New York: DK Publishing, 2005.

Murphy, Claire Rudolf, and Jane G. Haigh. *Children of the Gold Rush.* Boulder, CO: Roberts Reinhart, 2001.

Murphy, Jim. *An American Plague: The True and Terrifying Story of the Yellow Fever Epidemic of 1793.* Philadelphia: Clarion, 2003.

———. *The Great Fire*. New York: Scholastic, 1995.

———. *The Great Fire* (sound recording.). Northport, ME: Audio Bookshelf, 2003.

Nardo, Don. *Roman Roads and Aqueducts*. (Building History). San Diego: Lucent, 2001.

———. *The War of 1812*. (World History). San Diego: Lucent, 1991.

Nathan, Amy. *Count on Us: American Women in the Military*. Washington, DC: National Geographic, 2004.

Nelson, Derek. *Off the Map: The Curious Histories of Place Names*. New York: Kodansha, 1997.

Nelson, Robin. *From Cotton to T-Shirts*. (Start to Finish). Minneapolis, MN: Lerner, 2003.

Nemiroff, Mark A., and Jane Annunziata. *All About Adoption: How Families Are Made and How Kids Feel About It*. Washington, DC: American Psychological Association, 2003.

Nestor, Sandy. *Indian Placenames in America*. Jefferson, NC: McFarland, 2003.

Nicolet, Claude. *The World of the Citizen in Republican Rome*. Berkeley: University of California Press, 1988.

Nofi, Albert A. *Spies in the Civil War*. (Untold History of the Civil War). Philadelphia: Chelsea House, 2000.

Oatman, Eric. *Cowboys on the Western Trail: The Cattle Drive Adventures of Josh McNabb and Davy Bartlett*. (I Am American). Washington, DC: National Geographic, 2004.

O'Connor, Rebecca K., ed. *How Should the World Respond to Natural Disasters?* Farmington Hills, MI: Greenhaven, 2006.

Olesky, Walter G. *Maps in History*. (Watts Library). New York: Franklin Watts, 2002.

Olsen, Russell A. *Route 66, Lost and Found: Ruins and Relics Revisited*. Stillwater, MN: Voyageur, 2006.

Olson, Steven P. *Lincoln's Gettysburg Address*. (Great Historical Debates and Speeches). New York: Rosen Central Primary Source, 2005.

Orloff, Judith, and Darrell Mullis. *The Accounting Book: Basic Accounting Fresh from the Lemonade Stand*. Naperville, IL: Sourcebooks, 1998.

Orr, Tamra B. *Prohibition*. (People at the Center Of). San Diego: Blackbirch, 2004.

Osborne, Mary Pope, and Natalie Pope Boyce. *Pilgrims: A Nonfiction Companion to Thanksgiving on Thursday*. (Magic Tree House Research Guide). New York: Random House, 2005.

Owsley, Frank Lawrence. *King Cotton Diplomacy: Foreign Relations of the Confederate States of America*. Chicago: University of Chicago Press, 1959.

Paine, Albert Bigelow. *Thomas Nast, His Period and His Pictures*. New York: Macmillan, 1904. Reprint, Princeton, NJ: Pyne, 1974.

Parker, David L. *Stolen Dreams: Portraits of Working Children*. Minneapolis, MN: Lerner, 1998.

Parks, Carmen. *Farmers Market*. Orlando, FL: Harcourt, 2002.

Parks, Rosa, with Gregory J. Reed. *Quiet Strength: The Faith, the Hope, and the Heart of a Woman Who Changed a Nation: Reflections by Rosa Parks*. Grand Rapids, MI: Zondervan, 1994.

Parks, Rosa, with Jim Haskins. *Rosa Parks: My Story*. New York: Scholastic, 1992.

Parnam, Vanessa Roberts. *The African-American Child's Heritage Cookbook*. South Pasadena, CA: Sandcastle, 1993.

Parry, Ann. *Red Cross*. (Humanitarian Organizations). Philadelphia: Chelsea, 2005.

Partners for Livable Communities. *The Livable City: Revitalizing Urban Communities*. Blacklick, OH: McGraw-Hill, 2000.

Pascoe, Elaine. *Building America: The Brooklyn Bridge*. Woodbridge, CT: Blackbirch, 1999.

Patchett, Kaye. *Eli Whitney: Cotton Gin Genius*. (Giants of Science). San Diego: Black Birch, 2004.

Patrick, Denise Lewis. *Jackie Robinson: Strong Inside and Out*. (Time Life Books). New York: Harpers, 2005.

Patrick, John J. *The Bill of Rights: A History in Documents.* (Pages from History). New York: Oxford, 2003.

Payan, Gregory. *The Federalists and Anti-Federalists: How and Why Political Parties Were Formed in Young America.* (Life in the New American Nation). New York: Rosen, 2004.

Payment, Simone. *American Women Spies of World War II.* (American Women at War). New York: Rosen, 2004.

Pendergast, Sara, and Tom Pendergast, eds. *Bowling, Beatniks and Bell-bottoms: Pop Culture of 20th Century America.* Vol. 4, *1960's and 1970's.* Detroit: UXL: 2002.

Perl, Lila. *The Ancient Maya.* (People of the Ancient World). New York: Franklin Watts, 2005.

Peters, Russell. *Clambake—A Wampanoag Tradition.* (We Are Still Here). Minneapolis, MN: Lerner, 1992.

Petersen, Christine. *Rosie the Riveter.* (Cornerstones of Freedom). New York: Children's Press, 2005.

Pflueger, Lynda. *Thomas Nast, Political Cartoonist.* (Historical American Biographies). Berkeley Heights, NJ: Enslow, 2000.

Phillips, Larissa. *Women Civil War Spies of the Confederacy.* (American Women at War). New York: Rosen, 2004.

Pigache, Philippa. *ADHD.* (Just the Facts). Chicago: Heinemann, 2004.

Pisano, Dominic. *Charles Lindbergh and the* Spirit of St. Louis. Washington, DC: Smithsonian Air and Space Museum, 2002.

Plimouth Plantation. Mayflower *1620: A New Look at a Pilgrim Voyage.* Washington, DC: National Geographic, 2003.

Poleskie, Stephen. *The Balloonist: The Story of T.S.C. Lowe, Inventor, Scientist, Magician and Father of the U.S. Air Force.* Savannah, GA: Frederic C. Bell, 2006.

Pollard, Michael. *The Mississippi.* (Great Rivers). New York: Benchmark, 1997.

Poolos, J. *The Mayflower: A Primary Source History of the Pilgrim's Journey to the New World.* (Primary Sources in American History). New York: Rosen Central Primary Sources, 2004.

Popcorn Park Puppets. *Groark Learns About Prejudice* (videorecording). (Getting Along with Groark). San Francisco: Live Wire Media, n.d.

Powell, Anton. *Ancient Greece.* (Cultural Atlas for Young People). New York: Facts on File, 1989.

Powell, J. H. *Bring Out Your Dead: The Great Plague of Yellow Fever in Philadelphia in 1793.* (Studies in Health, Illness and Caregiving). Philadelphia: University of Pennsylvania Press, 1993.

Price Hossell, Karen. *The United States Constitution.* (Heinemann Know It. Historical Documents). Chicago: Heinemann, 2004.

Quigley, Mary. *Mesa Verde.* (Excavating the Past). Chicago: Heinemann, 2005.

Quinn, Bill. *How Wal-Mart Is Destroying America and What You Can Co About It.* Berkeley, CA: Ten Speed, 1998.

Quiri, Patricia Ryon. *The Declaration of Independence.* (True Books). New York: Children's Press, 1999.

Raatma, Lucia. *Great Women of the Civil War.* (We the People). Minneapolis, MN: Compass Point, 2005.

Radlauer, Ruth. *Mesa Verde National Park.* Chicago: Children's Press, 1989.

Ray, Delia. *A Nation Torn: The Story of How the Civil War Began.* (Young Readers History of the Civil War). New York: Lodestar, 1990.

Redmond, Shirley Raye. *Patriots in Petticoats: Heroines of the American Revolution.* New York: Random House, 2004.

Reier, Sharon. *The Bridges of New York.* Mineola, NY: Dover, 2000.

Rendon, Marcie R., and Cheryl Walsh Bellville. *Farmer's Market: Families Working Together.* Minneapolis, MN: Carolrhoda, 2001.

Ring, Susan. *Election Connection: Official Nick Guide to Electing the President.* San Francisco, Chronicle, 2004.

Rivera, Shiela. *The Assassination of John F. Kennedy.* (American Moments). Edna, MN: Abdo & Daughters, 2004.

Roberts, Russell. *Rulers of Ancient Egypt.* (History Makers). San Diego: Lucent, 1999.

Roberts-Davis, Tanya, ed. *We Need to Go to School: Voices of the Rugmark Children.* Toronto: Douglas & McIntyre, 2001.

Robinson, Jackie. *I Never Had It Made: An Autobiography of Jackie Robinson.* New York: Harper, 2003. Originally published by Putnam, 1972.

Robinson, Sharon. *Jackie's Nine: Jackie Robinson's Values to Live By: Courage, Determination, Teamwork, Persistence, Integrity, Citizenship, Justice, Commitment, Excellence.* New York: Scholastic, 2001.

———. *Promises to Keep: How Jackie Robinson Changed America.* New York: Scholastic, 2004.

Rosen, Daniel. *Independence Now: The American Revolution 1763–1783.* (Crossroads America). Washington, DC: National Geographic, 2004.

Rossi, Ann. *Created Equal: Women Campaign for the Right to Vote, 1840–1920.* (Crossroads America). Washington, DC: National Geographic, 2005.

Rowsome, Frank. *Verse by the Side of the Road: The Story of the Burma Shave Signs and Jingles.* New York: Stephen Greene Press, 1990.

Rozema, Vicki. *Voices from the Trail of Tears.* (Real Voices, Real History). Winston-Salem, NC: J.F. Blair, 2003.

Rumford, James. *Sequoyah: The Cherokee Man Who Gave His People Writing.* Boston: Houghton Mifflin, 2004.

Russell, Jerry L. *1876 Facts About Custer & the Battle of the Little Big Horn.* (Facts About). Reading, MA: Perseus, 1999.

Ruth, Amy. *Growing Up in the Great Depression, 1929 to 1941.* (Our America). Minneapolis, MN: Lerner, 2003.

Ryan, Bernard. *Protecting the Environment.* (Community Service for Teens: Opportunities to Volunteer). Chicago: Ferguson, 1998.

Sacks, David. *Encyclopedia of the Ancient Greek World.* 2d ed. New York: Facts on File, 2005.

Sakaney, Lois. *Women Civil War Spies of the Union.* (American Women at War). New York: Rosen, 2004.

Sanford, William R. *The Chisholm Trail in American History.* (In American History). Berkeley Heights, NJ: Enslow, 2000.

Santella, Andrew. *The First Thanksgiving.* (Cornerstones of Freedom). New York: Children's Press, 2003.

———. *Roosevelt's Rough Riders.* (We the People). Minneapolis, MN: Compass Point, 2006.

SatterField, Katherine Hoffman. *Benjamin Franklin: A Man of Many Talents.* (Time for Kids). Scranton, PA: HarperTrophy, 2005.

Savage, Jeff. *Cowboys and Cow Towns of the Wild West.* (Trailblazers of the Wild West). Springfield, NJ: Enslow, 1995.

Savageau, David, and Ralph D'Agostino. *Places Rated Almanac.* Indianapolis, IN: Macmillan, 1981– .

Save Our Land, Save Our Towns (videorecording). Reading, PA: Bullfrog Films, 2000.

Scarf, Maggi. *Meet Benjamin Franklin.* New York: Random House, 2002.

Schnyert, Mark. *Women of the Vietnam War.* (Women in History). Detroit: Lucent, 2005.

Schoen, Douglas. *On the Campaign Trail: The Long Road of Presidential Politics, 1860–2004.* New York: Regan, 2004.

Schomp, Virginia. *New York.* (Celebrate the States). New York: Benchmark, 2006. (Try other books in this series.)

Schor, Juliet. *Born to Buy: The Commercialized Child and the New Consumer Culture.* New York: Scribner, 2004.

Schubert, Frank, ed. *Voices of the Buffalo Soldier: Records, Reports, and Recollections of Military Life and Service in the West.* Albuquerque: University of New Mexico Press, 2003.

Seidman, David. *Young Zillionaire's Guide to Supply and Demand.* (Be a Zillionaire). New York: Rosen, 2000. (Try other books in this series.)

Shearer, Benjamin F., ed. *The Uniting States: The Story of Statehood for the Fifty United States.* 3 vols. Westport, CT: Greenwood, 2004.

Shepherdson, Nancy. *Ancestor Hunt: Finding Your Family Online.* Danbury, CT: Franklin Watts, 2003.

Sherman, Josepha. *The Constitution.* (Primary Source Library of American Citizenship). New York: Rosen, 2004.

Shuker-Haines, Frances. *Rights and Responsibilities: Using Your Freedom.* (Good Citizenship Library). Austin, TX: Raintree Steck-Vaughn, 1993.

Silate, Jennifer. *Mayor: Local Government in Action.* (Primary Source Library of American Citizenship). New York: Rosen, 2004.

Simmons, Rachel. *Odd Girl Speaks Out: A Girl Writes About Bullies, Cliques, Popularity and Jealousy.* Orlando, FL: Harcourt, 2004.

Simon, Charnon. *Molly Brown: Sharing Her Good Fortune.* (Community Builders). New York: Children's Press, 2000.

Sinnott, Susan. *Doing Our Part: American Women on the Home Front During World War II.* (First Book). New York: Franklin Watts, 1995.

Sioux, Tracee. *Immigration, Migration, and the Growth of the American City.* (Primary Sources of Immigration and Migration in America). New York: PowerKids, 2004.

———. *Immigration, Migration, and the Industrial Revolution.* (Primary Sources of Immigration and Migration in America). New York: PowerKids, 2004.

Slavens, Elaine. *Peer Pressure: How to Deal with It Without Losing Your Cool.* (Deal with It). Toronto: J. Lorimer, 2004.

Smith, Tom. *Discovery of the Americas, 1492–1800.* (Discovery & Exploration). New York: Facts on File, 2005.

Snyder, Inez. *Oranges.* (Harvesttime). New York: Children's Press, 2004.

Somervill, Barbara A. *Votes for Women: The Story of Carrie Chapman Catt.* Greensboro, NC: Morgan Reynolds, 2003.

Sonneborn, Liz. *The War of 1812: A Primary Source History of America's Second War with Britain.* (Primary Sources in American History). New York: Rosen, 2004.

Spangenburg, Ray, and Kit Moser. *Teen Fads: Fun, Foolish or Fatal?* (Teen Issues). Berkeley Heights, NJ: Enslow, 2003.

Speaker-Yuan, Margaret. *Philip Pullman.* (Who Wrote That?). Philadelphia: Chelsea House, 2006.

Spencer, Lauren. *The Assassination of John F. Kennedy.* (Library of Political Assassinations). New York: Rosen, 2002.

St. George, Judith. *The Brooklyn Bridge: They Said It Couldn't Be Built.* New York: Putnam, 1982.

Stanley, George Edward. *The New Republic, 1763–1815.* (A Primary Source History of the United States). Milwaukee, WI: World Almanac, 2005.

Stanley, Jerry. *Children of the Dust Bowl: The True Story of the School at Weedpatch Camp.* New York: Crown, 1992.

———. *Cowboys & Longhorns.* New York: Crown, 2003.

Stearman, Kaye. *Why Do People Live on the Streets?* (Exploring Tough Issues). Austin, TX: Raintree-Steck Vaughn, 2001.

Stein, R. Conrad. *The Battle of the Little Bighorn.* (Cornerstones of Freedom). New York: Children's Press, 1997.

———. *The Declaration of Independence.* (Cornerstone of Freedom). New York: Children's Press, 1995.

———. *The Great Chicago Fire.* (Cornerstones of Freedom). New York: Children's Press, 2005.

———. *The Great Depression.* (Cornerstones of Freedom) Danbury, CT: Children's Press, 1993.

———. *The Industrial Revolution: Manufacturing a Better America.* (American Saga). Berkeley Heights, NJ: Enslow, 2006.

———. *The Story of Mississippi Steamboats.* (Cornerstones of Freedom). Chicago: Children's Press, 1987.

Steinbeck, John. *Harvest Gypsies.* Berkeley, CA: Heyday, 2002 (reissue). (Now known as *The Grapes of Wrath.*)

Stewart, George R. *American Place-names: A Concise and Selective Dictionary for the Continental United States of America.* New York: Oxford University Press, 1985.

Stokes, Samuel N., A. Elizabeth Watson, and Shelley Smith Mastran. *Saving America's Countryside: A Guide to Rural Conservation.* (National Trust for Historic Preservation S.). Baltimore, MD: Johns Hopkins University Press, 1997.

Store Wars: When Wal-Mart Comes to Town (videorecording). Produced by Teddy Bear Films. Oley, PA: Bullfrog Films, 2001.

Streissguth, Thomas. *The Greenhaven Encyclopedia of the Middle Ages.* San Diego, Greenhaven, 2003.

Sundel, Al. *Christopher Columbus and the Age of Exploration in World History.* (In World History). Berkeley Heights, NJ: Enslow, 2002.

Sutherland, Anne. *Kidfluence: The Marketer's Guide to Understanding and Reaching Generation Y—Kids, Tweens and Teens.* New York: McGraw-Hill, 2003.

Swain, Gwyneth. *Dred and Harriet Scott: A Family's Struggle for Freedom.* St. Paul, MN: Borealis, 2004.

Talwar, Jennifer Parker. *Fast Food, Fast Track: Immigrants, Big Business and the American Dream.* Boulder, CO: Westview, 2002.

Tattersall, Clare. *Young Zillionaire's Guide to Money and Banking.* (Be a Zillionaire). New York: Rosen, 2000.

Taylor, Maureen Alice. *Through the Eyes of Your Ancestors.* Boston: Houghton Mifflin, 1999.

Teitelbaum, Michael. *The Bill of Rights.* (Our Government and Citizenship). Chanhassen, MN: Child's World, 2005.

Theunissen, Steve. *The Battle of the Little Bighorn.* (The American West). Broomall, PA: Mason Crest, 2003.

Thomas, Keltie. *The Kids' Guide to Money Cent$.* Tonawanda, NY: Kids Can Press, 2004.

Thomas, Mary Martha. *Riveting and Rationing in Dixie: Alabama Women and the Second World War.* Tuscaloosa: University of Alabama Press, 1987.

Thomas, Susanna. *Hatshepsut: The First Woman Pharaoh.* (Leaders of Ancient Egypt). NY: Rosen, 2003.

Thompson, Linda. *The California Gold Rush.* (Expansion of America). Vero Beach, FL: Rourke, 2005.

Thompson, William. *The Spanish Exploration of Florida: The Adventures of the Spanish Conquistadors.* (Exploration & Discovery). Broomall, PA: Mason Crest, 2002.

Thurber, James, and Candice Nelson. *Campaigns and Elections American Style.* (Transforming American Politics). Boulder, CO: Westview, 2004.

Tibbets, Alison Davis. *Henry Clay: From "War Hawk" to the "Great Compromiser."* (Historical American Biographies). Berkeley Heights, NJ: Enslow, 2003.

Time-Life Books. *What Life Was Like on the Banks of the Nile.* (What Life Was Like). Alexandria, VA: Time-Life Books, 1996.

Tobin, Jacqueline, and Raymond G. Dobard. *Hidden in Plain View: The Secret Story of Quilts and the Underground Railroad.* New York: Anchor, 2000.

Tracy, Kathleen. *The Fall of the Berlin Wall.* (Monumental Milestones). Hockessin, DE: Mitchell Lane, 2005.

Trout, Lawana Hooper. *The Maya.* (Indians of North America). New York: Chelsea House, 1991.

Trueit, Trudi Strain. *ADHD: Attention-Deficit/Hyperactivity Disorder.* New York: Franklin Watts, 2004.

———. *The Boston Tea Party.* (Cornerstones of Freedom). New York: Children's Press, 2005.

Tucker, Phillip Thomas. *Cathy Williams: From Slave to Female Buffalo Soldier.* Mechanicsville, PA: Stackpole, 2002.

Tym, Kate, and Penny Worms. *Coping with Families: Guide to Taking Control of Your Life.* (Get Real). Chicago: Raintree, 2005.

Understanding Government: The Legislative Branch (videorecording). Thousand Oaks, CA: Goldhill, 2000.

Valdez, Angela. *We the People: The U.S. Government's United Response Against Terror.* (United We Stand). Philadelphia: Chelsea House, 2003.

Vieira, Linda. *The Mighty Mississippi: The Life and Times of America's Greatest River.* New York: Walker, 2005.

Volo, Dorothy Denneen, and James M. Volo. *Daily Life During the American Revolution.* (Daily Life Through History). Westport, CT: Greenwood, 2003.

Wagner, Heather Lehr. *Charles Lindbergh.* (Famous Flyers). Philadelphia: Chelsea House, 2003.

Walker, Nickie. *Colonial Women.* (Colonial People). New York: Crabtree, 2003.

Walsh, Frank. *The Montgomery Bus Boycott.* (Landmark Events in American History). Milwaukee, WI: World Almanac, 2003.

Wandberg, Robert. *Volunteering: Giving Back.* (Life Skills). Mankato, MN: Capstone, 2002.

Webb, Alex. *Crossings: Photographs from the U.S.-Mexico Border.* New York: Monacelli, 2003.

Webster, M. L. *On the Trail Made of Dawn: Native American Creation Stories.* North Haven, CT: Linnet, 2001.

Weiner, Vicki. *The Brooklyn Bridge: New York City's Graceful Connection.* (Architectural Wonders). Chicago: Children's Press, 2004.

Weiss, Harvey. *Cartoons and Cartooning.* Boston: Houghton Mifflin, 1990.

Whitcraft, Melissa. *Seward's Folly.* (Cornerstones of Freedom). New York: Children's Press, 2002.

Whitelaw, Nancy. *Andrew Jackson: Frontier President.* (Notable Americans). Greensboro, NC: Morgan Reynolds, 2001.

Whiting, Jim. *The Cuban Missile Crisis: The Cold War Goes Hot.* (Monumental Milestones). Hockessin, DE: Mitchell Lane, 2006.

Williams, Donnie. *The Thunder of Angels: The Montgomery Bus Boycott and the People Who Broke the Back of Jim Crow.* Chicago: Lawrence Hill, 2006.

Williams, Jean Kinney. *Empire of Ancient Greece.* New York: Facts on File, 2005.

Williams, Julie. *Attention Deficit: Hyperactivity Disorder.* (Diseases and People). Berkeley Heights, NJ: Enslow, 2001.

Wilson, Antoine. *The Assassination of William McKinley.* (Library of Political Assassinations). New York: Rosen, 2002.

Wittmann, Kelly. *Explorers of the American West.* (Exploration and Discovery). Broomall, PA: Mason Crest, 2005.

Wolf, Robert V. *The Jury System.* (Crime, Justice and Punishment). Philadelphia: Chelsea House, 2002.

Wolfson, Evelyn. *From Abenaki to Zuni: A Dictionary of Native American Tribes.* New York: Walker, 1988.

Wood, Peter H. *Strange New Land: Africans in Colonial America.* New York: Oxford, 2003.

Wood-Trost, Lucille. *Native Americans of the Plains.* (Indigenous Peoples of the Plains). San Diego: Lucent, 2000.

Woog, Adam. *A Sweatshop During the Industrial Revolution.* (Working Life). San Diego: Lucent, 2003.

Woolf, Alex. *Why Are People Terrorists?* (Exploring Tough Issues). Chicago: Raintree, 2005.

Worth, Richard. *Mexican Immigrants.* (Immigration to the United States). New York: Facts on File, 2005

———. *Ponce de Leon and the Age of Spanish Exploration in World History.* (In World History). Berkeley Heights, NJ: Enslow, 2003.

Wucovits, John F. *Flying Aces.* (American War Library). Farmington Hills, MI: Lucent, 2002.

Yellin, Emily. *Our Mother's War: American Women at Home and at the Front During World War II.* New York: Free Press, 2004.

Yenne, Bill. *Santa Fe Chiefs.* (Great Passenger Trains). St. Paul, MN: Motorbooks International, 2005.

Yolen, Jane, and Heidi Elisabet Yolen Stemple. *The Salem Witch Trials: An Unsolved Mystery from History.* New York: Simon & Schuster, 2004.

Yorinks, Adrienne. *Quilt of States.* Washington, DC: National Geographic, 2005.

Zelon, Helen. *The Endeavour SRTM: Mapping the Earth.* (Space Missions). New York: PowerKids, 2002.

List of Illustrations

Section in "Suggestions for Class Projects"	Illustration Credit
"Life in the Middle Ages"	Dürer, Albrecht. "The Peasants' Dance," engraving, 1514. In Cardini, Franco. *Europe 1492* (New York: Facts on File, 1989).
"The Age of Exploration"	"Captain Cook," statue. Gisborn, New Zealand, 1994.
"Broadsides of the Civil War"	"Recruitment Poster for Tuckerman's Company D," poster, 1863. *The Civil War Letters of Cyrus D. Hardaway.* Unadilla Valley History. http://external.onenta.edu.
"Westward Expansion"	"Law West of the Pecos—Judge Roy Bean's Courthouse and Saloon, Langtry, Texas," photograph, 2000. From the authors' collection.
"Children at the Turn of the Century"	Bain, George Grantham. "Child Labor in the Textile Mills. The Lawrence Textile Strike Was a Strike of Immigrant Workers in Lawrence, Massachusetts in 1912 Led by the Industrial Workers of the World." (Library of Congress Prints & Photographs Division. Lot 10878).
"Mid-Century America"	"Peggy Whitley (author) and Friends," from the authors' collection.
"Creating a Digital Story"	"Michael Makes an A+: The Story of Success in the Library," photograph collage, 2006. From the authors' collection.
"You Are There"	"Twins," photograph, from the authors' collection.

Jumpstart	Illustration Credit
9/11	Watson, Jim, Photographers Mate 2nd Class. "A New York firefighter looks up at what remains of the World Trade Center after its collapse during a Sept. 11 terrorist attack," photograph, 2001. *United States Navy News* no. 010913-N-1350W-003. www.news.navy.mil/.
13 Original Colonies	Map of the 13 original colonies.
Abigail Adams	Stuart, Gilbert. "Abigail Smith Adams," oil on canvas, 1815 (Washington, DC: Library of Congress Prints & Photographs Division. Reproduction number LC-USZ62-10016 DLC).
Aboard the *Mayflower*	Currier, Nathaniel. "Landing of the Pilgrims at Plymouth 11th. Dec. 1620," lithograph, 1858.

Jumpstart	Illustration Credit
All Roads Lead to Rome	Augustus Caesar, Primaporta Statue. 20 BC (Rome). d'Hancarville, Pierre François Hugues. "copy of an antique vase," engraving, in *Collection of Etruscan, Greek, and Roman Antiquities*. Naples: François Morelli, 1766–1767. (University of Chicago Library).
The American Industrial Revolution	Sheppard, William L. "First Cotton Gin," wood engraving, 1869 (Washington, DC: Library of Congress Prints & Photographs Division. Reproduction number LC-USZ62–103801).
American Sweatshops	Hine, Lewis. "Folding paper box company," photograph, 1908 (Washington, DC: Library of Congress Prints & Photographs Division. Reproduction number LC-USZ62–68452).
America's Melting Pot	"Faces of America," collage of photographs from the Library of Congress Prints & Photographs Division, 2006.
Ancient Greece	Constantine, Dimitris. "Parthenon from N.W.," albumen print (1850–1880) (Washington, DC: Library of Congress Prints & Photographs Division. Reproduction number LC-USZ62-108930). Constantine, Dimitris. "Part of Frieze, Parthenon," albumen print (1850–1880) (Washington, DC: Library of Congress Prints & Photographs Division. Reproduction number LC-USZ62-108933).
Atchison, Topeka, and Santa Fe Railroad	"North Conway Scenic Railway," 1982. From the authors' collection. "Atchison, Topeka and Santa Fe Railway logo." In *Santa Fe: The Railroad Gateway to the American West*, Vol. 1, by Donald Duke (San Marino, CA: Golden West, 1995).
Banking	"Mock Banknote Drawn on the Fictitious Humbug Glory Bank," lithograph, 1837. www.loc.harpweek.com.
Battle of New Orleans	Hall, H. B. "The Battle of New Orleans," engraving, 1815 National Archives & Records Administration.
Becoming a Citizen	Aumuller, Al. "America Gains a Famous Citizen," photograph, 1940 print (1850–1880) (Washington, DC: Library of Congress Prints & Photographs Division. Reproduction number LC-DIG-PPMSCA-05649). Loeffler, A. " Immigrant Landing Station, NY," photograph, 1905 (Library of Congress Prints & Photographs Division. Reproduction number LC-USZ62-37784).
Becoming a State	Map of the 50 United States.
Benjamin Franklin, Statesman	Duplessis, Joseph. "Portrait of Benjamin Franklin," oil painting, appr. 1800 (National Archives and Records Administration. 1907 Photograph from Prints and Photographs Division of the Library of Congress Reproduction number LC-USZ62-831).
Border Patrol	"Border Patrol Agent," 2005. From the authors' collection.

Jumpstart	Illustration Credit
Boston Tea Party	Currier, Nathaniel. "Boston Tea Party," lithograph, 1846. Revere, Paul. "The Bloody Massacre Perpetrated in King Street, Boston, on March 5, 1770," line drawing, 1770 (National Archives & Records Administration III-SC-92632).
Brooklyn Bridge	"View of Bridge from New York," engraving from a photograph by Theodore Gubelman, 1883. *Harper's Monthly* (May 1883). "Bridge at Lake Houston State Park," 2002. From the authors' collection.
Buffalo Soldiers	"Company D, 8th Illinois Volunteer Regiment," photograph, 1899 (Washington, DC: Library of Congress Prints & Photographs Division. Reproduction number LC-USZ62-109102). Remington, Frederic. "Buffalo Soldiers in Camp," 1889.
Business of Doing Good	"Caring for Small Children: Lori and Gilly," 2006. From the authors' collection.
Cattle Drives	Russell, Charles Marion. "Roping," 1919. Photograph (retouched), 2005, from the authors' collection.
Changing Family	"Williams Family," 1958. From the authors' collection. "Whitley Wedding," 2000. From the authors' collection.
Charles Lindbergh: *The Spirit of St. Louis*	"Charles Lindbergh," photograph, 1927. (Library of Congress Prints & Photographs Division. Reproduction number LC-USZ62-115128)
Child Labor	Hines, Lewis Wicks. "Group of Breaker Boys. Smallest Is Sam Belloma, Pine Street. Location: Pittston, Pennsylvania," photograph, 1911 (Library of Congress Prints & Photographs Division. Reproduction number LC-DIG-nclc-01137.) Hine, Lewis Wicks. "Map," collage of photographs, 1914 (Library of Congress Prints & Photographs Division. Reproduction number LC-DIG-nclc-04986).
Civil War Spies	"Secret Service by Wm. Gillette," lithograph, 1896. Cinti, NY: Strobridge Lithograph Co. (Washington, DC: Library of Congress Prints & Photographs Division. Reproduction number LC-USZ62-99701).
Cold War	Flag of the Union of Soviet Socialist Republics. "The Dreaded KGB Building in Moscow," 2004. From the authors' collection.
Colonial Williamsburg	Hollen, Howard R. "The Governor's Palace, Williamsburg, VA," photograph, 1943 (Washington, DC: Library of Congress Prints & Photographs Division. Reproduction number LC-USW36-755). "Hornbook," printed paper affixed to wooden paddle. http://faculty.luther.edu/.

Jumpstart	Illustration Credit
Columbus Discovers America	Currier & Ives. "The Landing of Columbus at San Salvador, October 12, 1492," lithograph, 1876 (Washington, DC: Library of Congress Prints & Photographs Division. Reproduction number LC-USZ62-105062).
Coming to America	"New York—Welcome to the Land of Freedom—An Ocean Steamer Passing the Statue of Liberty: Scene on the Steerage deck," wood engraving, 1887. *Frank Leslie's Illustrated Newspaper*, July 2, 1887 (Washington, DC: Library of Congress Prints & Photographs Division. Reproduction number LC-USZ62-38214).
Cultures and Cuisines	Ryûryûkyo Shinsai. "Icefish Cooking," color woodblock print, 1820 (Library of Congress Prints & Photographs Division. Reproduction number LC-USZC4-8433).
Custer's Last Stand	Brady, Mathew. "Major General George Custer," photograph, 1865. http://www.sonofthesouth.net/. Goff, Orlando Scott. "Officers and Wives at Ft. Lincoln," photograph, 1873. Custer standing, without hat; Mrs. Custer standing on bottom step on left. http://www.wyomingtalesandtrails.com.
Dealing with Disaster	Munson, J. G. "Block of Burned Buildings in San Francisco after the 1906 Earthquake with Fire Truck Spraying Water on Them," photograph, 1906 (Washington, DC: Library of Congress Prints & Photographs Division. Reproduction number LC-USZ62-113371).
Declaration of Independence	Trumbull, John. "The Declaration of Independence," oil painting, 1876 (U.S. Capitol rotunda, Washington, DC). Currier and Ives. "The Declaration Committee," lithograph, 1876. (Library of Congress Prints & Photographs Division. Reproduction number LC-USZ62-820).
Donkeys and Elephants	Nast, Thomas. "Stranger things have happened. Hold on, and you may walk over the sluggish animal up there yet," *Harper's Weekly*, November 17, 1877. http://www.harpweek.com/.
Doughboys, Flying Aces, and Hello Girls	"1778–1783 America Owes France the Most Unalterable Gratitude—1917—French Comrade, Your Children Shall Be as Our Children," lithograph, 1918 (Washington, DC: Library of Congress Prints & Photographs Division. Reproduction number LC-USZC2-4114). "World War I Era Aerial Photography with a Side Mounted Camera and Open Cockpit Plane," photograph (NOAA Photo Library, number geod2049). http://www.photolib.noaa.gov/.
Dust Bowl	Marsh, George E. "Dust Storm Approaching Stratford, Texas. Dust Bowl Surveying in Texas," photograph, 1935 (NOAA Photo Library, Historic NWS collection). http://www.photolib.noaa.gov/. Rothstein, Arthur. "Farmer and Sons Walking in the Face of a Dust Storm, Cimarron County, Oklahoma," photograph, 1936 (Washington, DC: Library of Congress Prints & Photographs Division. Reproduction number LC-USF34-004052).

Jumpstart	Illustration Credit
Election of Abraham Lincoln	"Lincoln Taking the Oath at His Second Inauguration, March 4, 1865," woodcut, 1865. *Harper's Weekly*, March 18, 1865 (Library of Congress Prints & Photographs Division. Reproduction number LC-USZ62-2578). French, Benjamin Brown. "Inauguration of President Lincoln, March 4, 1861," photograph, 1861 (Library of Congress Prints & Photographs Division. Reproduction number USZ62-48090).
Fighting Prejudice	Nast, Thomas. "The Union as It Was: The Lost Cause, Worse Than Slavery," wood engraving, 1874 (Library of Congress Prints & Photographs Division. Reproduction number USZ62-128619).
The First Amendment	United States Constitution, pen and ink, 1787 (National Archives, Washington, DC). http://www.archives.gov.
Flower Children	"Bell Bottoms, 1973." From the authors' collection. "At the Renaissance Festival, 1973." From the authors' collection.
The Fountain of Youth	"Painting of Juan Poncé de Leon," graphic, 15 (Florida Memory Project number RC09544). http://ibistro.dos.state.fl.us/. Gutierrez, Diego. "Americae sive quartae orbis partis nova et exactissima description," map, 1562 (Library of Congress, Geography and Map Division). http//:www.loc.gov/.
Go West, Young Man	Waud, A. R. "Pilgrims of the Plains," wood engraving, 1871 (Library of Congress Prints & Photographs Division. Reproduction number USZ62-133214).
Going to Market: From Seed to Sale	Mee, Arthur, and Holland Tompson, eds. "To Market, to Market, to Buy a Fat Pig," The Book of Knowledge (New York: Grolier, 1912).
Gold Rush	Grabill, John C. H. "We Have It Rich," photograph, 1889 (Library of Congress Prints & Photographs Division. Reproduction number USZ62-7120). "Mining Life in California—Chinese Miners," wood engraving, 1857. *Harpers Weekly*, October 3, 1857 (Library of Congress Prints & Photographs Division. Reproduction number USZ62-130289).
Great Chicago Fire	"The Great Fire at Chicago: Scene in Wells Street—The Terrified Populace in Front of the Brigg's House, Which Has Just Caught Fire," wood engraving, 1871. *Harpers Weekly*, October 28, 1871 (Library of Congress Prints & Photographs Division. Reproduction number USZ62-109590). Hine, C. C. "Mrs. Leary's Cow: A Legend of Chicago." New York: Insurance Monitor, 1872. http://www.chicagohs.org/.
The Great Depression	Lange, Dorothea. "Destitute Peapickers in California; a 32 Year Old Mother of Seven Children, February 1936," photograph, 1936 (Library of Congress Prints & Photographs Division. Reproduction number LC-USF34–009058-C). Portrait shows Florence Thompson with several of her children in a photograph known as "Migrant Mother."

Jumpstart	Illustration Credit
History of Main Street	Hine, Lewis Wickes. "The Wagon That Delivers Home Work to Somerville, Mass.," photograph, 1912 (Library of Congress Prints & Photographs Division. Reproduction number LC-DIG-mcla-04224).
I Am the Pharaoh	Frith, Francis. "Colossus of Ramses II, Abû Sunbul, Egypt," photograph, (1840–1860) (Library of Congress Prints & Photographs Division. Reproduction number USZ62-108986). "Tutankhamen Death Mask," 1327 BCE. Reproduction from the authors' collection.
I Want That! Needs vs. Wants	"Cookies, Fruit, and Candy," 2005. From the authors' collection.
Indian Tribes in Your State	Winter, Lloyd, and E. Percy Pond. "Chilkat Indians in Dancing Costumes, Alaska," photograph, 1895 (Library of Congress Prints & Photographs Division. Reproduction number USZ62-101325).
Jackie Robinson Breaks Baseball's Color Barrier	Hassan, Rania. "Jackie Roosevelt Robinson," White House Dream Team baseball card, from http://www.whitehouse.gov/. "Baseball." From the authors' collection.
John Muir	"John Muir, Full-length Portrait, Facing Right, Seated on Rock with Lake and Trees in Background," photograph, 1902 (Library of Congress Prints & Photographs Division. Reproduction number USZ62-52000). Clark, William. "An Elkskin-bound Journal of American Explorer William Clark Is Open to the Entry of October 26, 1805," photograph, 1805. http://www.woodriver.org/.
Jury System	Peale, Rembrandt. "Thomas Jefferson," oil painting, 1805 (New York Historical Society). Photomechanical print (1890–1940) (Library of Congress Prints & Photographs Division. Reproduction number LC-USZC4-2474).
King Cotton	Homer, Winslow. "Cotton Pickers," oil on canvas, 1876 (Los Angeles County Museum of Art).
Lewis & Clark Expedition	Strickland, William. "Meriwether Lewis in Shoshone Indian Dress," engraving, c. 1816. *Analectic Magazine and Naval Chronicle.*
Life Along the Nile	"Cairo: the Sphinx," photograph (1860–1890) (Library of Congress Prints & Photographs Division. Reproduction number LC-USZ62-104866). Oxen pulling a plow during planting, from the tomb of Sennedjem on the West Bank at Thebes, 1224 BCE.

Jumpstart	Illustration Credit
Life in the Middle Ages	Lydgate, John. "Pilgrims Traveling to Canterbury," Miniature, Fifteenth Century. *Canterbury Tales*. In Cardini, Franco. *Europe 1492* (New York: Facts on File, 1989). "Saint Birgitta." *Revelationes*. Nuremberg: Anton Koberger, September 21, 1500 (Rosenwald Collection, Rare Book and Special Collections Division, Library of Congress). http://www.loc.gov/.
Lives and Times of My Grandparents	"Mom's Mom with Sarah," 2004. From the authors' collection.
Making Maps	Collins, Marjorie. "Putting the Finishing Touches on a Map of the World, Showing Routes of Early Explorers," photograph, 1942, taken at the Lincoln School of Teachers' College, Columbia University (Library of Congress Prints & Photographs Division. Reproduction number LC-USW3-009902-E). Meeker, Ezra. "Line of Original Emigration to the Pacific Northwest Commonly Known as the Old Oregon Trail," *The Ox Team or the Old Oregon Trail 1852–1906*, 4th ed. (1907).
Making Money	"1/3 of a Continental Dollar," February 17, 1776, printed by David Hall and William Sellers, Philadelphia. http://www.loc.gov/. "United States Coins," photograph, 2007. From the authors' collection.
Man on the Moon	"Apollo 17: Last on the Moon," 1972, National Aeronautic and Space Administration. http://antwrp.gsfc.nasa.gov/
Marketing to Kids	"Toys," 2006. From the authors' collection. "Piggy Bank," 2006. From the authors' collection.
Mayan Mathematicians	"Huejotzingo Codex of 1531", painting on Amatl, 1531 (Library of Congress) http://www.loc.gov/.
Mesa Verde Cliff Dwellings	Ansel Adams. Untitled. Mesa Verde National Park, Colorado. 1941. http://www.archives.gov/. "Cliff Palace, Mesa Verde, Colorado," photograph, 1911 (Library of Congress Prints & Photographs Division. Reproduction number LC-USZ62-116571).
Mighty Mississippi	Palmer, Fanny. "The Champions of the Mississippi," lithograph. New York: Currier & Ives, 1866 (Library of Congress Prints & Photographs Division. Reproduction number LC-USZC2–3743). Map of the Mississippi River and its watershed. National Park Service, U.S. Department of the Interior. http://www.nps.gov/.
Missouri Compromise	Kaufmann, Theodor. "Effects of the Fugitive Slave Law," lithograph (New York: Hoff & Bloede, 1850) (Library of Congress Prints & Photographs Division. Reproduction number LC-USZC4-4550).

Jumpstart	Illustration Credit
Oklahoma Land Rush	"Auction in Progress in Lumber Company Booth. Temporary Bank Buildings and the Beginnings of a Lodging House Nearby. Oklahoma. Anadarko Townsite," photograph, 1901 (National Archives, record number 48-RST-7B-80) http://www.archives.gov/. " First Train and Wagons Leaving the Line North of Orlando for Perry (Oklahoma Territory), Sept. 16, 1893" (National Archives, record number 49-R-7) http://www.archives.gov/.
Oldest Person in Town	Professor Ed Peniche, photograph, 2005. From the authors' collection.
Peer Pressure	"Four Friends," 1983. From the authors' collection.
Pilgrim Harvest	Ferris, Jean Leon Gerome. "The First Thanksgiving 1621," oil painting, 1915 (Washington, DC, Smithsonian). In *The Pageant of a Nation* (Cleveland, OH: Foundation Press, 1932) (Library of Congress Prints and Photographs Division, Reproduction number USCZ4-4961).
Place Names	"Prickett's Fort, West Virginia," 1993. From the authors' collection.
Political Cartoons	Currier & Ives. "An Available Candidate: The One Qualification for a Whig President," lithograph, 1848 (Library of Congress Prints & Photographs Division. Reproduction number LC-USZ62-5220).
Poverty in America	Lange, Dorothy. "Migrant Agricultural Worker's Family, Nipomo, California," photograph, 1936 (Library of Congress Prints & Photographs Division. Reproduction number LC-USZ62-58355).
The President Has Been Shot!	"President John F. Kennedy Speaking at Los Alamos Lab," photograph, 1962. http://www.lanl.gov/.
Prohibition and Gangsters	[New York City Deputy Police Commissioner John A. Leach, right, watching agents pour liquor into sewer following a raid during the height of prohibition], photograph, 1921 (New York World-Telegram and the Sun Newspaper Photograph Collection, Library of Congress Prints & Photographs Division. Reproduction number LC-USZ62-123257). "Two Mug Shots of Al Capone, One Facing Front, the Other Facing [Left]," photograph, 1931 (New York World-Telegram and the Sun Newspaper Photograph Collection, Library of Congress Prints & Photographs Division. Reproduction number LC-USZ62-123223).
Religions of the World	"The Floating Church of Our Savior for Seamen," steel engraving, 1844 (Library of Congress Prints & Photographs Division. Reproduction number LC-USZ61-1258).
Reshaping the Land	"Hoover Dam," 1978. From the authors' collection.

Jumpstart	Illustration Credit
Riding in the Back of the Bus	Mrs. Rosa Parks being fingerprinted in Montgomery, Alabama, gelatin silver print, 1956. New York World-Telegram & Sun Collection (Library of Congress Prints & Photographs Division. Reproduction number LC- USZ62-109643) Leffler, Warren K. "Civil Rights March on Washington, DC," photograph, 1963 (Library of Congress Prints & Photographs Division. Reproduction number LC-U9-10364-37).
The Right to Vote	Waud, Alfred Rudolph. "The First Vote," wood engraving, 1867. *Harper's Weekly,* November 16, 1867 (Library of Congress Prints & Photographs Division. Reproduction number LC-USZ62-19234). "Voting Machine," photograph, 2004.
Rosie the Riveter	Miller, J. Howard. "We Can Do It!," poster, 1943 Office for Emergency Management War Production Board (Still pictures records LICON, Special media archives services division, College Park, MD. National Archives ARC identifier 535413).
Rough Riders	Dinwiddie, William, "Colonel Roosevelt and His Rough Riders at the Top of the Hill, Battle of San Juan," photograph, 1898 (Library of Congress Prints & Photographs Division. Reproduction number LC-USZC4-7934.)
Route 66	Route 66 highway marker. Map of the contiguous United States showing Route 66. Edwardsville, IL, Route 66 bridge.
Salem Witch Trials	Crafts, William A. "Witchcraft at Salem Village," in *Pioneers in the Settlement of America* by William A. Crafts. Vol. I. (Boston: Samuel Walker & Company, 1876).
Seward's Folly	"Dog Sled Arriving from Iditarod; ¾ Million Gold from Iditarod Arr. Knik Jan 12/12," photograph, 1912 (Library of Congress Prints & Photographs Division. Reproduction number LC-USZ62-131849).
Social Security	Image of the original Social Security card in 1935. The card has changed very little today. http://www.ssa.gov/.
Stocks and Bonds	Underhill, Irving. "New York Stock Exchange, Broad Street," photograph, 1908 (Library of Congress Prints & Photographs Division. Reproduction number LC-USZ62-112785).
Supply and Demand	Excel graphic created for this book.
Taxes	"Home of the American Citizen after the Tax Bill Has Passed," wood engraving, 1862. *Frank Leslie's Illustrated Newspaper,* 14:355, July 19, 1862 (Library of Congress Prints & Photographs Division. Reproduction number LC-USZ62-133072).
Telling America's History with Photographs	"Fair Oaks, VA. Prof. Thaddeus S. Lowe Observing the Battle from His Balloon 'Intrepid'," glass stereograph, 1862 (Library of Congress Prints & Photographs Division. Reproduction number LC-DIG-cwpb-01560).

Jumpstart	Illustration Credit
Trail of Tears	Johnson, Kerry. "Cherokee Rose," photograph, 2004. Home Gardening, Mississippi State University Extension Service. http://msucares.com/. National Park Service. "Trail of Tears. National Historic Trail," map. http://www.nps.gov/.
Underground Railroad	Rowse, Samuel. "The Resurrection of Henry Box Brown at Philadelphia," lithograph, 1850 (Library of Congress Rare Book and Special Collections Division, Broadside Collection, portfolio 65, no.16). Jacob's Ladder quilt block.
Wal-Mart Comes to Our Town	Photographs, 2006, by the authors.
Where Cities Bloom	"Cloudless Earth Night," 2000. National Aeronautics and Space Administration. www.nasa.gov/.
Who Runs Our Town?	Rogers, William Allen. "Tammany Workers at the Polls in Pell Street, New York—The Beginning of a Free Fight," wood engraving, 1889. *Harpers Weekly*, November 16, 1889 (Library of Congress Prints & Photographs Division. Reproduction number LC-USZ62-108119). Hadra, E. "Our Boss," tobacco label, 1869 (Library of Congress Prints & Photographs Division. Reproduction number LC-USZ62-90688).
Women at War	"Harry T. Buford, 1st. Lt. Indpt. Scouts, CSA and Madam Velazquez in Female Attire," in *The Woman in Battle: A Narrative of the Exploits, Adventures, and Travels of Madame Loreta Janeta Velazquez, Otherwise Known as Lieutenant Harry T. Buford, Confederate States Army* (Richmond, VA: Dustin, Gilman and Co., 1876).
Women Get the Vote	"Mrs. Suffern with a Home-made Banner in the Parade," photograph, 1914 (Library of Congress Prints & Photographs Division. Reproduction number LC-USZ62-135533). Harris & Ewing. "National Anti-Suffrage Association," photograph, 1911 (Library of Congress Prints & Photographs Division. Reproduction number LC-USZ62-25338).
Women on the Home Front	"Production. Aircraft Engines. Reconditioning Used Spark Plugs for Reuse in Testing Airplane Motors . . . ," photograph, 1942 (Farm Security Administration, Office of War Information Photograph Collection. Library of Congress Prints & Photographs Division. Reproduction number LC-USE6-D-005578) Jacobs, Leonebel. "The Fruits of Victory," photomechanical print, F. M. Lupton, 1918 (Library of Congress Prints & Photographs Division. Reproduction number LC-USZC4-5561).
Writing the Constitution	Christy, Howard Chandler. "Scene of Signing of the United States Constitution," oil painting, 1940 (U.S. Capitol rotunda, Washington, DC). (Library of Congress Prints & Photographs Division. Reproduction number LC-H8-CT-P03-001).

Jumpstart	Illustration Credit
Yellow Fever Attacks Philadelphia	Sully, Thomas. "Benjamin Rush," oil painting, 1812 (Government Archives number 148-CP-200). Benjamin Rush. *An Account of the Bilious Remitting Yellow Fever* (Philadelphia: Thomas Dobson, 1794).

Subject Directory

Index

Entries that are the titles of Jumpstarts are in boldface type.

ABOUT THE AUTHORS

   PEGGY WHITLEY and SUSAN GOODWIN are librarians with master's degrees in library science and many years' experience in teaching research. Peggy is currently Dean of Educational Services at Kingwood College in Houston, Texas. She has taught in and been a librarian in public schools from elementary through high school. Susan has worked in public as well as in business libraries. She is currently a reference librarian at Kingwood College. Both authors have received the coveted Faculty Excellence Award. They have won writing and other awards for the popular Nineteenth and Twentieth Century American Cultural History Web sites at kclibrary.nhmccd.edu/decades. html. They are very interested in information literacy and work toward teaching community college students how to find and evaluate information for research assignments. Recently Susan won third place for a photograph in the Greater Houston Partnership photography contest. Peggy has earned the National Council of Exemplary Initiatives award for the past two years for professional development programs, *Scholarship of Teaching,* and *The Leader in Me.* Peggy and Susan are the authors of three other books in the 99 Jumpstarts series: *99 Jumpstarts to Research: Topic Guides for Finding Information on Current Issues* (with Catherine Olson), *99 Jumpstarts for Kids: Getting Started in Research,* and *99 Jumpstarts for Kids' Science Research.*